Dear

grateful for the great
friendship & the values
we share,

Peace to you,

Duncan

The Radical Teaching of Jesus

The Radical Teaching of Jesus

A Teacher Full of Grace and Truth:
An Inquiry for Thoughtful Seekers

Duncan S. Ferguson

WIPF & STOCK · Eugene, Oregon

THE RADICAL TEACHING OF JESUS
A Teacher Full of Grace and Truth: An Inquiry for Thoughtful Seekers

Wipf & Stock
An Imprint of Wipf and Stock Publishers
199 W. 8th Ave., Suite 3
Eugene, OR 97401

www.wipfandstock.com

PAPERBACK ISBN: 978-1-4982-3379-8
HARDCOVER ISBN: 978-1-4982-3381-1

Manufactured in the U.S.A.   01/11/2016

There are innumerable books about Jesus. The reason is obvious: we can never finish with him, and every age must encounter him anew.

—Gerhard Lohfink, *Jesus of Nazareth: What He Wanted, Who He Was*, xi

With gratitude to honest and thoughtful writers and teachers who
have sought to understand Jesus

Contents

Preface

THERE ARE NUMEROUS AND excellent resources available for the study of the Gospels and the life of Jesus. One might legitimately ask whether another resource is necessary. It is a good question and could be answered either way, but I think the better answer is a tentative yes. One fundamental reason is because Christians of every generation and culture generally feel that they must make an effort to understand the life and teachings of Jesus within their framework. His importance for each generation and setting is hard to overstate, and the meaning of Jesus must be claimed and owned as each generation engages in worship, study, and reflection. Others outside of the Christian family also want credible and contemporary accounts of this extraordinary person. It appears that there is always a new perspective that can be helpful and enlightening.

It is the case that a conscientious seeker can generally find these excellent resources; they are available in the great libraries and even online, although some guidance for finding the resources may be a requirement.[1] These resources are vast, located in many places, and written in several languages, and it is not easy to gain access to them all in one place. Even as one uses world-class libraries, it is difficult to know just what to select to answer one's questions and inquiries.[2] Still another part of an affirmative answer about the need for new resources is that nearly every book about Jesus has a particular point of view, growing out of a specific time and place, and they are usually targeted toward a particular audience. For example, one may find a book written by a scholar on an important but narrowly focused

1. Broad-based summaries of the resources are available in several places. An example is the work by Theissen and Merz, *Historical Jesus*. Even this volume has a clear point of view in suggesting what resources to consult.

2. I learned this lesson in the marvelous library of Princeton Theological Seminary.

subject designed for other scholars.[3] Or one may find a book for lay people designed to nurture faith, but lacking the details of historical background and context.[4] There are many fine books designed for a particular culture or ethnicity suggesting the relevance of the teaching of Jesus for the particular setting.[5] Or, one may find a book that attempts to invite the contemporary and thoughtful reader into the range of difficult, even overwhelming issues, which surround any attempt to interpret the life of Jesus.[6]

The category in which I would like to make a contribution is the teaching of Jesus, although in this category there is an abundance of thoughtful works.[7] I have been greatly informed and enriched by them, and to a large extent, my dedication is to these authors and teachers. For the past several decades, there has been a multitude of books about Jesus and his teaching that take into account the complex issues of the intricate balance of faith and history, the rise of a new consciousness, and the resulting phenomenon of the emerging church (nearly a new Reformation). These books continue to be published, but more recently with slightly less frequency.[8] My goal is to put the emphasis on Jesus the Teacher (Rabbi) and enable the thoughtful seeker to discover this wealth of information and insight found in the teaching of Jesus. I will stress the charismatic nature of his teaching, but will also suggest that Jesus is a compassionate healer and radical prophet who taught in these roles as well.[9] My hope is that readers may find a way of understanding Jesus of Galilee and his extraordinary teaching that has integrity, is credible, and is life-giving. From this base, good decisions about Jesus can be made.

While the book is for everyone with an interest, I do hope to reach a particular group of people, those who struggle with affirming orthodox creedal statements about Jesus, but still want to pursue a religious life and

3. See, e.g., the superb work of Brown, *Birth of the Messiah*. A more recent book is one by Allison, *Constructing Jesus*.

4. See the more popular book in the framework of American evangelicalism, Keller, *Jesus the King*.

5. See, e.g., Prothero, *American Jesus*.

6. See the monumental work of Meier, *Marginal Jew*, in 4 vols.

7. Among them is the fine book of Abernathy based on the lectures series of Perrin, *Understanding the Teaching of Jesus*. The classic work by Manson, *Teaching of Jesus*, remains a reliable guide.

8. An exceptional recent work is by Lohfink, *Jesus of Nazareth*. Still another book, published in 2013, has received the attention of many readers. It is by Aslan and entitled *Zealot: The Life and Times of Jesus of Nazareth*. Aslan draws more upon the history of the time of Jesus than he does upon the New Testament documents as he develops his views.

9. With Jesus, the medium is often the message.

to find a way to understand Jesus that *works* for them. Partly out of personal choice and because of my work as both an academic in the field and a minister to "cultured despisers"[10] or at least cultured doubters, I encounter many who cannot accept traditional ways of understanding the Christian faith. Many of these people are in the church, but troubled by the categories in which the Christian faith is framed and the dated sound of the liturgy. Of course there are many outside of the Christian family who struggle as well and long for a satisfying spirituality and a possible connection with transcendence.[11] These cultured doubters are asking whether they can, with integrity, stay in the Christian family, and others who are seeking a credible spirituality but unable to find Christian churches which provide them with what they consider to be an authentic pathway. It is on the pathway and the *practice* that Jesus offers where I put the emphasis.

The purpose of this book is therefore twofold. It is first to assist Christians who are seeking a deeper and more profound faith and way of life. It is to help those within the Christian family who are searching to find a way to understand and follow Jesus. They want a way that is informed by the classical understandings of Jesus and, at the same time, one that comes to the quest for understanding with a twenty-first-century consciousness and a desire to practice the teachings of love and compassion. They want to find a way that enables them to have integrity in their lifestyle and coherence in their worldview. Second, it is to assist those pilgrims outside of the Christian family searching for a spiritual center and hoping and willing to find guidance from Jesus whose universal teachings on truth and love attract them. The book is not essentially an *apologia* nor is it polemical in tone, although it has a positive spirit about the value of knowing about Jesus. It is essentially an attempt to offer credible information and thoughtful perspectives that will help readers make good decisions regarding their interpretation of Jesus, and, in many cases, about life.

The book, then, is based upon an informed understanding of the Bible and recent historical scholarship, a careful description of Jesus as a compassionate healer, charismatic teacher, and radical prophet, and sensitivity to the content and intellectual currents of contemporary life. The goal is to present the material in an accessible way for the educated reader. It will be relatively brief and succinct, avoiding unnecessary academic detail, although

10. The phrase is borrowed from Schleiermacher, the great theologian of the nineteenth century, who desired to reach out to honest doubters who had trouble accepting the Christian faith and religion in general. See *On Religion: Speeches to Its Cultured Despisers*.

11. I have a particular interest in writing about Jesus in a way that is interesting and helpful to the religiously unaffiliated.

my goal is that the finest scholarship will guide what is written. There is a sincere effort to have integrity with the historical challenge of gaining access to the Jesus of history, to enable the thoughtful seeker to understand the life, teachings, and interpretations of Jesus, and to offer a helpful way to assist those who seek to build a life based on the one who is described by the Gospel of John as filled with "grace and truth." I will place this person, Jesus, in the context of first-century Galilee in a Jewish setting, a context that is broader that the village of Nazareth and yet not fully Jerusalem. Rome is in the background, and context is very important in grasping his life and teachings.

I have been writing this book for about fifty years, as a campus minister in my early career, as an academic for many years which involved teaching courses on Jesus, and as an administrator in the church structures and higher education. In all of these settings, the model of Jesus as one filled with "grace and truth"[12] has been a guide. This phrase captures my presuppositions and shapes my hermeneutical method.

The book unfolds in the following way. Section 1 will focus on how to navigate the difficult terrain of history. It will speak to the ways we gain access to Jesus by a careful study of the Gospels, the historical context of the life of Jesus, and how Jesus understood his vocation as intimately connected with the kingdom of God. In section 2, we will go directly to the teaching of Jesus and explore his method of teaching, the topics in his teaching, and the radical character of his teaching. In section 3, we will attempt to translate the teaching of Jesus for our time and place in history by reviewing his teaching about how God intersects with world, the nature of the human response, and how it is that we are able to sustain a love-centered life.

I have lived with some fear and trembling in writing about Jesus. The topic is so important, and for me, at least, quite difficult. It is important to me in that I want to find a credible and satisfying way to understand the life and teachings of Jesus, in part through my writing, but also to assist others as they seek a well-informed and authentic way of understanding the person of Jesus. I have some fear that I might fail in these endeavors, especially in reference to others who may not appreciate an orientation that is open and searching rather thoroughly confessional in tone. I am keenly aware that in using methodologies and suggesting ways of understanding Jesus that are not always traditional I run the risk of harsh judgment by those who are deeply committed to traditional views. Of course, I run the risk in the other direction as well in that I do attempt to find a way to stay in the Christian family. It does seem to be the case that our religious feelings and convictions

12. John 1:14.

are very intense, and to offer alternative views may threaten and offend. I have no desire to cause discomfort to those for whom I have great respect and love although some discomfort leads to learning. I hope for open and free conversation in a safe place as together we seek to find our way.

I will primarily use the New Revised Standard Version of the Bible for quotations, although on occasion I will use other translations that seem more accurately to capture the meaning of a verse or section of the Bible. I will use CE or Common Era instead of AD, and BCE instead of BC for dates, and generally refer to the Old Testament as the Hebrew Bible, although there may be times in treating traditional Christian views that I will use the term Old Testament.

SECTION 1 —————————————————

The Terrain

Gaining Access to the
Teaching of Jesus

SECTION 1, IN THREE chapters, will address the challenge of gaining access to the historical Jesus. The terrain is complex and demanding. Nearly all agree that a full understanding of the Christian faith and ways of living the Christian faith are linked to the Jesus of history. At an earlier time in history, it was thought that this access came almost exclusively through the reading of the New Testament. This collection of writings is essential to understanding Jesus, but it is now widely accepted that most of these writings came years after the time Jesus lived. The writers' primary goals were not essentially biographical in character, nor did they possess the contemporary tools of historical scholarship. What they wrote were more like extended sermons designed to inform and nurture the early followers of Jesus. Chapter 1 explores how this change in historical understanding meant that the search for the historical Jesus began to look behind and through the New Testament and other sources to gain access to the Jesus of history. Chapter 2 continues the quest by exploring the historical setting in which Jesus lived. It is out of this context that his teaching was shaped and framed. In chapter 3, we turn more directly to the person of Jesus and give attention to his sense of vocation centered in his understanding of the kingdom of God. His teaching grows out of Jesus's understanding of his life mission. Historical study of the Gospels, an exploration of the context of first-century Palestine, and an attempt to understand the vocation of Jesus represent the challenging terrain that must be crossed to gain a trustworthy understanding of his teaching.

> *In the beginning* was the performance; not the word alone, not the deed alone, but both, each indelibly marked with the other forever. He comes as yet unknown into a hamlet in Lower Galilee. He is watched by the cold, hard eyes of peasants living long enough at subsistence level to know exactly where the line is drawn between poverty and destitution. He looks like a beggar, yet his eyes lack the proper cringe, his voice the proper whine, his walk the proper shuffle. He speaks about the rule of God, and they listen as much for curiosity as anything else.[1]

---

1. Crossan, *Historical Jesus*, xi.

1

Accessing the Teaching of Jesus
The Possibilities and Limitations of History

The Difficulties of Access

HISTORICAL STUDY IS A complex undertaking resting on a rocky terrain that makes our trek to the teaching of Jesus demanding. There is a popular view of history that suggests that historians are expected just to tell us what happened in the past. In part, that is what they do, and at an earlier time in history, there was movement within the discipline of history, based in Germany, which maintained that historians should describe the past "as it actually happened." The motivation behind this movement was admirable in that it called upon historians to tell the story of history objectively and without the interference of bias, unfettered as they often said. Historians have heeded this guidance, but the challenge of following it, as most historians have discovered, is very difficult and not always the only goal of writing history.

The reasons for the difficulty are many and varied. The *first* and most obvious one is that those who do the work of history bring their own *pre-understanding* to their work.[1] They read the records of history through the

1. The study of pre-understanding or prior assumptions that shape the work of the historian became a critical issue in the middle of the twentieth century, especially in reference to the history of the Bible. Polanyi, in his book *Tacit Dimension*, argued that we bring our presuppositions to the work of interpreting the past. I trace this hermeneutical issue in reference to biblical interpretation in *Biblical Hermeneutics*. I also maintain that even the historical methods, designed to be free of prior assumptions, have presuppositions within them. For example, these presuppositions are clearly evident when the historian may wish to defend or to discount traditional beliefs.

3

"sun glasses" of their own outlook. This reality becomes especially evident in dealing with religious history and in particular for those religions which are based on events in history and the recordings of these events. The records of these events have become foundational for belief and practice. The Abrahamic religions, Judaism, Christianity, and Islam, are rooted in people and events of the past and affirm that these people and events carry divine significance. Those who read the accounts of Moses, Jesus, or Muhammad, especially if they are adherents to the faith traditions that formed around these figures, have a clear point of view. Faith enters into the reading of the life and teachings of these great religious leaders. As faith entered into the discussion, the issue of the nature and interpretation of history became a fundamental concern, and hermeneutics, the study of interpretation, became a separate discipline.[2]

At stake was the question of whether historical study could accommodate the notion of the supernatural entrance into the flow of history. If the work of history is to describe as accurately as possible what has occurred, and to base the description on natural causes and conditions, then it becomes difficult to say, on the basis of history, that an event happened because of divine intervention and that God sent the resulting religious truth for the good of humankind. For example, the historian may say that Moses taught ethical principles in the Ten Commandments, but finds it difficult to say on historical grounds that Moses received from God the plates at Mt. Sinai on which the Ten Commandments were listed. A historian might say that Jesus was crucified, but apart from the presupposition of faith, one cannot on the basis of historical study say "for your sins." It is equally difficult for the historian, apart from a faith orientation, to say that Muhammad received the Word of God in his trances in a dark cave in the hills above Mecca, but a historian could say that Muhammad and his followers believed that he did.

If the presence of presuppositions in the work of a historian makes the task of historical study complex, so too does a *second* factor, namely that history is written in a particular time and place and *is generally targeted toward a well-defined audience.* The words of the historian or commentator on the meaning of events are shaped by the needs, assumptions, and understandings not only of the author, but also the reading public. Winston Churchill's several-volume history of the Second World War has a distinctly

2. The presence of presuppositions, and in particular the outlook of faith, raised the issue of hermeneutics to the forefront of biblical interpretation. It was basic to the writing of Bultmann, a prominent New Testament scholar in the early to mid-twentieth century. Gadamar's book *Jesus and the Word* spoke openly about the outlook of faith in understanding Jesus. Gadamar, *Truth and Method*, became required reading for biblical scholars as did a multitude of other works on the subject of hermeneutics.

British point of view, and he writes to help the British people understand the nature and causes of this many-faceted conflict. For our purposes, as we explore the teaching of Jesus, it is important to realize that the New Testament documents are written to guide and nurture the new Christian community. The Gospels, Matthew, Mark, Luke, and John, while intimately connected with the life of Jesus, are not biographies disciplined by the methods of contemporary historical scholarship, but extended sermons to bring guidance and faith to the Christian church that was forming. Faith is clearly present as a presupposition, and the events recorded allow for divine intervention and include what are called miracles or events that are outside of scientific ways of description and explanation. A. E. Harvey's book *Jesus and the Constraints of History* underlines this point and even captures the message in the title of the book.[3] As a way of compensating for this tension, theologians and biblical scholars spoke about two kinds of history, sacred and secular.[4] It was possible in the category of sacred history to postulate the entrance of the divine into the flow of human history, and much of the Christian theology in the middle of the twentieth century spoke directly about God's acts in history, a story told in both the Hebrew Bible and the New Testament.

A *third* complicating factor in the writing of history is the *scarcity and complex character of historical records*. It is difficult to find sufficient records to trace fully what actually happened prior to the age of the audio-visual recording of the history with direct access to decision-making in councils and parliaments, influential speeches, and key events. But even with modern technology that records in sight and sound major historical events, it is still not easy for the historian to discern all that happened and to ascertain the full meaning of the events. For example, we do have several recordings of the shooting of President John F. Kennedy, but there is still a measure of doubt about who was behind the murder and how it may have influenced the pattern of American life.

For our purposes, we must face these challenges in our goal to access the teaching of Jesus. For centuries, the Christian community and most of Christendom accepted the accounts as recorded in the four Gospels as being an accurate account of what he said and did. With the rise of the historical-critical method in historical research, beginning in the late eighteenth century and reaching maturity in the nineteenth and twentieth centuries, it wasn't long before the New Testament and the Gospels in particular began

---

3. I will occasionally use the phrase "the life and teaching(s) of Jesus" but want to underline that a full biography of Jesus is not possible given the records we have.

4. See, e.g., Richardson, *History Sacred and Profane*, and McIntire, *God, History, and Historian*. German authors used the words *historisch* and *heilsgeschichte* to distinguish between the two types of history.

to be studied using the methodologies of critical-historical research. There were those within the Christian community who continued to maintain that the records were accurate, and in fact were divinely guided and protected so that there would be a trustworthy account. According to the view of this more conservative tradition, the Scriptures were understood, at least in their original form, as being divinely inspired and in some cases even inerrant. There are many evangelical and orthodox Christians who still maintain this "high" view of Scripture and of the New Testament in particular. In fact there is a whole spectrum of positions in regard to the level at which the Bible and the New Testament in particular records and preserves for the believing community a trustworthy record and an authentic interpretation of the life and teachings of Jesus. The Bible continues to be the authority on matters of belief and practice.[5]

The mainstream of New Testament scholarship, while fully appreciating the New Testament as a source of information about the life and teachings of Jesus, view the record as having the limitations of a human effort to record sacred events for the benefit of the new Christian community. Those with this perspective would view, for example, that one basic task of New Testament scholars is to attempt to discern which of the words that are recorded in the Gospels as coming from Jesus were originally spoken by him or were inserted by others who thought they best represented what he said.[6] The answers vary across the spectrum. The other Abrahamic "cousins," Judaism and Islam, deal with the same issue. The Jewish community speaks about the authenticity of Torah (Law, or first 5 books of the Hebrew Bible) and the Muslim community trusts the record of the Qur'an. Indeed, the faithful followers of Islam believe that the Qur'an *is* the Word of God.

For many still faithfully engaged in Christian churches and mission, it has been difficult not to take into account the work of the critical-historical study of Scripture and of the Gospels in particular. This more progressive side of the Christian community acknowledges the human character of the Bible, but believes it still points to the foundational belief that God spoke to the human family in many ways and especially in Jesus.[7]

5. Reventlow addresses the issue of the authority of the Bible in matters of faith in *Authority of the Bible*.

6. I will speak more about this task of deciphering which sayings come directly from Jesus and which ones are inserted to meet the needs of the new Christian churches. The Jesus Seminar, more central to New Testament studies a decade or two ago, received a great deal of attention as it endeavored to determine which sayings attributed to Jesus in the Gospels came directly from him. See, e.g., Funk, *Honest to Jesus*.

7. A good representative of this point of view comes from a distinguished scholar, Wright, whose works include *Who Was Jesus?* and *The Original Jesus*. Again, there is a whole spectrum of positions and outcomes and enough books to fill a small library. The

Methods of Historical Study

A very brief summary of the range of research strategies in the historical-critical approach to the New Testament and especially the Gospels might be helpful at this point.[8] There are the usual disciplined inquiries that one does for nearly any historical study. To understand the events and literature of the past, it is necessary to understand the *historical context* that enables the reader to discern the point of view and line of thought of the writer and the historical events that are described. In a sense, there are two contexts which need examination, first, that of the writer and, second, that of the events which the writer describes. The writer's work is examined *internally* in terms of how a particular passage fits into the piece of writing and links to the chapter, page, and preceding and following paragraphs. There is a study of the language used by the writer, and it is examined from the perspective of the philosophy of language, linguistics, the meaning of words, and the syntax and details of grammar. In addition, there is the study of the trends of thought that may have influenced the writer, with an eye on assumptions and point of view. Then, there is a careful scrutiny of the *external* context that includes the time and place in history of the events described. Did the writer's point of view cause a partial distortion of the historical events being described or did it open up a valuable perspective on these events? What do other historians say about the same period of time? Historical study, as does all critical inquiry, has built into it a check and balance system, with historians carefully scrutinizing the work of their colleagues.

There are other research strategies that are more specific in character than the general study of context. They are not exclusively orientated to biblical study but are closely associated with the study of the Bible. The list is long, but let me mention five in particular.[9] The first is *textual criticism*, the task of sorting through the available copies of the texts that exist and seeking to find the most authentic text.[10] In some cases, the best text may be the oldest one and therefore closer to the time of the original writing, but its age does not always assure that it hasn't been changed by scribes who have copied the text. Part of the task is to find a text that does not appear to be

former Pope Benedict XVI (Joseph Ratzinger) also takes this position in his beliefs and writing. See *Jesus of Nazareth*, vol. 2, *Holy Week*.

8. See Ferguson, *Biblical Hermeneutics*, 68–78. See also the excellent summary by Powell, *Jesus as a Figure in History*, 31–50.

9. On occasion, different terms are used to describe these historical methods, and there is often some overlap.

10. A good account of this form of historical study of the Bible is Ehrman, *Misquoting Jesus*.

altered either because of an honest mistake such as missing a line, or one that has been altered to represent better a particular theological perspective. Examples of both accidental and purposeful change of the texts of the New Testament are numerous.

Another historical method is the study of the writing as a literary work of art, an approach that is called *literary criticism*. More recently as it developed exclusively in reference to the study of Gospels, two subcategories have emerged called *narrative criticism* and *social-scientific criticism*. Literary criticism is a more general term and often contains aspects of the other historical-critical approaches. It attempts to establish the meaning of a text by a careful study of the historical and literary environment. For example, a historian might study how the author of Matthew's Gospel was influenced by references in the Hebrew Bible. Or, on a slightly different tack, the historian might study how the King James translation was shaped by the English used at the time of the translation of the Bible.[11] The subjects of this study are to determine authorship, the resulting issue of authenticity, collaboration and derivative sources, revision, chronology, genre and even such details as the use of words, sentence structure, and paragraph construction. Because of the wide range of concerns grouped under the category of literary criticism, the term does carry some ambiguity. The terms, narrative criticism and social-scientific criticism narrow the scope of this strategy somewhat. For example, narrative criticism focuses on the literary dimensions of the individual Gospels with an emphasis on the place of story, including the metaphors and symbols of the story, as a means of articulating an important religious truth. A theological orientation, called narrative theology, grew out of this emphasis. One reputable scholar maintains that we should avoid the tendency to just look at an individual verse or saying of Jesus and miss the larger flow of the narrative. He argues that in an oral society, the narrative was told to the new Christian community, but unlikely read because of illiteracy. It was the meaning of the story, not just a key verse, which was central.[12] Social-scientific criticism studies the Gospels from the perspective of their social world.[13] A well-received and widely read book by John Dominic Crossan, *The Historical Jesus: The Life of a Mediterranean Jewish Peasant*, as the title implies, uses the social-scientific methodology and places Jesus in the first-century context of the peasant class.

The mention of dependence between the Gospels leads to another historical methodology called *source criticism*. The objectives of this aspect

---

11. Nicolson, *God's Secretaries*.

12. Horsely, *Prophet Jesus and the Renewal of Israel*, 95–100.

13. Tatum, *Quest of Jesus*.

of historical research are primarily three in number: (1) to trace the de-velopment of the document, observing how various sources contributed to the document's final form, as for example Mark's influence on Matthew and Luke, and Luke's acknowledgement of using sources in the writing of his Gospel (Luke: 1:1–4); (2) to evaluate the historical accuracy of the writing in light of its dependence on and reliability of sources, as for example how an-other source, perhaps the earliest source, often called Q (German for *Quelle* or source), may have shaped the Synoptic (Greek for "viewed together") Gospels; and (3) to determine the interdependence of the documents, as for example in the case of the Synoptic Gospels.

Another historical research methodology is called *form criticism*. Its goal in the study of the Gospels is to analyze the way that human experience is verbally expressed. This strategy uses a methodology that is common in understanding folk material and focuses on how the patterns of commu-nication govern human experience. The premises are that folk memory is both the primary vehicle of tradition and is preserved in small units. Iso-lating these units (forms) of the primitive tradition and discovering their usage in the life of a community (life situation) have the potential of reveal-ing how the Bible came to be in its present form. Smaller units (pericopes) have been cast in several forms including a pronouncement (often following a miracle), a narrative such as a story or parable, a legend, an aphorism, and a myth.[14] The scholars who contributed the most to this methodology are Martin Dibelius and Rudolf Bultmann, both influential New Testament scholars in the early to mid-twentieth century.[15]

I will mention one other research methodology used in many areas but essential in biblical study. It is called *redaction criticism* or the study of the way that the biblical authors and the scribes who copied the manuscripts edited and revised the manuscripts on which they were working. It is ap-parent that the material they received has been arranged and altered to fit an ordered structure to express their own theology or that of the church of their day and in some cases changing the original quite substantially.[16] One example is the way that the final chapter of the Gospel of Mark essentially closes (or the original has been lost) at 16:8, but additional verses have been added (vv. 9–20). It is also the case that the authors of Matthew and Luke redact the account from Mark that they use in their accounts.

With these various methodologies, biblical scholars attempt to ac-cess the life and teaching of Jesus. The outcomes of these disciplined and

---

14. Other terms are used to describe the nature of a particular form of expression.

15. Dibelius, *Jesus*; and Bultmann, *History of the Synoptic Tradition*.

16. See Perrin, *What Is Redaction Criticism?*

thoughtful quests, across decades and even centuries, have been very helpful although quite varied.[17] As I have briefly introduced thoughtful students and laypersons to these historical methodologies and inquiries, I have discovered a range of responses. Some, heavily invested in the life of the church, are somewhat threatened and want to stay well within traditional Christian teaching, and I have referred them to excellent scholars who continue to maintain that historical scholarship does not necessarily challenge a faith orientation and in fact can make it more credible as one adjusts to the "constraints of history."[18] Others have said that they do find it more difficult to affirm traditional creedal statements about Jesus, but nevertheless find insightful and helpful resources within Gospels as they seek a spiritual pathway and a foundation for their ethical convictions. Still others just want to learn, letting the facts speak for themselves, and they ask if there are other resources beside the Gospels for learning about the life and teachings of Jesus.

Sources apart from the Gospels

In answering this last inquiry, I always mention the references to Jesus in the New Testament apart from the Gospels and note Paul's writing in particular. It would be hard to overstate the influence Paul has had on the understanding of Jesus, and a multitude of books have been written describing and interpreting Paul's views.[19] It is important to note that Paul emphasizes in his writing the "Christ of faith" or the post-Easter Jesus. He is more interested in interpretation and the meaning of what Jesus said and did than he is in biographical facts of the life of Jesus. But there are many references to the humanity of Jesus in Paul's writing. For example, Paul speaks of the birth of Jesus (Rom 1:4; Gal 4:4), that Jesus was fully human (Phil 2:6), and gives considerable attention to his death (Gal 1:3; Rom 5:6–18; 1 Cor 1:30; 5:18; 15:3). Paul builds his theology on the resurrection of Jesus (1 Cor 15:5–9) that underscores the problem of historical study in treating events outside of the natural cause and effect sequences of historical description. For Paul,

17. There are many thoughtful summaries of the historical quest for Jesus. Among them are Grant, *Historian's Review of the Gospels*; Powell, *Jesus as a Figure in History*; and Theissen and Winter, *Quest for the Plausible Jesus*. In addition, there are volumes that attempt trace the interpretation of Jesus across the centuries: e.g., Pelikan, *Jesus through the Centuries*; Duling, *Jesus Christ through History*.

18. See Johnson, *Real Jesus*.

19. There are many classic works on Paul. Two more recent ones are Crossan and Reed, *In Search of Paul*, and Borg and Crossan, *First Paul*. One author, Davies, in *First Christian*, represents the view that Paul went well beyond the message of Jesus to found Christianity.

this event happened in time and space, as did the healings and miracles. Of course, he makes reference to the ethical teaching of Jesus as well and speaks directly about loving one's neighbor (Rom 13:9–10; 15:1–3). There are references as well to the important events that have become sacraments in the Christian church such as the last supper (1 Cor 11:23–26). Other writers of the New Testament documents apart from the Gospels also speak directly about the life and teaching of Jesus. For example there are references to the humanity of Jesus in the book of Acts (1:1–2), in Hebrews (2:14), and in 1 John (1:1–3 and 4:2) just to mention a few.

Of particular importance is perhaps the oldest source of information, called Q, that was used by the authors of Matthew and Luke.[20] Unfortunately, the Q documents are not available, but it is clear that these writers used Q as they describe similar events in the life of Jesus and record sayings of Jesus. At many points, these two Gospels differ from each other, but when there is agreement in the accounts it is likely that they drew upon the material in Q. The Q material tends to picture Jesus as a prophet who has come to announce the end of the present age and the coming of God's kingdom for which the followers of Jesus should be prepared. It would not be accurate to describe Q as another Gospel that has been lost but rather a collection of sayings that can only be inferred from other writings. But because Q antedates the Gospels, it is of great importance as it stresses the themes of the renewal of the covenant community and pictures Jesus as God's appointed prophet to call for renewal of first-century Judaism. As one reads the apocalyptic passages in the sayings of Jesus, some of which are in Q, it is possible to interpret them in way that maintains that Jesus was pointing to the end of history. A strong case can be made for this point of view, but I follow Richard Horsely in maintaining that Jesus spoke more directly in them about the renewal of Israel.[21]

In my teaching in higher education and the church community, I have also received many inquiries about whether there are references to Jesus near the time he lived that are not in the New Testament. It might be well, at this point, to mention these other resources and add these perspectives to the biblical accounts in order to learn as much as possible about the teachings of Jesus. These references are somewhat limited and also may have been altered some, but they do help confirm the historicity of Jesus.[22] Josephus, a Jewish historian who lived from the mid-thirties to the end of the first

---

20. Allison, *Constructing Jesus*, 23–25.

21. Horsely, *Prophet Jesus and the Renewal of Israel*, 79–94.

22. There are those who have questioned the historicity of Jesus. A thoughtful book that reviews this issue is Ehrman, *Did Jesus Exist?*

century CE, makes reference to Jesus in his *Antiquities of the Jews*. There is some reason to think that the manuscript of Josephus was altered in order to have this Jewish author make reference to Jesus in a positive manner, but the reference is important to confirm that Jesus lived and taught in first-century Palestine. The text reads in the following way: "About this time (i.e. while Pontius Pilate was governor of Judea, A.D. 26–36) there lived Jesus, a wise man, if indeed one ought to call him a man. For he was one who wrought surprising feats and was a teacher of such people as accept the truth gladly. He won over many Jews and many of the Greeks. He was the Messiah."[23] Whether this reference came from Josephus has been debated, but it is an early reference to Jesus and his character.

A Roman governor, Pliny, writes to the emperor Trajan in about 110 CE with some worry about the new Christian movement. However, following an investigation, he finds the movement somewhat harmless, though caught up in superstition. He does commend the founder of this new movement, Jesus, for teaching moral values and giving women an important leadership role. Suetonius (ca. 70–122 CE), also a Roman author, writes in *Lives of the Twelve Caesars* that the Jewish community during the reign of Emperor Claudius (41–54 CE) has been divided "at the instigation of Chrestos," a probable reference to the Greek form of Christ spelled Christos. Tacitus (ca. 55–117 CE), also a Roman historian, writes in his *Annals* that Christians were to blame for the fires that Nero was supposed to have set and refers to the Christian founder as Christus. The *Annals* also reference that Pontius Pilate put Jesus to death. These Roman references say little about the life and teachings of Jesus, but do speak of his influence.

There are a few comparable references to Jesus in early rabbinical sources and in the Dead Sea Scrolls, but little that gives us direct information about the teaching of Jesus. There has been some discussion about the possible influence of the Essene community, described in the Dead Sea Scrolls, upon Jesus, and there is evidence that Jesus was exposed to this movement. But there is little to indicate that Jesus endorsed the more sectarian strains in the Essene way of life. In summary, these sources not linked to the New Testament do confirm the existence of Jesus, the loyalty of his followers, his great influence even following his death, and the growth of the Christian movement that penetrated into the social strata of the Roman Empire.

There were also a number of writings within the larger Christian community that did not become a part of the New Testament. In some instances, these writings add valuable information about the teachings

---

23. *Antiquities* 18.63, quoted by Kee, *What Can We Know*, 7. Kee traces these early references to Jesus (6–19), as does Ehrman, in *Does Jesus Exist?*, 35–68.

of Jesus, although in many cases they are interpretations that grow out of later developments in smaller segments of the Christian movement. Many of them take the form of Gospel portrayals and often attach the names of the disciples of Jesus or other titles to their writing that would give them credibility. Among those that take the form of a narrative Gospel are the *Infancy Gospel of Thomas* and the *Infancy Gospel of James*. The narrative that carries the name of Thomas contains stories about the miraculous acts of the young Jesus and includes stories about how Jesus cursed one of his friends, a description that affirms his special powers but does not match the behavior we associate with the loving Jesus. The one with the name of James relates stories about the birth of Mary, the mother of Jesus, and her early life of dedication to temple worship and her marriage at the age of twelve to Joseph, an older widower with children from a prior marriage. Other writings in the genre of Gospel are the *Gospel of the Ebionites*, the *Gospel of the Hebrews*, and the *Gospel of the Nazoreans*, writings that are referenced by early church leaders, but which do not add vital information about the teaching of Jesus.[24]

Three others, the *Secret Gospel of Mark*, the *Gospel of Peter*, and the *Gospel of Thomas*, have received careful scrutiny by scholars who have attempted to discern if these accounts may have sayings that could be traced back to Jesus or helpful perspectives about the life of Jesus. In the case of the *Secret Gospel of Mark*, there is a letter of Clement of Alexandria (died ca. 215 CE) that was discovered in 1958. The letter contains two passages about Jesus which are not in the Gospel of Mark, and these passages speak about a person rising from the dead and about a young man with similarities to the one mentioned in Mark 14:51–52, often thought to be Mark, the disciple of Jesus. The *Gospel of Peter*, discovered in Egypt in 1886 and probably dating back to the eighth or ninth century CE, contains an account of the death and resurrection of Jesus. The author purports to be Peter, and he assumes the role of storyteller. The Gospel is likely an account based on the canonical Gospels, although the biblical scholar John Dominic Crossan has argued that there is an earlier account of the passion, called the Cross Gospel, which may have contributed to the accounts in the canonical Gospel that has received the most attention.[25] It is perseved in Coptic, but was thought to be originally written in Greek. The prologue in this writing claims an association with Thomas, one of the twelve, and speaks of the secret sayings that Jesus spoke. Jesus is portrayed in the writing as a gnostic

24. Tatum, *In Quest of Jesus*, 79–82.

25. Grant and Freedman, *Secret Sayings of Jesus*, provides a modern translation with commentary on the *Gospel of Thomas*.

wisdom teacher whose words lead to eternal life, and many of the sayings have parallels in the four canonical Gospels.[26]

What Can We Know?

The brief summary of the sources available for accessing the teaching of Jesus and the challenges raised by the "constraints" of history suggest a fundamental question to which we now turn. It is: What then can we know about the life and teaching of Jesus? At an earlier point in New Testament scholarship, from the beginning of the twentieth century until mid-century, there were outstanding scholars who doubted whether the New Testament sources available to us, written many years after the life of Jesus, infused with cultural and theological presuppositions, and layered as they are with copying and translations, could reveal very much about Jesus and his teaching.[27] But more recent biblical scholarship has maintained that we can know a significant amount about the context, the life, and the teaching of Jesus, although such knowledge is always obtained with care and discipline in the search.[28] A look at the search over time and its current status will place us on a more firm foundation as we prepare ourselves to understand the teachings of Jesus.

The Life of Jesus: What We Can Know

We turn first to what we can know about the life of Jesus. As we go along, we will provide more information about the life of Jesus, but at this point our goal is to summarize current research and to demonstrate that we can know a sufficient amount about his life on which to have a credible foundation for a faith commitment and an authentic spiritual pathway. It is the case that Christians live "by faith and not by sight"[29] but the leap of faith is best taken from a reliable base. Over the past several decades, New Testament scholars have worked diligently to establish that base and to provide a good option for launching our faith inquires and spiritual practices.[30]

---

26. See Pagel's book *Gnostic Gospels* for a full account of the *Gospel of Thomas* and its importance in understanding the teaching of Jesus.

27. Bultmann, *Jesus and the Word*, 11–19.

28. See, e.g., Keck, *Future for the Historical Jesus*, and Eckardt, *Reclaiming the Jesus of History*.

29. 2 Cor 5:17.

30. See the excellent account of the search in Dawes, *Historical Jesus Quest*. See also Theissen and Winter, *Quest for the Plausible Jesus*.

At the beginning of the twentieth century, based largely on the pivotal work of Albert Schweitzer, it was widely held that many of the histories (Lives) of Jesus, written in the previous centuries, were largely shaped by the history and culture out of which the author came and wrote.[31] While many of these lives of Jesus had good historical information in them and were often informative and inspiring, they were partially limited by inadequate historical information, not because the authors did not make a sincere effort to do historical study, but because new historical information and methodologies were not always available.[32] Many, of course, were written out of a faith orientation with the purpose of nurturing faith, and most of these interpreters of Jesus continued to *maintain* a relatively orthodox understanding of the "Christ of faith." *To maintain and sustain a traditional faith understanding is one clear choice and option to the historical challenge of accessing Jesus and his teaching.* This point of view is often built upon a high level of trust in the accounts in the Synoptic Gospels, and in most cases, these studies target a Christian community that holds the common assumptions of a particular time and place in history. One author, who has great respect for these accounts, nevertheless, after reviewing these writings, wisely recommends caution about "modernizing Jesus."[33] It is a part of the Christian way to bring the life and teachings to a place of intersection and relevance to a setting in which people struggle to find meaning and guidance; it is integral to the teaching and preaching mission of the church. But it is always a risk as we so easily create Jesus in our own image and fail to deal directly with this first-century Jewish teacher and prophet whose history, culture, and ways of understanding the world were quite different from our own.

In part influenced by the paradigmatic work of Schweitzer and many critical studies leading up to his work, other biblical scholars branched out in several directions. Another strategy, beyond maintaining classical orthodox views was *to reaffirm the "historic biblical Christ,"* not merely because the Bible and church tradition "tell me so" but by exploring ways to argue that the so-called quest of the historical Jesus was a "blind alley,"[34] at

31. Schweitzer, *Quest of the Historical Jesus.*

32. In my early interest in this subject, I read with great interest the classic works of Edersheim, *Life and Times of Jesus the Messiah*; Farrar, *Life of Christ*; and Renan, *Life of Jesus*; and the popular work by Sheldon, *In His Steps.* Because of my Scottish heritage and education, I read and was influenced by Baillie's *God Was in Christ*; Barclay's *Mind of Jesus*; and Stewart's *Life and Teaching of Jesus.*

33. Cadbury, *Peril of Modernizing Jesus.*

34. Dawes, *Historical Quest,* 216–38, quoting from Kahler, *So-Called Historical Jesus.*

least for finding a foundation for faith. The German scholar Martin Kahler (1835–1912) was an important spokesperson for this strategy, one that was not just a conservative and polemical attempt to preserve the historic faith, but one which raised a serious question about whether the quest for the historical Jesus would uncover accurate and trustworthy information and whether what was discovered would provide a foundation for faith.

Kahler's thoughtful questioning of the assumptions of the so-called quest for the historical Jesus opened the door for two of the most influential Christian scholars of the early to mid-twentieth century to probe the issues. There were Rudolf Bultmann (1884–1976) and Karl Barth (1886–1968), one an influential New Testament scholar and the other a distinguished theologian. Rudolf Bultmann, the German New Testament scholar recognized how difficult it was to find one's way back to the historical Jesus. He maintained that our New Testament records are limited and that they are documents designed to sustain the faith of the early Christian community. Further, they have mythological assumptions about the world and divine activity in history. He suggested that the inherent worldview of the New Testament needs to be demythologized, and he maintained that we could know very little about the Jesus of history. As one writing from within the Christian family, he affirmed that the Christ of faith comes to us not through historical inquiry, but through the proclamation of the gospel. His method is fully aware of the historical realities, and his position, in large measure because of the limits of historical information, becomes essentially theological in character; God speaks to us in the kerygmatic proclamation that we hear and claim by faith.

Swiss theologian Karl Barth also recognized the challenge of finding the hidden Christ buried in the pages of the New Testament and lurking behind the historical events of first-century Palestine. He believed that historical scholarship surrounding the events of the life of Jesus was important, but he, like the Apostle Paul, devotes little attention to the historical Jesus, in large part due to his theological convictions about the way of the divine revelation. There is, says Barth, an "infinite qualitative distinction between time and eternity" implying that no human claim to know God is possible which includes an effort based solely on historical study. Barth says that we should say a decisive "no" to human quests to find God, but an enthusiastic "yes" to the revelation of God. In this way, he deals with the all too human character of the Bible and of the New Testament in particular. He avoids the simple identification of the Bible with revelation, but does see the Bible as "containing" that revelation. The Bible does tell a trustworthy and compelling story about how revelation occurs, pointing to the divinely appointed prophets and apostles. We read the text to learn about and know God, but we pay attention to the subject of the text, not its human limitations. It is the Bible that points us to the personal incarnation of God's Word, the coming of Jesus Christ, and the revelation of God's will and way in the world.[35] God speaks to us through the Bible, and therefore Barth can speak of the Bible as "the Word of God," but it is the message of God coming to the human family through Abraham and the great prophets, and ultimately in the person of Jesus Christ. Barth's position was often referred to as neo-orthodoxy in that it was a reaffirmation of traditional Christian belief.

Bultmann (Lutheran) and Barth (Reformed) spoke for the whole Christian family, but came to their task from Protestant backgrounds. Roman Catholic theologians also spoke eloquently about how it is possible to reaffirm the central tenets of the Christian faith, even with the challenges presented by historical study. The distinguished Catholic theologian Edward Schillebeeckx undertakes this task in his extraordinary two-volume study, *Jesus: An Experiment in Christology* and *Christ: The Experience of Jesus as Lord*. The work is comprehensive and complex and merits careful study. But suffice to say for our purposes, Professor Schillebeeckx argues for a "post-critical, narrative history."[36] Like Karl Barth, he is more concerned with the story that is told in the Gospels than he is with the work of critical study. "What matters is the truth of the story itself, that is, whether it 'turns us on,' strikes home and makes us the active subject of a new story."[37] His concern is with the identity of Jesus, not with the fact that the story is told by those who lived and wrote in a precritical era. The New Testament must be searched for clues that may be able to guide the human quest for salvation, and he *reaffirms* that we discover and claim by faith God's definitive saving activity in Jesus of Nazareth. Schillebeeckx's contemporary Bernard Lonergan undertakes a careful analysis of critical historical study.[38] He too, without discounting the realities of critical historical study, is able to affirm with integrity the reality of God's disclosure in Jesus of Nazareth.

In this period of the mid- to late twentieth century, there was also a turn toward liberation theology, a movement that understood the Jesus of history as a model for the pursuit of justice. The movement, originating in Latin America, had great influence all across the Christian world. It argued persuasively that we must understand the historical circumstances of Jesus

35. See Dawes, *Historical Jesus Quest*, 268–75, and Barth, *CD*, vol. 1, *Doctrine of the Word of God*, pt. 2.

36. Schillebeeckx, *Jesus*, 77–102.

37. Ibid., 77.

38. Lonergan, *Method in Theology*, 153–85. See also Tracy, *Analogical Imagination*, 248–304; Rahner, *Foundations of Christian Faith*, 178–321; and Küng, *On Being a Christian*, 228–321.

and use the understanding of the age of Jesus and the model of Jesus to challenge the unjust social structures that exist in the present world. It is the life of Jesus, about which we know a sufficient amount, which should guide the current mission of the Christian church.[39]

The quest for the historical Jesus does not end with Bultmann's inclination to say that we can know little about Jesus and Barth's affirmation that the historical text is less important than the message. Nor does it end with the finest expression of Roman Catholic thought in second half of the twentieth century, which finds a way through the historical underbrush to reaffirm the New Testament's message that the Jesus of history is integral to the foundation of Christian faith. The influence of these great theologians of the past generation was extraordinary and will continue. But their foundational work did not prevent the continuing quest for the historical Jesus and the many questions that it raises. *A third response to the challenge of history was the new quest for the historical Jesus.* It became a central focus of both New Testament scholars and indeed, of the entire Christian church. This trend, which took expression in stages, was firmly committed to understanding the life and teaching of Jesus. In many cases, these efforts were undertaken without the presupposition of a faith orientation or the motive to guide the Christian community.

W. Barnes Tatum, in his excellent history of the quest of Jesus, articulates several stages to the quest. He provides the following outline:[40]

Period 1: Pre-Quest (before 1778), period of precriticism

Period 2: Old Quest (1778–1906), period of source criticism

Period 3: No Quest (1906–1953), period of form criticism

Period 4: New Quest (1953–1985), period of redaction and
    narrative criticisms

Period 5: Post-Quest (since 1985), period of social-scientific criticism

Professor Tatum makes it clear in his discussion that the Post-Quest era since 1985 did not mean the quest was over, but that its original strategies have morphed into new approaches. The focus continues to be on the Jesus of history that is entirely justified. But the motive for the quest tends to

---

39. A pivotal book in the movement of liberation theology is Gutierrez, *Theology of Liberation.* A very thoughtful book by Echegaray, *Practice of Jesus,* goes directly to the life of Jesus, assuming that one can know how he lived and what he taught. See also Boff, *Jesus Christ Liberator;* Bonino, *Faces of Jesus;* and Sobrino, *Christology at the Crossroads.*

40. Tatum, *In Quest of Jesus,* 87–109.

be more theologically neutral and less driven by the need to help the Christian community find a way to manage the challenge of history. However, there continues to be writing which attempts to help Christians understand and be comfortable with the challenges of history,[41] and some authors focus on the need to help "true believers" recover from the disillusionment of discovering that the Bible is a quite human book.[42]

A brief discussion of the new quest in its several forms may be helpful at this point as a way to move to a discussion of gaining access to the teaching of Jesus. Those who had been students or influenced by Bultmann and Barth initially led the new quest. Hans Conzelmann, a former student of Rudolf Bultmann, published an essay in 1953, which he had prepared for the occasion of a meeting of Bultmann's former students.[43] It became a call to resume the study of the historical Jesus. The new effort was not aimed at writing a biography of Jesus nor did it seek to understand the psychology of the development of Jesus. It was clear from the start of the new quest that there is not sufficient historical information to merit these inquiries. The separation of the Jesus of history and the Christ of faith would be acknowledged, but in his essay is the clear desire to establish continuity between the Christ of faith and the Jesus of history. Certain historical conclusions could be reached and provide a means to make the leap of faith from the historical Jesus. Other scholars followed Conzelmann's outline including another one of Bultmann's students, Günther Bornkamm.[44] Professor Bornkamm avoided the attempt at a biography and focused on the message of Jesus, and his book became a model for the new quest. American scholar James M. Robinson, in his essay "New Quest," gave a name to the movement.[45] The new quest and new patterns of the quest continue into the present. Occasionally, New Testament scholars will speak of a second or even a third new quest, each with a slightly different approach and emphasis. Different views of Jesus had developed, but nearly all of them have put the emphasis on Jesus as a historical person, a first-century Jew who lived in Palestine and who taught and acted in dramatic and influential ways.

41. There are many examples that help Christians find their way. Borg's *Meeting Jesus Again for the First Time* is a good example.

42. Meyers, *Saving Jesus from the Church*, and Bawer, *Stealing Jesus*, are sincere efforts to help those who struggle with earlier beliefs and hope to find a new place to stand.

43. Conzelmann, *Jesus*.

44. Bornkamm, *Jesus of Nazareth*. This volume had a great influence on my development.

45. Quoted by Tatum, *In Quest of Jesus*, 101. Robinson's essay is entitled "New Quest of the Historical Jesus."

The Teaching of Jesus

Among the legacies of the new quest, continuing to the present, was the challenge of determining which material in the Gospels was authentic. Did it originate with Jesus and remain essentially intact primarily in oral form across the decades between the ministry of Jesus and the time it took written form in the Gospels? Certain criteria have been developed in New Testament scholarship to discern which of the recorded sayings of Jesus may be considered authentic and which were redacted or added in order for the author of the Gospels to structure and order the story and to express a theological point of view. A review of these criteria and the results of the inquiry will move us forward in our trek to the teaching of Jesus.

Several criteria have developed over the past several decades as historians have attempted to determine whether or not the actions and teaching of Jesus, which are attributed to him, actually occurred as they have been recorded the Gospels. The inquiry has a measure of sensitivity in that many of the events and sayings of Jesus have been questioned. In some cases, an action or unit of teaching may be judged as having a historical core, but the expansion and interpretation of the acts and words may not have been present in the moment, but expanded to express a point of view and to guide the new Christian community. In other cases, an event or a pericope may be judged to not have occurred, but inserted to give the oral tradition and the subsequent writing needed structure and theological perspective.

A good example, expressed recently by the former pope, Joseph Ratzinger, is whether the infancy narratives in Matthew and Luke are historical accounts or theological reflections.[46] Was Jesus born in Bethlehem or was he Jesus *of Nazareth*? Did Matthew, drawing heavily upon his desire to place Jesus in the lineage of David, put the place of the birth of Jesus in Bethlehem as the family home of King David? It did cause a bit of a stir to have the pope raise questions about the stories of Christmas and their importance to us for the traditional celebrations of our most important Christian holiday.

Those of us on this side of the revolution in critical historical inquiry might ask why Matthew and Luke were not more concerned with historical accuracy. Our answer is that they were not critical historical scholars, but interpreters of the meaning of the coming of Jesus. They had both oral tradition and some written material in front of them, and they used what they had to tell their story. For Matthew, the goal was to understand Jesus as part of God's ongoing redemptive work with and through the children of

---

46. Ratzinger, *Jesus of Nazareth: The Infancy Narratives*, 58–66.

Israel, and in Luke's Gospel the goal was to speak of a universal message for all people, including Gentiles whom we call the "three wise men."

One can appreciate the universal message of the Gospel accounts, but it does not prevent us from asking the historical questions. As we ask these questions, we do so with a sincere desire to know and understand, and, with the methodologies now at hand, to enable us to better access a "plausible Jesus."[47] Many approaches in searching for a plausible Jesus have been used, and they are generally referred to as the criteria for access. These criteria might be grouped in five major categories.

The first, called the *criterion of dissimilarity*, holds that the sayings and teachings of Jesus in the Gospels might be judged as authentic if they are not like sayings of the early church, on one hand, or of the contemporary Judaism of the time of Jesus on the other hand.[48] To use this criterion assumes a full knowledge of early church history and ancient Judaism. The goal is to find those sayings of Jesus which are distinctive and integral to *his teaching and understanding*, not ones that have been attributed to him, often sincerely, in order to give authority to the emerging theology of the church and to separate Jesus from the Judaism of his time. One theme that has been underlined as directly from Jesus is his teaching on the kingdom of God, and its unique character as being both present and future. Even the phrase "the kingdom of God" is not as central in Judaism or in the thought of other early Christian leaders such as the Apostle Paul. Also mentioned is the way that Jesus speaks about the ethical norms in the Torah without referencing a precedent, which was always present in the teaching of other rabbis, the way he speaks of God intimately as *Abba*, and his use of parables.[49] Such a criterion, if used wisely and well, allows us to claim a great deal of what is attributed to Jesus as authentic, that is, as coming from him and not inserted by an author with good intentions, but without the foundation of history.

A second criterion and one more accessible to the thoughtful reader and not exclusively the purview of the New Testament scholar is called *multiple attestation*. The goal of this strategy suggests that if sayings and actions of Jesus are found in several sources, such as Mark, Q, Matthew, Luke, and John, then there is the likelihood that it is something that Jesus said or did. These several sources, each in their own way, describe Jesus as one who spoke in parables, reached out to those who were discriminated against

47. Theissen and Winter, *Quest for the Plausible Jesus*, speaks directly to this concern.

48. Theissen and Winter make the criteria of dissimilarity the main theme in their book *Quest for the Plausible Jesus*.

49. Tatum, *In Quest of Jesus*, 106–7. I will follow Professor Tatum's listing the five criteria. One recent study of Jesus, Allison's *Constructing Jesus*, employs all of these criteria in a persuasive way.

and lived on the margins, challenged the religious leaders of his time, and engaged in acts of healing and exorcism. This method has been used even before the rise of the historical criticism of the biblical accounts, but has been continued and increased in importance with the emergence of the use of nonbiblical sources, such as Q and the *Gospel of Thomas*.

A third criterion is called by different names, but one common title is the *criterion of embarrassment*. The thesis of this criterion is the affirmation that those sayings and actions of Jesus that would have been seen as an embarrassment for the church would not have been made up by the church and inserted into the manuscript. Among those actions and sayings of Jesus in this category is the baptism of Jesus by John, an act of repentance and cleansing which goes against the claim that Jesus was sinless. Another is the conflict that Jesus has with his family as he begins his ministry in Nazareth, but later his mother Mary and his brother James are prominent in the life of the church. Other examples are Peter's denial of being a follower of Jesus at the time of crucifixion and the betrayal of Jesus by Judas, both signs that Jesus may have not always chosen the best people to be his disciples.

A fourth criterion, more of a historical check than a positive attribute, is often called the *criterion of language and environment*. The goal of using this criterion is to judge whether the sayings and actions of Jesus match the culture of first-century Palestine. It provides a way of discerning whether a saying or an action of Jesus was said or done by Jesus or whether, again perhaps with the best intentions, it has been inserted by an author to provide context and character to the description of Jesus.[50] Linguists and historians, to discern whether these events in the life of Jesus were authentic, scrutinized many of the foundational sayings and actions of Jesus. This criterion also crosses languages as discernment is made whether the statement might be compatible with the common language of Jesus, Aramaic.

A fifth and final criterion that has been used widely and has similarities to one or two of the other criteria (e.g., multiple attestations) is what is called the *criteria of coherence*. The goal in the application of this criterion is to place many of the events in the life of Jesus alongside those that are considered authentic and if they address similar themes, do they cohere with those that are judged to be activities of the historical Jesus? Using this criterion with care and discipline does expand the amount of material in the Gospels that may be judged to be authentic sayings and actions of Jesus. Not infrequently, this criterion is applied to some of the titles used to describe Jesus, and in particular the title of "Son of Man." Do the many uses of the

---

50. Several contemporaries of Bultmann, while respectful of his work, nevertheless continued in the quest of the historical Jesus. Among them are Dodd, *Founder of Christianity*, and Jeremias, *Parables of Jesus*.

phrase attributed to Jesus on several occasions have a common meaning? There continues to be some debate about the meaning and use of the title by Jesus. But it is the most common title used by Jesus to refer to himself and when it is attributed to Jesus in a passage, it increases the likelihood that the passage is authentic. The general consensus of New Testament scholarship is that the phrase is consistently used by Jesus as a way of speaking about the futuristic and apocalyptic dimensions of the kingdom of God. The conversation continues on this issue, but it does illustrate the way in which the criterion of coherence is applied.

One Part of the Terrain

Our goal in this chapter has been to describe one part of our quest to access and understand the teaching of Jesus. We have described it as a trek across the unpredictable terrain of history, a trail that must be followed if we are to arrive at our destination. Fortunately, other good and gifted people have crossed this terrain and recorded guidelines for us to follow. We have excellent maps and much to draw upon as we begin our arduous hike. In the records of those who have gone before us is a range of viewpoints, not unexpected in that all of us see different sights as we walk. These different sights give us marvelous perspectives and shades of meaning, and they enable and invite us to put our impressions together in different ways. But as we do, we discover that there is a common core, a set of historical events that provide us with a foundation, a base from which to take our leap of faith.[51]

We know, for example, that Jesus was born in Palestine and reached maturity in the village of Nazareth. Near the age of thirty, he sensed an emerging vocation, left Nazareth, and had contact with John the Baptist, the prophet who called his listeners to repentance and renewal. John baptized Jesus, an event Jesus understood as a time of commitment to his life's vocation. Jesus then began his public ministry, returning to the region of Galilee, and made the village of Capernaum his base. There he called men and women to follow him, and selected a special group of twelve to assist him in his mission. He engaged in healings and exorcisms and proclaimed the nearness, and even the presence of the kingdom of God. He embodied grace and truth and people sought access to him. He taught that God was personal and loving, and sensed that he was God's son, calling God *Abba*. He taught an ethic of love, love for God and love for one's neighbor. In time, with his disciples, he traveled to Jerusalem where he boldly challenged the temple system, was arrested by Roman authorities, and eventually died by

51. Charlesworth, *Jesus within Judaism*, 169.

crucifixion. Those who followed him, believing that he rose from the dead, began a movement that was to become the Christian church.

It is this history that we seek to understand, and in this endeavor, we must now engage in a historical inquiry about the setting in which Jesus taught and healed. We continue our trek to the teaching of Jesus with the conviction that both the content and method of his teaching were intimately related to his historical context.

Study Resources

Discussion Questions

1. What are the challenges and responsibilities of the historian in framing a picture of a past event or era?

2. In what ways does the biblical record of the life and teachings of Jesus provide a reliable foundation on which to pursue a religious life?

3. What are the limitations of the biblical record as an authoritative guide for belief and practice?

4. In what ways are we able to find guidance from the teachings and traditions of the Christian church as we seek to understand the life and teachings of Jesus?

5. In what ways might a community of people with common beliefs and practices assist us in our trek over the unpredictable terrain of following the pattern of life taught and modeled by Jesus?

Terms and Concepts

1. Pre-understanding: The assumptions about reality that we bring to the goal of making sense out of what we experience and encounter.

2. Textual Criticism: The task of sorting through the several records of historical events in order to find the one that is most likely to reflect an account of what actually happened.

3. Constraints of History: The fact that it is not easy to recover the past in that we read the records through our presuppositions, have limited and conflicting records, and are unable to use the natural cause and effect logic of history to deal with events that claim divine intervention.

4. Q (German word for *Quelle* or source): A resource of possible sayings and actions of Jesus, now lost, but which are in evidence in the Gospels of Matthew and Luke.

5. Criterion of Dissimilarity: A view that maintains that the teachings of Jesus may be more authentic if they are not the teachings of the early church or the Judaism of the time of Jesus; they are unique to Jesus.

Suggestions for Reading and Reference

Borg, Marcus J. *Jesus: Uncovering the Life, Teachings, and Relevance of a Religious Revolutionary*. San Francisco: HarperSanFrancisco, 2006.

Harvey, A. E. *Jesus and the Constraints of History*. Philadelphia: Fortress, 1982.

Johnson, Luke Timothy. *The Real Jesus: The Misguided Quest for the Historical Jesus and the Truth of the Traditional Gospels*. San Francisco: HarperSanFrancisco, 1997.

Powell, Mark Allan. *Jesus as a Figure in History: How Modern Historians View the Man from Galilee*. Louisville: Westminster John Know, 1998.

Tatum, W. Barnes. *In Quest of Jesus*. Nashville: Abingdon, 1999.

Theissen, Gird, and Dagmar Winter. *The Quest for a Plausible Jesus: The Question of Criteria*. Translated by M. Eugene Boring. Louisville: Westminster John Knox, 2002.

2

Accessing the Teaching of Jesus
The Historical Setting

WE CONTINUE OUR DEMANDING trek across the rocky terrain of historical study with the goal of arriving at our destination with a better understanding of the teaching of Jesus. We noted in the preceding chapter that our challenge is spanning the gap of two thousand years, across history, languages, and cultures and attempting to discover what he *said and did*. He taught, as all great teachers, in both word and deed. We focused in chapter 1 on the records of his life and teaching with special attention to the Gospels. We identified the components of the challenge and the strategies suggested by critical-historical study to maximize the information that can be obtained from the written records. We called attention to the following challenges:

1. These records and in particular the Gospels were written many years after the life of Jesus by people who shared the worldview of their time.

2. These records were not based on or informed by historical-critical study nor were they attempts to write biography. Historical and biographical information are present, but the genre is *gospel* or good news to nurture and guide an emerging Christian community.

3. These primary records, the Gospels, were written in *koine dialektos*, the common language of Greek spoken in the Hellenistic world and the language of the New Testament. Aramaic, spoken by Jesus, is in the background. They have been translated and copied and have been changed in this process. We have no access to the original writings.

4. We read these records, even if we are self-aware regarding our presuppositions, through the lenses of our time and place in history, our values and beliefs, and the rich and many-faceted character of the traditions of interpretation, and especially the Christian understanding of their meaning and importance.

5. We noted that there are other documents, often referred to as gnostic or wisdom writings, and that the *Gospel of Thomas* in particular is important to the quest to understand Jesus.[1]

Our task of interpreting these records has these challenges. The records do not prevent access to Jesus but do invite a measure of humility and care as we read the records in the Gospels and the other literature of the time of Jesus. We listed ways that New Testament scholars have utilized in order to find their way across this terrain and listed several historical strategies that aid in finding the best record. We began by saying that all historical documents are better understood when there is a thorough study of the context and language in which they were written and an inquiry regarding the purposes of the author. We went on to describe several more detailed methods, including:

1. Textual criticism: the effort to find the most trustworthy texts, the ones which reflect most accurately the intent of the original author;

2. Literary criticism: the study of the nature (genre) of the literature, the use of language, and the intended purpose of the writing. We identified two more specialized approaches within the general category of literary criticism, one focusing on the narrative or the story and how it communicates a message, and the other probing the historical setting from a social-scientific perspective to understand the customs and culture of Jesus.

3. Source criticism: the identification of the sources which may have been used by the author and the reliability of these sources;

4. Form criticism: exploring the way that the Gospels often come to us in small units called periscopes. These units express human experience in particular ways or "forms" in a life situation and the method is much like that of an anthropologist who works with folk literature and artifacts.

1. Bourgeault, *Wisdom Jesus*, is especially cogent in making the case that Jesus was exposed to the wisdom tradition.

5. Redaction criticism: the ways the manuscripts have been altered either by accident or by intention to steer the literature in a way that organizes the writing and expresses a point of view.

We utilize these historical strategies and are guided by them in our reading as we attempt to learn about the life and teachings of Jesus. In short, we learn about the teaching of Jesus by reading the Gospels in an informed way. But we do not discount other more common ways of reading the Gospels such as seeking inspiration, ethical guidance, and spiritual nurture. We went on to describe several ways that scholars have used to identify those sayings, attributed to Jesus in the Gospels, which clearly have their origin in what actually occurred and what he likely said. We spoke about five criteria which are often used in this endeavor: the criterion of dissimilarity, the criterion of multiple attestation, the criterion of embarrassment, the criterion of language as common in the setting and environment, and the criterion of coherence.

We implied that a more general study of context would also help us gain access to the teaching of Jesus and give us a better understanding of what he said and how he said it. We learn by a thorough study of his historical setting. Our assumption is that even the great teachers and sages who point beyond the limitations of their time to that which is universal nevertheless frame their teaching within the language and culture of their moment in the flow of history. They act and speak out of historical circumstances. The teaching of Jesus, while radical and challenging many of the assumptions and social circumstances of his historical context, still comes to us in the language and thought of first-century Judaism in the land of Palestine. The goal of this chapter is to explore the way the extraordinary teaching of Jesus is shaped by his world.

The World of Jesus: The Land[2]

It is easy to forget, as we are caught up in the Gospel accounts of the life of Jesus that he was born in a small province of the Roman Empire, Palestine, and inherited a Jewish legacy filled with the stories of Abraham, Moses, kings such as David, and the great prophets. He came to an environment with an identity, beliefs, and values and to a home where he was cared for in

---

2. Connick, in his book *Jesus: The Man, the Mission, and the Message*, 107, describes the context of the life and teaching of Jesus. I will occasionally follow Connick's discussion of the world of Jesus.

his infancy, was taught as a boy, and matured. As Luke says, he "increased in wisdom and in stature, and in favor with God and people."[3]

The land in which he was born has many names, Canaan (lowland), and within the religions that honor the events which occurred there, the Promised Land and the Holy Land. Its most common name is Palestine, although this name has political nuances for the Jewish citizens of Israel because it generally refers to the Arab-Palestinian population. The southern part of the region is called Judea and the northern part is referred to as Galilee. Galilee is often divided into three regions: Upper Galilee (with mountains and streams), Lower Galilee, which is hilly, and the land around the Sea of Galilee. The majority of the area in which Jesus lived is within the current national boundaries of modern-day Israel. He also taught and healed in the outlying areas in the West Bank and perhaps Gaza, areas that are now often referred to as the Palestinian territories.

The leaders of Rome may have thought of the region as a distant and unimportant corner of the empire. But in spite of the stereotype of the region by some Roman leaders, the area was in fact very strategic, linking three continents (Europe, Asia, and Africa) and serving as a crossroads for armies seeking power and influence. The boundaries of the region at the time of the birth of Jesus were somewhat porous and stretched from north to south approximately 150 miles with a width from 35–50 miles. Modern-day Lebanon, where Jesus may have also been present, is to the north, Syria to the northeast, Jordon to the east, the Arabian Desert and the Sinai Peninsula to the south, and the Mediterranean Sea to the west.

The topography of the region is diverse, with coastal plains and ports, desert regions, fertile farmland, and highlands to the north. The Jordan River, flowing north to south, is often thought of as a boundary; hence the region is called the "West Bank" or west of the Jordan River.[4] The Lake of Galilee was and continues to be a source of food from fishing. The Dead Sea is toward the southern edge. The climate has similarities to the climate of parts of California, with warm summers, cooler winters, and limited rainfall. The area became the setting for the life and teachings of Jesus, and his teaching is full of references to the land that was his home.

3. Luke 2:52. The Greek word *anthropos* is translated as "men" in some versions, but I have chosen "people" in that it speaks of Jesus being respected by all of those around him.

4. See Crossan's discussion of the role of the Jordon River in section 2, entitled "The Jordon Is Not Just Water," in *Jesus: A Revolutionary Biography*, 29–53.

Levels of Government and Leadership[5]

The region with its nearly three million people had overlapping governments, as evidenced by the way Jesus was tried and convicted.[6] The story
of Jesus begins approximately at the time of Herod the Great's death in 4
BCE. The Romans gave Herod, an Idumean ruler outside of the Jewish inner
circle, the authority to rule over Palestine.[7] The Romans had given him the
authority to select his successor, and he chose to divide the region between
his sons. Archelaus was appointed king of Judea in the south, Antipas was
designated as tetrarch of Galilee and Perea, and Philip became tetrarch of
the region northeast of Galilee. These appointments needed the approval
of Rome and approval was sought from Augustus. After some turmoil and
rebellion, Augustus essentially approved these appointments with the exception of the demotion of Archelaus to the title of ethnarch, a title that
lacked the status of king. His leadership was ineffective, and he often of-
fended Jewish values. The situation got out of control when he married his
brother's widow while he was still in a marriage relationship. Augustus sent
him away to Gaul and put in a Roman procurator to rule the region, one of
whom we meet later in the story, Pontius Pilate, who ruled the region from
26–36 CE. Jesus, at the point of his arrest and trial, encountered these two
layers of government—Herodian and Roman. Across the formative years
of the life of Jesus, he observed how these governments functioned and the
ways in which the occupied territory of Palestine was governed. Rome did
allow for local rule, and it is accurate to say that the government systems
had a *modest* measure of justice. However, Jesus saw injustice especially in
reference to the poor. He did strongly react when Antipas decapitated John
the Baptist. John had denounced Antipas, the ruler of Galilee, regarding his
marital practices and Antipas, fearing John's power with the masses, took
this action.

A third level of government, centered in Jerusalem, was the home rule
of the Sanhedrin, a Jewish ruling council of seventy people that functioned
much like a high court. It was made up of the leaders of the Jewish community and decided on disputed points of the law, and more generally the
life and customs of the Jewish people. Within the Sanhedrin were several
religious leaders. There were *priests* who served the people in their places
of worship. They cared for the sanctuary, presided at the altar of the temple,
and guided the people in their spiritual practices. They were especially

5. Connick, *Jesus*, 38–57.

6. See Ratzinger, *Jesus of Nazareth: Holy Week*, 167–201.

7. Idumaea was the Greek name given to the region in Judea from Beth-zur to
south of Beer-sheba.

concerned about the purity and holiness of the people and performed the rites of atonement. Jesus raised questions about whether the current religious practices led to vital religious life, and in part because of his penetrating questions, there was some tension as he later encountered members of the Sanhedrin and the high priest in his trial.

There was a second group of people who belonged to a religious order called the *Levites*. They served as temple assistants and were often thought of by those present in the temple as priests, although they did not have the full authority of priests. A third group, *scribes*, many of whom were priests, had a special responsibility. Their function was less priestly in character and more concerned with understanding the Torah. They were experts on what it said and were dedicated to ensuring that its message was understood and not in any way denigrated. Jesus encountered these religious leaders and had a range of conversations and complex encounters with them. Priests, Levites, and scribes would be present, both in the temple, the center of the religious life of the people, and occasionally in synagogues that were present to serve people who were not in Jerusalem. The synagogues functioned as centers of religious education, and it is possible that Jesus may have received part of his education in a synagogue.[8]

There were also several groups of Jewish leaders who formed around common interests and convictions, not unlike political parties.[9] These groups had representation in the Sanhedrin and strong opinions about religious ideas and practice. They were also concerned about the presence of an alien government and its influence on the Jewish way of life. Perhaps the largest political party was the *Pharisees* who were descendants of the Hasidim or "pious ones" and deeply committed to spiritual practices. They were concerned about following the Law (Torah), especially the Levitical requirements which separated them from those whom they judged to be unclean. They believed that the Law should apply to all of life and developed ways about how the Law should be applied to new situations. In time, a tradition of interpretation of the Law developed that was later codified in the Mishnah and the Talmud. Their interpretations were occasionally quite detailed, as for example the list of the thirty-nine kinds of work banned on the Sabbath. The list of prohibitions evolved to six hundred and thirteen, a large number that was quite confusing to laypeople. Jesus encountered many Pharisees in his public ministry.[10] The Gospels, and especially Matthew, de-

---

8. Mark 6:1; Matt 13:54; Luke 4:16.

9. See Theissen and Merz, *Historical Jesus*, 137–41.

10. Ibid. See the section entitled "How Does Jesus Relate to the Three Religious Parties?," 141.

scribe Jesus raising questions about the religious system of the Pharisees, but there is also evidence that Jesus had respect for their dedication.[11]

A second group, the *Sadducees*, had influence disproportionate to their size. The membership included leaders of the priestly class and those with wealth and power. Unlike the Pharisees, they resisted interpreting the Law in new ways for changing circumstances and tended to be conservative in their outlook. Only the Pentateuch (the first five books) was thought of as Scripture. They did not believe in the developing array of doctrines affirmed by the Pharisees. For example, they rejected the belief in eternal life, angels, and spirits. Their interpretation of the Torah was quite narrow and their religious life was centered in the temple in Jerusalem. There were inevitable conflicts between the Pharisees and the Sadducees, and the Sadducees, too, were suspicious of the outspoken prophet from Nazareth.

Another group, not mentioned in the New Testament, but perhaps influential in the thought of John the Baptist and whose ideas were likely familiar to Jesus, was the *Essenes*. We know about this group and their convictions from the Dead Sea Scrolls and the description in the scrolls of their separatist community called Qumran.[12] Like the Pharisees, they were dedicated to the spiritual life as they understood it and believed that true spiritual practice required living in a separate community. They lived by a guide, called the *Rule of the Community*, and took vows to follow its requirements. The Essene community was motivated by the conviction that the people in the mainstream of Judaism, represented by the religious establishment in Jerusalem, had lost their way. The Essenes lived in the hope that Messiah would come and lead them to a validation of their beliefs and practices, partly through a Holy War. A war did come, but not with the outcome for which they hoped. In fact, the Romans in about 68 CE slaughtered the majority of the Essenes. Scholars continue to debate how much John the Baptist and even Jesus may have been influenced by this movement.

One other group deserves to be mentioned, and it is the group known as the *Zealots* who were dedicated to challenging the Roman rule of Palestine. They were people committed to following the Torah, not unlike the Pharisees. They were extreme patriots, especially sensitive to Roman oppression, and believed it should be resisted with military force. One of the disciples of Jesus, Judas, may have been influence by the Zealots and felt betrayed when Jesus did not lead in establishing a political kingdom with the goal of ending Roman rule in Palestine.

11. Matt 5:20: "For I tell you, unless your righteousness exceeds that of the scribes and Pharisees, you will never enter the kingdom of heaven."

12. Charlesworth, *Jesus within Judaism*, describes the possible influence of the Dead Sea Scrolls on Jesus (ch. 5, "Jesus and the Dead Sea Scrolls," 54–75).

Of course, the great masses of people who were contemporaries of Jesus were not political or religious leaders or members of these different groups and parties. They were common people, attempting to find a good life in spite of their poverty and the ubiquitous presence of hunger and illness. It was this vast array of people who sought to hear Jesus and be healed by him. It was this group whom Jesus loved, spending more time with their needs and concerns than he did with Sabbath observance and ritual purity.

The Religious Context: The Core Beliefs and Practices

The radical teaching of Jesus is deeply rooted in the land, the culture, the economy, and the socio-political environment of first-century Palestine. The people of Palestine depended upon the land for basic sustenance and for many of its residents farming was a way of life. Jesus makes reference to the land frequently in his teaching, calling attention to its fundamental importance and to its beauty as he illustrates a spiritual insight. There is, for example, the parable of the sower,[13] the parable of the weeds among the wheat,[14] and the parable of the mustard seed.[15] He speaks of the lilies of the field and how even Solomon in all his glory was not clothed as beautifully as the lilies.[16] It is fair to say that undergirding the teaching of Jesus is the phrase, "We belong to the land."

He speaks frequently of cultural norms, referencing practices concerning divorce and the place of oaths.[17] He often challenges the prevailing cultural paradigm, as for example the inherent patriarchy in the region. Jesus challenges it and demonstrates respectful behavior toward women and treats them as equals. The economy is also present in many of his teachings. For instance he speaks with compassion for the poor[18] and cautions his listeners about the treasure they may accumulate.[19] He demonstrates wisdom and poise when challenged about government authority and the payment of taxes, quieting those who questioned him.[20]

Jesus is perceptive about the world around him. He observes the Roman provincial government and its practices. He is keenly aware of the

13. Matt 13:1–9.

14. Matt 13:24–31.

15. Matt 13:31–32.

16. Matt 6:28.

17. Matt 5:31–32, 5:33–37.

18. Matt 25:42–43.

19. Matt 6:19–21.

20. Luke 20:20–26.

social divisions, the distinctions between slave and free, and rich and poor; the importance of birth; the difference between Jew and Gentile; and one's rank in the family. He understands the social status attributed to where one lives and the gulf between town and country. The cities were the centers of wealth, trade, and industry whereas the rural areas were isolated and perceived as provincial.[21] Jesus lived in a setting in which power was precariously balanced between the established families and the customs and laws of Judaism and the Roman governor. There was tension between those who farmed and lived in the country and those who controlled the wealth in the cities, between those who spoke Greek and adopted the values of Hellenism and those who spoke Aramaic and remained within the framework of a Jewish way of life.[22] Justice does not prevail in the complex governmental system of Palestine, and Jesus, the radical prophet is sensitive to various forms of oppression and speaks truth to power.[23]

The caring and compassionate Jesus brings his religious heritage and convictions to the context of first-century Palestine. He addresses with courage and boldness in his teaching and actions the injustice of the legal systems, the poverty of the people, the suffering of the marginalized,[24] and the inadequacies of the religious teaching and practices. Jesus, immersed in certain core beliefs and practices that were fundamental to his Jewish faith, draws upon this rich tradition to speak and act for the welfare of others.

At the heart of his beliefs and convictions were the basic teachings of Judaism. Yes, there were differences between religious teachers and the groups to which they belonged. But there was sufficient agreement about the core beliefs and practices to influence the mind and spirit of Jesus, and it was these core beliefs and practices that motivated him and called him to his vocation as a compassionate healer, charismatic rabbi, and a radical prophet. Again and again, he references these core beliefs and practices and resists those who, in attempting to clarify their application to every aspect of life, got bogged down in legalistic detail. In one of these conversations, a debate about what activities are legitimate on the Sabbath, Jesus reminds them, "The Sabbath was made for humankind, not humankind for the Sabbath."[25]

---

21. Riches, *World of Jesus*, 14–21.

22. Ibid., 29.

23. Matt 23:23–24: "For you tithe mint, dill, and cumin, and have neglected the weightier matters of the law: justice and mercy and faith. It is these you ought to have practiced without neglecting the others. You blind guides! You strain out a gnat but swallow a camel."

24. Crossan, *Historical Jesus*, xi, speaks with careful definition to the status of Jesus as a peasant, sensitized to injustice, malnutrition, sickness, and agrarian oppression.

25. Mark 2:27.

What were these basic beliefs and practices that were shared by first-century Judaism? There are many, but let me mention four that are in evidence as we observe the life of Jesus through the Gospels. The foundational affirmation was the belief in a *personal God who entered into human life and the course of history*. God was not a vague principle, a tribal fetish, or a cultural icon, but a transcendent and omnipotent One (Yahweh) who had called the Hebrew people to a life of faith. Yahweh was the creator of the world and sovereign over the powers of evil. The faith of the Jewish people in the time of Jesus, while often accompanied by premodern superstitions, was profoundly monotheistic. The teaching of Deuteronomy 6:4–5 (Shema) was foundational: "Hear, O, Israel: The Lord is our God, the Lord alone. You shall love the Lord your God with all your heart, and with all of your soul, and with all of your might." In one incident, recorded in the three Synoptic Gospels, Jesus is asked which of the commandments is first and most important, and Jesus replies by quoting from the biblical text: "The first is, 'Hear, O Israel: you shall love the Lord your God with all your heart, and with all your soul, and with all your strength. The second is this: you shall love your neighbor as yourself. There is no other commandment greater than these.'"[26] Jesus, during the trying moment in the garden of Gethsemane, prays to God using the Aramaic term "Abba" suggesting familial intimacy.[27] For Jesus, God is personal, accessible, and engaged in human affairs.

A second foundational affirmation of the Jewish people of the first century was the belief that they had a *covenant relationship with Yahweh*. The covenant, a formal agreement or treaty between two parties, committed each party to some obligations. But unlike an official legal statement, the covenant was more personal and hinged upon a relationship of trust, spiritual practices, and obedience to Torah. In turn, God would bless the people of Israel and care for their welfare. Fundamental to the understanding of the covenant was the story of emancipation from Egypt and the action of Moses in the wilderness of Sinai. Moses encounters God and understands that God has delivered the people of Israel, and this story of deliverance and exodus becomes the paradigmatic narrative for the understanding of the covenant. "Then Moses went up to God; the Lord called to him from the mountain, saying, 'Thus you shall say to the house of Jacob, and tell the Israelites: You have seen what I did to the Egyptians, and how I bore you on eagles' wings and brought you to myself. Now, therefore, if you obey my voice and keep my covenant, you shall be my treasured possession out of all the peoples. Indeed, the whole earth is mine, but you shall be for me a priestly kingdom and

26. Mark 12:29–31.
27. Mark 14:36.

a holy nation. These are the words that you shall speak to the Israelites.'"[28]
There were also the stories of the early covenant with Abraham and the
promise of blessing to his descendants. In addition, there is the renewal of
the covenant with David. The sense of being called to a covenant relationship
with God became foundational for Jewish belief and practice.

The terms of the covenant evolved over time and took form in the
Hebrew Scriptures, and in particular the first five books of the Scriptures
that became *the* Law (Torah). The range of practices prescribed in the Jewish Scriptures was believed to be God-given, and the variety of practices
and customs which developed (circumcision, the temple, the priesthood,
etc.) became the guidance for following the will and way of God.[29] At the
heart of many of these guidelines are the practice of justice and the protection of those who might be oppressed by those with power. There are many
subjects covered, but what emerges for the Jewish people, learning from
their history, is the deep conviction that *God calls them to an ethical life*,
both as individuals and in the formation of the social order. It becomes clear
to them from exposure to the biblical narrative that individuals are to live in
ways that respect others and to participate in ways of creating a social and
legal system that insures justice and leads to peace. Perhaps the best known
listing of the teachings of Jesus about the ethical life is the Sermon on the
Mount, most likely a collection of sayings from several sources, but in its
form in Matthew, chapters 5–7, there is the calling to a profoundly ethical
life, one that many believe is next to impossible to follow.

In addition, as a fourth core belief and practice, the people of Israel, as
they reflected on their history, would *look to the future with hope*. They saw in
their historical narrative that God enters into human history to heal, redeem,
and guide. In this reflection on their own suffering, they developed empathy for the suffering of others and sought ways to relieve that suffering. They
would return to their belief that a loving God created life and that it is sacred
and to be hallowed; life can be lived with joy and purpose. As life is threatened
and circumstances become challenging, it is still possible to live in hope, not
despair, because the God who saved them in the past will guide them in the
present and restore them to a better life in the future. This particular affirmation became central to the life and teachings of Jesus, and it was his articulation of the kingdom of God that would be the expression of hope.

One historical development that occurred two centuries before the life
of Jesus (168–67 BCE), but most likely alive in the mind of Jesus and his
Jewish contemporaries, was the resistance to the Seleucids in Syria, which

28. Exod 19:3–6.

29. Riches, *World of Jesus*, 32.

were overlords of Palestine. As it was recounted in story form, it became a tangible expression of these four core values, and in particular the need to be faithful to the covenant and have hope in the intervention of God in a time of oppression and suffering. The Seleucid ruler Antiochus Epiphanes was insistent that the Jewish population adapt to the Hellenistic culture.[30] The Jewish population did attempt to make some accommodation to the demands of Antiochus Epiphanes, but drew a line in the sand when an altar erected to Zeus was placed in the temple.[31] A Jewish leader, Mattathias, with his sons, took exception to the altar to Zeus and in general to the faithlessness of the Jewish community. He refused to offer a sacrifice on the altar, attacked a Jew who was sacrificing on the altar, and killed him and the king's official. He and his sons fled to the rural hills, and the Maccabean revolt (named after Mattathias' son, Judas Maccabeus) ensued. This revolt is remembered and celebrated at the yearly festival of Hanukkah, a holiday inviting loyalty to God. The Jewish community would see in this story the call to worship the one true God, to live faithfully and ethically within the expectations of the covenant, and to live with hope that God will intervene in times of cultural and political threats.[32] Similar themes run through the book of Daniel, a book likely written in the same era.

Many other issues and questions emerged that were not unimportant. For example, there were questions about why God would allow suffering and the unrighteous to prosper. As in any human group, there were differences and conflicts, but the four affirmations of one almighty God, the creation of the covenant, the formation of the Law or Torah as an expression of God's will, and the presence of hope were foundational. These would be basic to the formation of the way Jesus viewed the world, and he would keep them paramount in his assessment of his setting and his calling.

Jewish Religion in the Region of Galilee

I often need to remind myself that Jesus was a first-century Jew who lived in the region of Galilee in ancient Palestine.[33] The teaching of Jesus grows out of

30. Some of these events are recorded in the first book of Maccabees. Hellenism may be understood as the influence of ancient Greek thought, culture, and customs.

31. 1 Macc 1:54–64.

32. Riches, *World of Jesus*, 37–42.

33. As one who has lived in the Christian church a good part of my life, I have had to be reminded from time to time that the Jesus of history was a first-century Jew. Surrounded as I was by titles such as Son of God and Lord, and the theologies of Paul and the cosmic vision of John's Gospel, I lived with the conviction Jesus was above the boundaries of time and place. But immersed as I have been these past few decades in

his understanding of this region and the ways that Judaism took form there in belief and practice. He learned about first-century Judaism through the customs and culture of the region of Galilee and in his interaction with the people of Galilee. He was also exposed to the slightly different forms of Judaism in the surrounding region, to the south in Judea and especially in Jerusalem.

As he left his family and work in Galilee and began his itinerant ministry with these influences, he invited others from the region to follow him. He went with his disciples and with deep convictions rooted in his Jewish faith. Over the weeks and months of his ministry, he became known as a compassionate healer, charismatic rabbi (teacher), and a radical prophet. What were the factors that called him from the life of a carpenter in the village of Nazareth to the courageous religious revolutionary "disturbing the peace" in Jerusalem? Unfortunately, we do not have his diary or writings; he left no manuscripts for us. We can only assume that his sensitivity and brilliance absorbed and massaged the beliefs and values of the region of Galilee. So we say that to a large extent it was his understanding of the life of the people in the region and the ways his understanding and faithful practice of the first-century Judaism called him to proclaim the kingdom of God and seek the well-being of his people.

There are the accounts of the birth of Jesus in Bethlehem that might suggest that Jesus was influenced by the beliefs and practices that prevailed in Judea. It is these accounts of the birth in Bethlehem that are celebrated at the Christmas season by Christians around the world.[34] These accounts should not be easily discounted, but the more important shaping influence on Jesus was the region of Galilee. Jesus came from Nazareth and was a Galilean.[35] In many ways, he was somewhat distant from Judea and from the primary leadership of Judaism. As a result, there were differences in perspective by the Galilean people that took the form of ethnic characteristics,

the literature about Jesus and travel to the region, I have reconnected in a profound way with the Jesus of history who was Jewish in his religious outlook. I have also reaffirmed what was only vaguely in the background, that history is important for the church and that accurate history is essential. It is only by rigorous historical scholarship that we can understand and proclaim the Christian message with integrity. Vermes, *Religion of Jesus the Jew*, and *Jesus in His Jewish Context*, have been especially helpful, as has Sanders, *Jesus and Judaism*, and dozens of others.

34. Matt 1:18—2:23 and Luke 2:1–40. These accounts are occasionally classified as legends with a spiritual message as opposed to accurate historical accounts. Ratzinger, in his book *Jesus of Nazareth: The Infancy Narratives*, created some stir by suggesting that these stories might be more theological reflections than historical accounts. But either way, I agree with him that the accounts are informative about early Christian belief.

35. Meier, whose four-volume study of Jesus is seen as excellent and thorough, labels his work *A Marginal Jew*.

cultural expression, and sociological structures and systems.[36] These variants often meant that a Jewish person might be more open to Hellenistic influences and a Jewish prophet less bound by the political and social conflicts of Judea. The population would be more mixed, with various non-Jewish tribal groups maintaining their own identity. Those from Galilee could be recognized by accent and custom, and there may have been a stigma attached to a prophet from Galilee. In the incident of Peter denying his association with Jesus, one bystander came up to Peter and said that Peter's accent betrayed him and linked him to Jesus, the Galilean.[37]

The Gospel record is clear that Jesus came from the village of Nazareth, and Mark and John assume that Jesus was born in Nazareth, although Matthew and Luke place the birth in Bethlehem and fill these stories with enchanting detail. Those in the Christian family continue to celebrate the birth of Jesus in Bethlehem, and numerous customs of celebration (the stable, the shepherds, the wise men, and the star) express the profound belief that this was special birth anticipated in the Hebrew Scriptures. There is a profound spiritual message in these birth accounts. But it is also important to note that the authors of Matthew and Luke have a point of view and link the birth of Jesus to the Davidic heritage with Bethlehem being understood as "the city of David." They also speak of Bethlehem as the birthplace of Jesus in fulfillment of the prophecy in Micah 5:1–2, which reads: "But you, O Bethlehem . . . from you shall come forth for me one who is to rule in Israel."

But even with these accounts in Matthew and Luke, it is accurate to say that Jesus *came from* Nazareth. Historians who write about Jesus and his life and teaching inevitably title their books or reference him in one way or another as Jesus of Nazareth.[38] It was a Jewish village in southern Galilee and somewhat cut off from the primary trade routes and therefore politically and economically of little significance. The relatively small population, with estimates ranging between one hundred and two thousand, was primarily engaged in agriculture and lived in quite primitive conditions. The village, however, was close to a large and flourishing city, Sepphoris, which had been destroyed in 4 BCE and then reconstructed. It had a diverse population and was influenced by Hellenistic culture. Jesus grew up within the sphere of influence of Sepphoris and may have practiced his skills as a craftsman in the rebuilding of the city. The biblical record is quiet about this phase of the life of Jesus, and we cannot say for sure in what ways the city

36. Theissen and Merz, *Historical Jesus*, 162–63. This volume informs me as I trace the ministry of Jesus.

37. Matt 26:73.

38. Bornkamm, *Jesus of Nazareth*, an influential study of Jesus in the mid-twentieth century, and Lohfink's more recent *Jesus of Nazareth* are two examples.

may have influenced him, but it is likely that his exposure to the culture of Sepphoris contributed to the ways he put his faith together.[39]

The Preparation for His Ministry: Baptism and Temptations

At about the age of thirty, Jesus left his family and work and began to pursue his vocation.[40] He traveled to the south into the desert of Judea east of Jerusalem and became associated with the fiery prophet, John the Baptist, who may have been a relative.[41] John the Baptist, though close in age to Jesus, had already begun his mission as a prophet. He had gone to the wilderness of Judea, "wore clothing made of camel's hair," and boldly proclaimed the coming kingdom of heaven.[42] Many from Jerusalem and the surrounding region went to hear him and responded to his message calling for repentance and to be baptized in the Jordon River. Jesus, also came to be baptized "to fulfill all righteousness" and in this experience felt the empowering presence and call of God to begin his life work.[43] The account in Matthew's Gospel speaks of the heavens opening, the Spirit of God descending like a dove, and a divine voice saying, "This is my Son, the Beloved, with whom I am well pleased." There has been much written about this story, some saying it should be read literally and others who understand it as a narrative filled with symbol and metaphor. Still others question the historicity of the event. The event is recorded in the other three Gospels, and it is probable that there is a historical event that forms the basis of these accounts. And it is likely that Jesus sensed the presence and call of God, although it is more difficult to speak of a literal dove and voice.

It is clear that when Jesus returns to the region of Galilee, the influence of John the Baptist and his outspoken style of preaching would have been fresh in his mind and heart. It is possible, though Jesus clearly has his own

---

39. Theissen and Merz, *Historical Jesus*, 164–66.

40. In ch. 3, we will explore the vocation of Jesus in some detail.

41. The account of the pregnancy and Mary and the birth of Jesus in ch. 1 of Luke's Gospel speak of Mary's relationship to Elizabeth, the mother of John the Baptist.

42. Matt 3:1–12.

43. Matt 3:13–17. Christian theologians have raised questions about the need for Jesus to be baptized if baptism implied the need for forgiveness of sins. If Jesus, according to orthodox Christian teaching was sinless, then his baptism must have had another meaning. It is the phrase "to fulfill all righteousness" that is often used to explain that Jesus was concerned to do all that God expects, and that the baptism was an expression of identification and solidarity with the people who were renewing their religious commitments.

charismatic style of teaching, that the first events of the ministry of Jesus in the region of Galilee may have been quite bold and dramatic, causing his family and acquaintances to be somewhat shocked by the proclamation of Jesus in the synagogue in Nazareth that he was fulfilling what was written in the scroll of Isaiah.[44] It is easy to understate the influence of John the Baptist upon Jesus because the biblical accounts are careful to speak of John as a forerunner.[45]

The styles of the two prophets differed, but they shared a common mission, that the Jewish people must change direction (repent) and prepare to receive and endorse the reign of God. Only by repentance and faithfulness to the covenant expectations would Israel be restored. Matthew's Gospel describes John's mission in the following way: "In those days John the Baptist appeared in the wilderness of Judea, proclaiming, 'Repent, for the kingdom of heaven has come near'" (Matt 3:1–2). Mark's Gospel is very direct in describing the start of the mission of Jesus: "The time is fulfilled, and the kingdom of God has come near; repent and believe in the good news" (Mark 1:15). We will say a good deal more below about the meaning of the term kingdom of God, but it is clear that this somewhat inclusive term has great meaning for John, Jesus, and their followers.

As mentioned above, it is also probable that Jesus understood his baptism by John the Baptist as another *moment* of calling to his vocation.[46] The aims of the Gospel writers must be taken into account in reading these narratives and historical questions remain. There is a clear movement from history to gospel, but it is largely accepted that John baptized Jesus. Mark wants to get Jesus on the way to his messianic ministry and its dramatic conclusion without excessive detail. Matthew wants to link the account to biblical prophecy, and Luke wants to place the account within a larger historical frame of reference. All may be accurate perspectives, and there is agreement among them that Jesus does sense or hear the Spirit and voice of God in the affirmation. Jesus has prepared himself, is ready to begin his ministry, and hears the affirmation of God, "You are my Son, the Beloved; with you I am well pleased."[47]

The Synoptic Gospels agree as well, most likely taking the cue from Mark's Gospel that following his baptism Jesus goes into the wilderness to prepare himself for the challenge of his calling.[48] Again, there are historical

---

44. See the account in Luke 4:16–30. See also the passage that Jesus quotes in Isa 61:1–2.

45. Luke 3:15–17. Matthew's Gospel treats this issue in some detail (Matt 3:1–17).

46. Theissen and Merz, *Historical Jesus*, 196–213.

47. Luke 3:22.

48. Mark 1:12–13; Matt 4:1–11; Luke 4:1–13.

questions about Jesus going into the wilderness of Judea to fast, meditate, pray, and reflect upon his vocation for forty days.[49] This period is framed within the concept of temptation, a concept that suggests that Jesus will be tested to see if he can remain faithful to his calling. Some see this account as a commissioning to his messianic ministry. The narrative is designed as a challenge to Jesus over whether to obey his sense of God's call to be a servant-messiah or to understand his messianic calling in terms of power, strength, and conquest. His disciples and others may have understood the calling of Jesus as a messiah being victorious in a military and political way rather than in terms of identification with the poor and marginalized. The wrong paths are present and offered in the account: the path of seeking physical gratification following a fast ("One does not live by bread alone"); the path of being powerful as one views the kingdoms of the world ("Worship the Lord God, and serve only him"); and the path of testing rather than trusting God ("Do not put the Lord your God to the test").

It is apparent that this account is a metaphoric narrative, teaching that Jesus was tempted by evil (Satan) to betray his understanding of his call. There are those who would interpret the passage as literal, received in story form and told by Jesus to his disciples. But most interpreters would see it as a didactic reflection helping the followers of Jesus to understand him and to follow his extraordinary example. The message to Jesus and his followers is that it is important that they should prepare themselves to honor their deepest values and live with integrity in reference to their faith.[50]

The Ministry in Galilee

Following his encounter with John the Baptist and his preparation in the wilderness of Judea, Jesus returned to the region of Galilee and entered into his life of teaching and healing. The center of his activity was the city of Capernaum on the north shore of the Sea of Galilee. It is probable that he was welcomed into the home of Peter and likely that the mission of teaching

49. Forty is a number used in other passages in which the faithful have been tested, e.g., Moses and the children of Israel, who spent forty years in the wilderness. Some scholars have raised questions about the amount of water and food necessary to survive and what wildlife might have been present. The account does not address these questions, and the forty-day time period may have been a convenient way to speak about an extended period of time for a spiritual retreat.

50. Just outside the city of Jericho there is a steep hill with a cave near the top. The cave does have a viewpoint that enables one to look across a wide section of land, and the sacred tradition is that it was this place where Jesus was taken to see "all the kingdoms of the world."

and healing was begun in that setting.[51] It was strategically located for the itinerant life of Jesus who walked the shores of Lake Galilee, and it provided easy access to the other regions of Galilee. The archeological remains of the city are quite revealing in terms of the mission of Jesus, with some evidence that there are the ruins of the synagogue where he taught and the so-called house of Peter where he came for rest.

It is from this base that Jesus becomes an itinerant preacher and travels, often with his disciples, across the region of Galilee and the surrounding area. He encounters a wide range of ethnic tensions, social and economic conflict between rich and poor and between those who rule and those subject to rule, and differences in religious understanding and practice. Once again, we observe Jesus as compassionate healer, charismatic preacher, and radical prophet. He brings his profound understanding of his Jewish faith and practice to bear upon a multitude of challenging encounters.

As Jesus undertakes his mission, he has already developed many relationships that were part of his life during his years of growing up and working as a carpenter in Nazareth. Of course there is his immediate *family* and most likely an extended family. The biblical account suggests some tension among his family given his dramatic turn toward a teaching prophet.[52] The Gospel of Mark speaks directly about members of his family describing Jesus as having gone too far, and they try to restrain him. At one point they try to speak with him while he is with a crowd of people. He is told that his mother and brothers are asking to see him, and Jesus uses this incident to teach that all people are his kindred.[53] At a later point, members of his family embrace his mission, and James, a brother becomes a leader in the church of Jerusalem, and other brothers and his mother become believers and devote themselves to prayer.[54] While some critics question the historicity of these incidents, it should be noted that Jesus faced the same difficulty that others have faced in leaving the family setting and business and launching out in new directions. This narrative in Mark does meet the criterion of embarrassment in that a more idealistic description of Jesus would leave this family tension out of the story.

In addition to his family, Jesus relates to many other groups: intimate followers called disciples; large crowds of people both curious and needy; women whom he treated with great respect; and of course those who oppose him. We will look briefly at each group. One of his first acts on returning

51. Matt 9:1 refers to Capernaum as Jesus' "own town."

52. Mark 3:21–22.

53. Mark 3:31–35.

54. See the account in Acts 1:14.

to Galilee was to call a group of *disciples*, an immediate group of men, but also a larger group that included women who were quite close to Jesus. Each of the Gospel writers describes the invitation to join Jesus in his mission in a particular way.[55] In Mark, the disciples are called directly by Jesus who spoke with messianic authority.[56] Peter, James, and John leave their fishing and literally follow Jesus. The passages in Matthew and Luke imply that the disciples choose to follow Jesus because of his charisma, message, and mission.[57] In John's Gospel, there is the pattern of following Jesus because a trusted relative or friend urges it.[58] It is likely that these disciples would have understood the invitation, although they would not be fully aware of the implications of saying "yes" to Jesus. Both rabbis (teachers) and prophets had disciples. It was an accepted pattern and there were expectations. Because of these expectations, there are those who say that they need to "take care of business" before they join the group. Jesus moves on to those ready to make the commitment.[59] Those who say yes soon discover that they will become known as followers of Jesus and may be harshly judged by those who oppose the mission of Jesus. They also discover that they will be engaged in ministry, to heal and caste out demons.[60] Life will change and not be easy, although they will share the joy and gratification of being included in what they understand to be a God-given mission. The biblical account says that twelve were chosen to serve as an immediate group (apostles), and the number twelve has been interpreted to refer to the ministry of Jesus to the twelve tribes of Israel. But a larger group shares the mission.

In the early stages of the ministry of Jesus, he is quite popular and large *crowds* come to hear him and many seek healing.[61] Over time, others come with mixed motives, perhaps to learn from this charismatic rabbi, but also to question the implications of this radical prophet. There were large groups of followers who remained loyal across the weeks and months of the itinerant ministry of Jesus, but as the mission continues, the crowds begin to get smaller, in part because they may have already seen and heard Jesus teach and heal, but especially as more understand the commitment required to become a follower. Jesus does become quite well known in the region of

---

55. Theissen and Merz, *Historical Jesus*, 213–17. This book informs me as I frame this section of ch. 2.

56. Mark 1:16–18.

57. Matt 8:19–22; Luke 9:59–62.

58. John 1:35–42.

59. Matt 8:19–22.

60. Mark 3:13–19.

61. Mark 3:7–12.

Galilee, and his reputation as healer, teacher, and prophet, and one with an alternative and radical point of view, goes beyond the region of Galilee.

There is a group of *women* in particular who find in Jesus one who challenges the prevailing patriarchal attitude and includes them in his inner circle.[62] Jesus addresses them directly with his message, not as those who must stay at home and be told what to believe and do by their husband. Jesus, defying custom, speaks with them as equals, invites them to be disciples, and heals them as well. For example, Mary of Magdala is cured of evil spirits and becomes a well-known disciple of Jesus.[63] The woman with an issue of blood suffers not only from her illness, but also the stigma attached to it. She breaks through the taboo of contact with Jesus, is healed, and acknowledged publically by Jesus.[64] Women are accepted and begin to follow him and they are accepted as those sharing in the ministry. What is also very noticeable and unusual for the time and place of his ministry is that Jesus illustrates his message and parables with examples of women. For example, there is the parable of the lost coin, and it is a woman who misplaces it.[65]

As the ministry of Jesus continues across the weeks and months and his reputation expands, there are those who see him as a potential threat and *begin to oppose him*. His style of teaching is different from that of the scribes and the Pharisees in that he speaks from within himself and not by quoting authorities to justify his comments, "for he taught them as one having authority, and not as their scribes."[66] He differs from them in his interpretation of Scripture and tradition. He often places human well-being rather than purity and custom as the focus and meaning of Scripture as he does in reference to eating practices and in honoring one's parents.[67]

Not only do the Jewish authorities that are Pharisees or Sadducees challenge Jesus, but also there are differences as well with the *Herodians*, especially in reference to unfair taxation. A group of both Pharisees and Herodians question and test him about paying taxes to Caesar (an alien and occupying government), and Jesus confounds them with his well-known and wise response when given a coin with the question about paying taxes to the emperor whose face was on the coin: "Jesus said to them, 'Give to the emperor the things that are the emperor's, and to God things that are God's.'

62. There are many examples, such as the anointing in Bethany (Mark 14:3–9).
63. Luke 8:2.
64. Mark 5:24–34.
65. Luke 15:8–10.
66. Matt 7:29.
67. Mark 7:1–17.

And they were utterly amazed at him."[68] The conflicts with these governments and religious groups become more intense, and they reach a climax
in the last week of the life of Jesus in Jerusalem.

Understanding Jesus in His World: His Identity

Jesus pursued his calling in the region of Galilee with wisdom, understanding, and commitment. As he did, he had categories from his religious heritage and the customs of the culture that described his various roles. Three
stand out, although it is likely that there were many phrases used to describe
him. The three roles I want to emphasize are healer, rabbi (teacher), and
prophet. As he traveled across the region of Galilee, he was comfortable
with these titles, as were those whom he encountered. So, too, were the immediate group who traveled with him and a much larger group of disciples.
It was within and through these three primary roles that he taught, and if
we are to understand his teaching, we must understand that what he taught
and how he taught were shaped by his self-understanding as a healer, a
rabbi (teacher), and a prophet. Later, as the young Christian community
reflected upon the life and teaching of Jesus, other titles would emerge, and
we will discuss these titles in chapter 3. One is especially important and will
be given special attention; it is the term messiah, which would have been
present during his active ministry, and in time it actually emerged as part
of his name in the Greek form, Christ.[69] But the terms of healer, teacher,
and prophet were immediately apparent to those who encountered him,
although many wondered if he might be the promised messiah. Healing,
teaching, and proclaiming God's will and way as a prophet are not inconsis-
tent with the expected messiah. But there were many visions of the expected
messiah and it was a term filled with mystery and hope. It may have been
easier for his contemporaries to identity him in the three roles that were
immediately present in their daily lives. There were healers, rabbis, and
prophets in their midst. Although we have no access to the inner thoughts
of Jesus, we assume that these three roles matched his self-understanding,
described what he did as he traveled, and what people saw when they met
him. His followers would likely use the categories of their culture that

---

68. Mark 12:17.

69. We will say more about whether Jesus understood himself as messiah, and if
so, which of the meanings of the term he may have endorsed. We will explore in ch. 3
the several titles that are used by his followers to try to explain his identity and mission.

helped them understand who he was and what he did.[70] What did these terms mean and imply?

Jesus as Compassionate Healer

In Mark's Gospel, the timeline for Jesus as he turns toward his public ministry is the baptism, the temptation, and the calling of his first disciples.[71] The next activities recorded are the healings of sick and troubled people. The author of Mark's Gospel may have had other reasons than chronology to place these accounts in the early part of his Gospel, but a careful reading of the Synoptic Gospels would suggest that there is more of a broad-based chronological order in Mark than in Matthew or Luke. Mark does place them up front and important in his narrative; and the order following the baptism, temptation, and calling of the disciples in Mark is as follows:

1. Jesus heals the man with an unclean spirit (Mark 1:21–28).

2. Jesus heals many at Simon's (Peter's) house (Mark 1:29–34).

3. Following a reference to Jesus going on a "preaching tour," Jesus cleanses the leper (Mark 1:40–45).

4. At the beginning of chapter 2, Jesus heals the paralytic (Mark 2:1–12).

By healing, we mean the restoration of health and the making of a person whole or well whether the ailment is physical, mental, or spiritual. Healing is an important topic in the Hebrew Bible, and Jesus would have been sensitive to its importance in his ministry. Even the broader term salvation implies being made healthy and whole, free from danger and distress, and restored to what God intends for one to be. Again and again, passages of the Hebrew Bible say that God desires that human beings be healed and that they can be healed through the power of God. Jesus, sensing the empowering grace of God, believes that healing is part of his calling and it becomes

---

70. E.g., in Luke 5:31, Jesus is quoted as saying that he is like a physician. The Pharisees and their scribes call into question why it is that Jesus is eating and drinking with tax collectors and sinners. He answers them: "Those who are well have no need of a physician, but those who are sick. I have come to call not the righteous but sinners to repentance."

71. Mark 1:9–20.

an integral part of his public ministry.[72] The word gets out that Jesus has the power to heal, and "people came to him from every quarter."[73]

There are several ailments which people have who seek to be healed by Jesus. Not all of the categories used in the Gospels to describe these illnesses would be the categories used by the medical profession today, but they were the way that the contemporaries of Jesus understood these illnesses. As one might expect, there are those within the Christian community who accept the terminology of the gospels and its implications in a quite literal way. An "unclean spirit" is an unclean spirit, not a prescientific way to speak about an emotional illness or a spiritual crisis. And we were not present when these incidents occurred, so we have the challenge of understanding and interpreting these events. My preference is to understand them in more contemporary terms, leaving room for the healing power of empathic care, transforming presence, and the flow of God's healing grace.[74] As he made healing possible, Jesus tapped into the flow of God's healing grace and strongly resisted the role of a magic faith healer, present in his time and ours.

There are at least three different types of ailments that people have who come to Jesus and ask for healing. There are the *physical ailments* such as blindness and deafness and injuries and birth defects that are disabling.[75] Jesus encounters many people with these ailments who feel trapped and see no options for a better life. Second, there are people who are *ill with a disease* such as leprosy or a "fever." The stories describe Jesus, drawing upon the power of God, healing these ailments.[76] Third, there are *emotional and spiritual ailments,* such as being overcome by fear and isolation that cause

72. Ps 41:2–3 and Ps 103:3 are two good examples of faith in God's healing power. Other references to heal and healing may be found in Isa 53:5; Jer 17:14; 33:6–8; and Hos 14:4. Each reference has its own nuance for the meaning of healing.

73. Mark 1:45.

74. The subject of spiritual healing by Jesus deserves a full treatment, well beyond our purpose in this chapter. I introduce the topic as a way of describing one way that his contemporaries and a way for Jesus to teach those who follow him understood Jesus. He becomes for them a person for others whose teaching about compassion is modeled in his life by healing those who suffer. The notion of healing apart from the use of medicine suggests that divine healing is an intervention of God in the flow of human activity; it is a supernatural miracle. This topic needs discussion, as well, and we will address it at a later point in this volume. Suffice to say that it is hard for us living in a scientific era to be comfortable with the notion of miracle, but there is evidence that healing occurred in the presence of Jesus. How it occurred is a subject for long discussions.

75. Mark 7:31–37 records the story of a deaf man who is cured by Jesus and there are several (13) similar narratives in the gospels.

76. For example, Jesus heals a man with a withered hand (Mark 3:1–6; Matt 12:9–14; Luke 6:6–11).

great suffering.[77] Often these illnesses may be what are now called profound psychological ailments and Jesus, using the language and categories of his time and place, heals these ailments as well. Frequently, the ailments, which might be categorized as mental or emotional breakdowns, are viewed as a spiritual crisis and the language of unclean spirit or demon possession is often used.[78] Jesus did heal them by exorcism, calling on the evil spirits to leave the ailing person.

The biblical authors ascribe to Jesus slightly differing motivations in his healing ministry, although compassion, the form that love takes in the presence of suffering, appears to be always present. Jesus cares deeply and profoundly about the suffering of those whom he encounters. Mixed with the compassion is a desire to teach those who are being healed and those who are present at the time of healing that faith in God's healing power assists in the healing.[79] Often, Jesus makes a pronouncement such as "your faith has made you well" following the healing, and in this way he is teaching in both word and deed as he heals.[80]

As the crowds surround Jesus and demand all of his time and energy, Jesus commissions his disciples to assist him and engage in healing and the other ministries they are learning to share with Jesus.[81] What is important to note about this commissioning as his disciples engage in healing is that it is the divine presence and power that heals and not the power a single individual that heals apart from divine grace. Even Jesus does not want to be thought of as a miracle worker with magical powers, a category that was present in his setting.[82] The message Jesus wants people to understand is that the saving and healing grace of God can flow through those who open their minds and hearts to God's presence and power.

---

77. Mark 5:1–13 describes a person whose illness has forced him out of society and into a cave or tomb. In the time of Jesus, sick and deformed people were removed from society. This illness is described as both psychological and spiritual.

78. Mark 5:1–20 describes the person to be healed as a demoniac.

79. Mark 10:52 describes a blind man who is healed and Jesus comforting him with the words, "Your faith has made you well."

80. Matt 10:52.

81. Matt 10:1–5; Mark 6:7–13; Luke 9:1–6.

82. Following the healing of young girl, Jesus "strictly ordered them that no one should know this" (Mark 5:43).

Jesus as Charismatic Teacher

I chose the word charismatic to describe the teaching of Jesus, in part because it is a word that has entered into our common language, but more importantly because it suggests that one has been gifted with a special talent and called to a particular responsibility.[83] Of all the terms used to describe Jesus, perhaps teacher is the most common and accurate. The emphasis on the centrality of teaching in the mission of Jesus emerged, though it was always in the Christian vocabulary, in the nineteenth century as liberal interpreters attempted to speak more about the life of Jesus. In time, this emphasis lost some of its credibility as critics pointed out that it was all too easy to create the Jesus of history out of the categories current in the time and place of the author.[84] Following these critiques, interpreters of Jesus began to question whether it was possible to go back behind the Gospel records and recover the true or real Jesus of history. Fortunately, for the last several decades, there has been a return to the view that Jesus can be accessed by historical study. The research and writing of these past decades warns the interpreter of Jesus against the risks of an uncritical reading of the Gospels, but affirms that there is much to learn about the Jesus of history.

Careful historical study argues that Jesus was a teacher *par excellence* who taught with charisma. He was a *gifted* teacher who expressed himself with authority, and he had the extraordinary power to attract learners. The author of Matthew, eager for others to understand both the way Jesus taught and the content of his teaching goes directly to the teaching. Not unlike Mark, Matthew lays the foundation for the ministry of Jesus. Matthew speaks of his birth, the escape into Egypt and return, the baptism by John the Baptist, the temptations, and the return to Galilee to begin his public ministry. As Mark's Gospel tends to lead with actions such as the healings, Matthew's Gospel goes directly to the teaching of Jesus. The author begins in chapter 5:1–2 with the following: "When Jesus saw the crowds, he went up the mountain; and after he sat down, his disciples came to him. Then he began to speak, and taught them, saying:" What follows is the Sermon on the Mount. Luke's Gospel speaks as well about the centrality of the teaching of Jesus in the Sermon on the Plain.[85]

In the next section, we will study in detail both the manner and content of the teaching of Jesus, but at this point, we emphasize the role of Jesus

---

83. Theissen and Merz, *Historical Jesus*, 185–239.

84. Bailey, *Jesus through Middle Eastern Eyes*, is very helpful in the effort to understand Jesus and his teaching in the context of his own culture.

85. Luke 6:17–49.

as a teacher or rabbi.[86] Rabbi in Hebrew has the connotation of "my great one" or "my teacher." It came to mean, as these different dimensions came together, a master or teacher of students. In the New Testament, Rabbi is used in direct address to Jesus, not as a title. For example, in John 1:38, we have the following discourse between Jesus and two disciples: "When Jesus turned and saw them following, he said to them, 'what are you looking for? They said to him, Rabbi, (which translated means Teacher), where are you staying?'" Jesus easily responds to the question when called Rabbi. He is comfortable with being called a teacher.

There are many qualities that make Jesus a distinctive and extraordinary teacher. I will address these qualities in some detail in section 2, but at this point, I want to stress how the role of rabbi shaped his teaching. It has to do primarily with the subjects of his teaching in that a rabbi is not unlike our understanding of a priest or pastor. He was not a teacher of the many subjects in a current university curriculum or even of the advanced learning in his time. He was rather a teacher about the *big questions*, the most important concerns of being human and navigating life. In unique and penetrating ways, he invites his listeners to understand the human drama. He speaks about the meaning of life, how to live in faithfulness to God, how to relate to others, how to live in an ethical way, how to deal with illness and suffering, and how to face death. He draws from the great insights of his Hebrew Bible and Jewish faith, but is not bound by authoritative interpretations. He speaks from deep inside of himself, as one with authority and with penetrating insight. People marvel, many are transformed, and yet some find what he says to be too hard to follow or threatening. The crowds come to hear and learn.

Jesus as Radical Prophet

There were many prophets in the Hebrew Bible, and no doubt Jesus learned about them as he was taught, possibly in the synagogue in Nazareth and in his associations with the priestly leadership of the Jewish community. He learned firsthand in his association with John the Baptist about the role of the prophet, and there were other contemporaries of Jesus who understood themselves as prophets.[87] The common understanding of the prophet was one who serves as a channel of communication between the human and divine world. In particular, the prophet's role was to proclaim the will of

86. Chilton chooses the title Rabbi as he writes about Jesus. See *Rabbi Jesus*.

87. E.g., Theudas and Judas the Galilean are mentioned as prophets in the time of Jesus in Acts 5:36–37.

God to the people and to speak about its urgency in the present and in the future.[88] There are those who have overly emphasized the predictive character to the prophet although this look into the future is often present as the prophet speaks. But in most cases the prophet points to the future with a warning. In many cases, the construct is that if you continue in your disobedient ways, violating the covenant, your future is in jeopardy. In other cases, the prophet brings hope, and the logic is if we turn to the ways of God, we will be blessed and have a good future. At times, the current situation looks so difficult that the prophet teaches that no human action will change the conditions and only the intervention of God will alter the current situation.

In addition, and especially in the case of Jesus, the prophet speaks with authority. His words are not mediated by reference to a past precedent or to a religious leader in Jerusalem. Further, Jesus bases his prophetic statements on his intimate relationship with God. Others may have felt very close to God as well, but few spoke with the authority and confidence of Jesus because of his sense of personal intimacy with the divine, his Father.[89] When he spoke, he spoke of the past to provide narratives as an example and to clarify the differences of interpretation of past precedents. He frequently begins his teaching with, "You have heard it said . . . but I say to you . . ." in order to give his comments context. For example in Matthew 5:43–44, we read: "You have heard that it was said, 'You shall love your neighbor and hate your enemy.' But I say to you, Love your enemies and pray for those who persecute you."

His subjects in his prophetic voice are many, but central to them is his teaching about the kingdom of God. Jesus speaks about this subject in all of its complexity, but underlines that the kingdom of God means the reign of God and the power and presence of God, which transforms individual lives and social conditions. We will expand on this concept in chapter 3, but two points might serve as an introduction. The first is that it has the structure of the past, the present, and the future. He speaks about the history of the Hebrew and their experience. He speaks about the current situation and its difficulties. And he speaks about the kingdom of God, now present in his ministry, but which will come in the future in a more dramatic and definitive form.

The second is that the reign of God expressed as the power and presence of God intersects with both individual lives and oppressive social conditions. A case in point might be the narrative in Luke 19:1–10 about the tax collector whose name was Zacchaeus. As Jesus comes to Jericho,

88. On occasion, the prophet is characterized as the one who speaks the word from God to the people, whereas the priest pleads the case of the people to God.

89. Sanders, *Historical Figure of Jesus*, 238–39.

the residence of Zacchaeus, he asks if he can spend the day with him. The conversation takes place and Zacchaeus is transformed as a person. In addition, the social conditions of oppression by Roman taxation and the corrupt practice of collecting taxes are challenged by the prophet from the peasant class who knew the meaning of poverty called Jesus. While oppressive social structures do not disappear, Zacchaeus does what he can to pay back what he has taken unfairly and which was justified by both government structures and the religious establishment. Jesus was a radical prophet who named injustice when he saw it.

In these three roles, that of compassionate healer, charismatic rabbi, and radical prophet, Jesus engages in teaching his followers about the most important issues of life. We turn now to expand on how his setting and these roles influenced his teaching. We will explore how he may have understood his vocation, and how others gave him titles of identity in an effort to learn what beliefs and values motivated this healer, teacher, and prophet. They sense, as his followers across the centuries have sensed that his identity and vocation shaped the manner and content of his teaching. We continue our trek across the rocky terrain toward the understanding of the teaching of Jesus.

Study Resources

Discussion Questions

1. How much does the study of the historical context in which Jesus lived tell us about him and his importance to Christians and others with a profound interest in Jesus?

2. How and why did Jesus relate to the government officials whom he encountered?

3. What differences in religious belief and practice did Jesus have with the religious leaders of his time?

4. How much was Jesus influenced by his religious heritage and how much did he move beyond it?

5. Which of the categories of understanding the Jesus of history (healer, teacher, and prophet) is most convincing and persuasive for you?[/NL]

Terms and Concepts

1. Pharisees: A large group of Jewish leaders who advocated a reinterpretation of the laws of Moses to guide Jewish believers in current situations and exigencies.

2. Sanhedrin: A Jewish ruling council of seventy leaders that functioned like a high court and decided on disputed issues and points of the law.

3. Yahweh: The Jewish name for God who is transcendent and omnipotent, the God who created the world and was sovereign of the power of evil.

4. Covenant: A formal agreement or treaty between 2 parties (Yahweh and the Jewish people) committing each party to certain obligations.

5. Prophet: One who serves as a channel of communication between the human and divine world; one who speaks the word of God to the people.

Suggestions for Reading and Reference

Charlesworth, James H. *Jesus within Judaism: New Light from Exciting Archaeological Discoveries*. New York: Doubleday, 1998.

Connick, C. Milo. *Jesus: The Man, the Mission, and the Message*. Englewood Cliffs, NJ: Prentice-Hall, 1974.

Crossan, John Dominic. *Jesus: A Revolutionary Biography*. San Francisco: HarperSanFrancisco, 1994.

Riches, John. *The World of Jesus: First-Century Judaism in Crisis*. New York: Cambridge University Press, 1990.

Sanders, E. P. *Jesus and Judaism*. Philadelphia: Fortress, 1985.

Vermes, Geza. *Jesus in His Jewish Context*. Minneapolis: Fortress, 2003.

3

Accessing the Teaching of Jesus
His Vocation

OUR GOAL IN THIS study is to understand more fully the radical teaching of Jesus. We spoke about the pursuit of this goal as a trek on demanding terrain; the teaching of Jesus is difficult to access. It is a movement back across two thousand years of history, culture, and languages, and the *primary records* we use as our map have a special character that must be factored into our journey. We must be good map readers. Chapter 1 was an introduction to the nature of these records, primarily the Gospels of the New Testament. The Gospels in particular and other parts of the New Testament are extremely helpful, but as we spoke about them, we urged that they be studied reflectively rather than naively, although a more devotional reading of them may provide spiritual guidance and be profoundly nurturing. We invited the use of several wisely developed and fine-tuned methods of historical study to help us access the teaching of Jesus. We were careful to acknowledge that history has its constraints, that it is a product of the imperfections of memory, the intrusion of presuppositions, and the inadequacies of documentation. In our trek through history we only get to the suburbs of truth and often find ourselves longing to get to the center of truth about what happened in the past. In our study of history, we learn that such a quest is difficult.

We continued our trek toward the goal of accessing the teaching of Jesus through history in chapter 2, believing that *the world of Jesus* would provide valuable guidance in both accessing and understanding his teaching. Jesus was a first-century Jew who lived in Palestine and was shaped by the rhythms of the region of Galilee. The time and place moved him and moved in him. He belonged to the land,[1] observed the governments and the power structures, pondered the nature of justice and oppression, and experienced first-century Judaism as a movement in crisis.[2] He sensed a divine call, left his work as a carpenter, visited the outspoken prophet, John the Baptist, and prepared himself in the wilderness of Judea for his work as a compassionate healer, charismatic teacher, and radical prophet. It was within this framework that he taught with profound wisdom and compelling insight about the most urgent questions of life and death.

One guiding theme for the study so far has been that history is of fundamental importance if we are to reach our goal of understanding the teaching of Jesus. We argued that we should attempt to study history with a sense of balance and proportion, with discipline, and openness to its factual and didactic nature. We underlined the importance of being self-aware about our own presuppositions and how they influence our reading of history. But even with these practices and this awareness, it is still a venture on to an unpredictable terrain. There are those who would argue, often persuasively that accessing Jesus is less dependent upon historical study and more a leap of faith. One may learn facts about Jesus through historical study, but a true relationship with Jesus is based on faith. It is more important to *know* Jesus than to know about him. I am sensitive to the importance of such a total commitment of trust, but maintain that there is wisdom in leaping with our eyes open, perhaps not fully aware of where we will land, but hoping that it is a leap based on a credible outlook and historical integrity, especially if we want to *access and understand the teaching of Jesus.* One might with the innocent faith of a child place one's life in the arms of loving parent or brother, but as we move from speaking like a child, thinking like a child, and reasoning like a child, we shift to adult ways.[3] We move from seeing in a mirror dimly to a better view.

We have argued that getting this better view comes with a careful study of the historical records and the Gospels in particular and in exploring the historical context in which Jesus lived, taught, and acted. There is one other point of view that will assist us in accessing Jesus and his teaching. It has to do with *understanding the person,* an exploration that is dependent upon the records and the historical setting, but goes beyond them to inquire about the way Jesus incorporated, internalized, and "owned" the values and beliefs of his historical circumstances. What was it that Jesus believed and valued?

1. Some have described Jesus as coming from the class called "the people of the land" and occasionally the concept of peasant is used, a concept that needs amplification. See Crossan, *Historical Jesus,* 24–136.

2. See Riches, *World of Jesus,* 10–29.

3. 1 Cor 13:11.

How did he understand his vocation and mission in life? What was his identity? As we probe for answers to these questions, we discover that once again we are on rocky terrain. From his time to ours, gifted, thoughtful, and faithful people have followed the trails through these mountains and valleys. The answers given to these questions are varied. I have learned a great deal from them for which I am grateful, but have found less unanimity than one might expect. I have learned that this search for answers about the identity of Jesus is a trek that is no easier than the earlier ones, the study of the records about Jesus and the exploration of the world of Jesus. But it is a trek that is crucial for us because *teachers teach out of their identity, values, and sense of calling.* And when one teaches about the most important questions of life, about relationships, ethics, meaning, and connecting with transcendence, one especially draws upon what gives life its center and coherence. Buddha did, Muhammad did, and certainly Jesus did with great conviction. What is his identity and mission? To these questions we now turn, with humility before their complexity.

The Vocation of Jesus

We observed in the previous chapter that Jesus is engaged in compassionate healing, taught with wisdom and insight, and prophetically challenged the systems and causes of suffering and oppression.[4] This is what he did during his public ministry in the region of Galilee and in his final days on his way to and in Jerusalem. What was motivating him and guiding him as he engaged in these challenging and remarkable activities? On this question, there is more agreement among New Testament scholars than on most questions regarding Jesus. They are careful to say that not enough is known to write an intimate biography, but what can be affirmed is that Jesus understood his vocation as *a calling to proclaim the kingdom of God and invite his followers and listeners to embrace the kingdom of God.* The author of Mark is clear: "The time is fulfilled, and the kingdom of God has come near; repent, and believe in the good news."[5] Of course this proclamation only raises more questions about what was meant by the kingdom of God, and once again, there are many points of view, and they come to us from the most gifted scholars of the ages.[6]

---

4. Matt 9:36: "When he saw the crowds, he had compassion for them, because they were harassed and helpless, like sheep without a shepherd."

5. Mark 1:15.

6. Albert Schweitzer devoted his attentions to the question in *The Mystery of the Kingdom of God.*

The Kingdom of God

The teaching of Jesus is full of metaphors and analogies. His use of them makes his teaching attention-getting, engaging, and compelling, and in many cases almost poetic.[7] His primary metaphor, which gives most of his teaching coherence, is the kingdom of God, and it would have been understood by his contemporaries as a way to talk about God; God's power is unlimited, not unlike that of a king. While the meaning of the term needed continual amplification (which Jesus did), his listeners would have understood the term's primary meaning to be the *reign of God, and the will and way of God at work in the world for good.*[8] His listeners would have heard his teaching as guidance, reflection, and comfort. They would understand that God will help the marginalized to be given their rights, the weak access to power, the ill the possibility of healing, and the lost and guilty forgiveness and redemption. They would have also heard about justice, accountability, and judgment.

Because Jesus taught about the kingdom of God in his itinerant ministry, he framed his comments in reference to the needs of his listeners and followers. His teaching was not in the form of an academic lecture based on a system of knowledge, but targeted toward the felt needs of the people who were present. In addition, the authors who record his teachings frame them in reference to the needs of the early Christian community. Therefore we do not have a systematic development of the concept, but a direct and engaging word of comfort and challenge. The author of Matthew's Gospel comes closest to an overview on the nature and expectations of the kingdom in the Sermon on the Mount, but even this section is set in the context of teaching to human need. What we have is immediate guidance and help, and as we are invited into these settings through the Gospels, we have questions. Does the kingdom point to the reign of God or is it about a place or setting where there is divine rule? Is the kingdom present or future or both? Is it about salvation or judgment or both? Is it the sole work of God or does it come through a messianic intermediary? Is it imposed or is there human freedom and participation? Is the kingdom about politics or being truly spiritual? Let's turn to these questions and others that will naturally follow.

Reign or Place? The message of the kingdom of God is primarily about *God's rule or reign* rather than a reference to a geographical place such as a city or state. The term kingdom does carry political overtones and, while it

---

7. Theissen and Merz, in *Historical Jesus*, have a chapter entitled "Jesus as Poet: The Parables of Jesus," 316–46.

8. See Rohr, *Jesus' Plan for a New World*, for a contemporary application of the kingdom of God.

has a very personal meaning, it has a corporate meaning as well. The goal is that the rule of God, which is to say the power and presence of God will reign in individual lives and in the corporate structures in which individuals live in order to ensure the well-being of all. He taught them to pray, "Your kingdom come. Your will be done on earth as it is in heaven."[9] Jesus teaches that those who have invited God's reign into their lives are truly blessed; they are pure in heart and will see God. But immediately following this pronouncement there is a reference to the peacemakers who are blessed, for they seek to build a just peace and shall be called the children of God.[10] The kingdom of God is about the transformation of individual lives and the social structures in which they live, made possible by the reign of God.

Present or Future? A second question that has been front and center in the debate about the meaning of the kingdom of God is whether it is present here and now for "subjects" who dwell in the kingdom or future in terms of divine action about the flow and end of history. The records indicate that Jesus taught that the kingdom of God is near and immediately present. He says, "The time is fulfilled and the kingdom of God has come near; repent, and believe in the good news."[11] Jesus embodies the message, and he urges his listeners to change direction and embrace the good news of God's reign. All of the signs point to the kingdom's nearness and power: "So also, when you see these things taking place, you know that it is near, at the very gates."[12] It is especially present for those who are persecuted: "Blessed are those who are persecuted for righteousness' sake, for theirs is the kingdom of heaven."[13]

The coming of the kingdom may start in a small way, and it might be easily missed. Jesus says that it is like a tiny mustard seed dropped in the ground, not immediately apparent, but which will grow to a tree big enough for a bird's nest. Or it might be compared to the woman who mixes yeast in her dough, and returns to find that the leavened dough became loaves of bread.[14] So the kingdom of God is present here and now, but will grow and have implications for the people of Israel and for all people. Because it might be easily missed, it is important to be prepared and anticipating its arrival. Jesus says: "Keep awake therefore, for you do not know on what day

---

9. Matt 6:10.
10. Matt 5:8–9.
11. Mark 1:15.
12. Mark 13:29.
13. Matt 5:10.
14. Matt 13:31–33.

your Lord is coming."[15] When the kingdom comes in its fullness, there will be both blessing and judgment, so keep awake and do not miss its coming which would be like a wedding in which the bridegroom was late and missed his opportunity to get married.[16] The kingdom is already present, but not yet fully realized. It is both present and future, and its full coming will be a dramatic divine intervention, often associated in Christian thought with the second coming of Jesus.[17] More likely, Jesus was not speaking about a second coming, but was pointing to God's intervention for the renewal of Israel.[18]

Salvation or Judgment? Once again, there have been those interpreters of the Gospel records that have stressed that the coming of the kingdom is good news that transforms one's life and makes it whole while others have stressed that there will be judgment with the coming of the kingdom. The records indicate that Jesus speaks of both salvation and judgment. For example, in reference to salvation, Jesus teaches that the kingdom brings abundant joy, like the fisherman who throws his net into the sea and catches fish of every kind.[19] This fisherman is not unlike others with need, such as the poor in spirit who now have full access to the transforming power of the reign of God, and those who mourn that will be comforted by the presence of God.[20] Jesus also speaks of judgment when he says that it is not unlike the harvest of wheat when both the grain and the weeds are harvested together: "Let both of them grow together until the harvest; and at harvest time I will tell the reapers, collect the weeds first and bind them in bundles to be burned but gather the wheat into my barn."[21] John the Baptist emphasized judgment in his preaching about the kingdom, but opened the door to salvation through baptism. The records suggest that Jesus often led with salvation but judgment is present in the background.[22]

God Alone or Others? The goal of the reign of God is to bring in the will and way of God. The records indicate that Jesus understands himself as the one who proclaims the arrival and presence of the kingdom of God. Luke

15. Matt 24:42.

16. Matt 25:1–13.

17. Matt 16:27–28. On this question, much has been written and there continues to be differences of opinion. See, e.g., the recent work by Allison, *Constructing Jesus*, 31–220. A conservative and thoughtful account of the kingdom as both present and future is Beasley-Murray, *Jesus and the Kingdom of God*. An earlier book by Ladd, *Critical Questions about the Kingdom of God*, maintains a similar point of view.

18. See Horsely, *Prophet Jesus and the Renewal of Israel*, 130–49.

19. Matt 13:47–49.

20. Matt 5:3–4.

21. Matt 13:30.

22. Theissen and Merz, *Historical Jesus*, 275.

writes that at the beginning of the Galilean ministry, Jesus rises to preach in the synagogue of Nazareth and proceeds to say that he has been called by God to fulfill what has been written, "The Spirit of the Lord is upon me, because he has anointed me to bring good news to the poor. He has sent me to proclaim release to the captives and recovery of sight to the blind, to let the oppressed go free, to proclaim the year of the Lord's favor."[23] Jesus understands that he is the one God has chosen (anointed) and he will be the intermediary to proclaim and embody the kingdom. It is also clear that Jesus invites a human response to the invitation. The kingdom is present in Jesus and he urges his listeners and followers to embrace the kingdom. In the proclamation of the coming kingdom, Jesus on occasion refers to one like the Son of Man who sows the seed. The term Son of Man often was just a reference to a human person but as Jesus speaks about the kingdom and uses the term, it is likely that he was pointing to a messianic intermediary referenced in the book of Daniel and was speaking about the future of the kingdom in apocalyptic images.[24] Either way, it is clear that Jesus teaches that there is need for a human response; an act of the will that affirms and says yes to the invitation. He says, "Let anyone with ears listen."[25]

Costly or Graciously Given? As before, this question is answered as more of a "both-and" than an "either-or." There is a cost, but it is not a cost in reference to money or possessions; the invitation is open to all, including those who are poor, meek, and marginalized. The good news of the kingdom, the transforming power and presence of God is available to all, but it means that we must change. "Then Jesus told his disciples, 'If any want to become my followers, let them deny themselves and take up their cross and follow me. For those who want to save their life will lose it, and those who lose their life for my sake will find it.'"[26] He goes on to say that we should not worry about what we should eat or what we should wear or for that matter about fame and fortune if we say yes to the invitation. The message is: "But strive first for the kingdom of God and his righteousness, and all these things shall be given to you as well."[27] In addition, we must receive the

---

23. Luke 4:18–19, quoting Isa 61:1–2.

24. Matt 13:41–42. See Dan 7:13–14, in which the Hebrew *bar adam* (Son of Man) is used, a term that may merely mean a human being, but I suggest it points to a special messenger. We will say more about the eschatological dimension of Jesus' teaching in section 2. See Zeitlin, *Jesus and the Judaism of His Time*, 121–25.

25. Matt 13:43.

26. Matt 17:24–25. We will expand on the meaning of these verses in the next section.

27. Matt 6:33.

kingdom without deceit and mixed motivations, but with the humility and
innocence of a child.[28]

Of Supreme Value or only One of Many Blessings? Jesus understands
that his vocation in life is to proclaim the message of the kingdom of God
and invite his listeners to "strive first for the kingdom of God and his righteousness." We should do anything and everything we need to do in order
to receive the power and presence of God into our lives and allow God's will
and way to reign. Matthew's Gospel records Jesus as saying: "The kingdom
of heaven is like a treasure hidden in the field, which someone found and
hid: then in his joy he goes and sells all that he has and buys that field." Further, he teaches: "Again, the kingdom of heaven is like a merchant in search
of fine pearls; on finding one pearl of great value, he went and sold all that
he had and bought it."[29]

Jesus as Messiah

Jesus understood his vocation as one who proclaims the kingdom of God,
invites people to change directions (repent), and receive God's power and
presence. He speaks of it as a transforming experience for individuals, but
also as divine power to transform social and political social structures to ensure justice and the well-being of all. It would have been natural for those who
saw him heal and heard him teach to ask whether he was the promised messiah. An alien government ruled the people of Israel and even their religious
faith seemed unable to give them comfort. Many hoped that a messiah would
come to deliver them. As they encountered Jesus they wondered if he might
be the anointed one, called by God to bring them deliverance and relief.

John's Gospel records that on a given day the Apostle John told others about Jesus and responded to people's questions about Jesus. Andrew
was with John and wanted his brother Simon (Peter) to meet Jesus. He
finds Simon and says, "We have found the messiah (which is translated
Anointed)."[30] In another incident, a critical one in terms of the decision to
go to Jerusalem, it is recorded that Jesus asks his disciples who people say
that he is. After some give and take, Peter answers, "You are the Messiah
(Christ), the Son of the living God"[31] and Jesus responds positively to Peter's
answer. Jesus is ready to culminate his ministry as the anointed one.

28. Matt 18:1–5.

29. Matt 13:44–46.

30. John 1:41.

31. Matt 16:16–17. There is, of course, some question as to whether these conversations actually took place, and, as we have suggested, a good historian will raise this

At this point, it is important to ask what was meant when the term messiah was used to describe Jesus. What did Peter have in mind if in fact those words were spoken approximately as they are recorded? It is also very important to note for our purposes of accessing and understanding the teaching of Jesus that his teaching would have been shaped by this identifying title. Did Jesus understand himself to be the promised Messiah? This question has extraordinary importance in understanding Jesus and his teaching, and scholars often refer to it as "the Messianic question."[32] My view is that it was most likely a term used by his followers, and in fact it became so common an appellation that it emerged as part of his name, Jesus *Christ*. The term messiah translates a Hebrew word, which means anointed, or more literally, one smeared with oil (lotion) as a symbolic appointment to a particular task. It appears in Greek as "Christos" and in English as "Christ."

Across the centuries, Christians have assumed that Jesus was the Messiah and it was and continues to be a commonly accepted way to describe Jesus within the Christian community. The global Christian church has generally accepted that the Gospel accounts in John 1 and Matthew 16 as well as other passages that refer to Jesus as the Messiah are accurate. But the Jewish community, both then and now has not accepted the title as an accurate description of the identity of Jesus. More neutral scholars point out that we cannot be sure that Jesus understood himself as the Messiah or whether his disciples thought of him as the Messiah. These scholars maintain that the references appear in passages that may not be linked to actual conversations and are used to develop the coordinating theme of their writing and to teach and guide a second generation of Christians. These positions must be factored into our treatment of the teaching of Jesus, but for now, I will focus on the different ways that the identifying label of messiah may have been understood in the time of Jesus.

The term was used in different ways in the time of Jesus, and it is difficult to be absolutely sure what may have been meant even if his contemporaries used the term to describe the identity of Jesus. But what can be affirmed is that it was one way of speaking about hope, that there was one who was anointed that would come and deliver an oppressed people. A brief review of Hebrew hopes in reference to the term messiah will shed some light on why Jesus was identified as Messiah by so many.[33]

---

question. It is true that the authors of both the Gospels of John and Matthew are inserting a point of view. But it is still likely, given the teaching and actions of Jesus, that many of his followers would think of him as the Messiah.

32. Connick, *Jesus*, 285–312. I am helped by his discussion and will draw upon it in this section about Jesus as messiah.

33. Zeitlin, *Jesus and the Judaism of His Time*, 115–26.

The Hebrew people articulated their hope in a messiah in a variety of ways. There were those at one extreme, in strong opposition to an alien government's oppression, who thought in terms of the political restoration of Israel with a descendent of King David sitting on the throne. The coming kingdom, ushered in by a messianic king would be a political state. Another less political and more spiritual hope was that all those within Israel would turn to God and ask God to be supreme in their lives; a message preached by John the Baptist. People from a distance as far away as Jerusalem came to hear John proclaim his message. The logic of the message was: if you obey the terms of the covenant, God will surely bless us. Still another expression of hope was that this messiah would prophetically challenge injustice by speaking truth to power regarding unjust social structures. The messiah would bring in a reign of peace and justice.

However, these hopes did not always include the special role of a messianic figure that would bring about the changes. In fact, Jewish hope was more deeply rooted in God, rather than an intermediary figure that would be honored as kingly and would bring about the new age. Further, Hebrew hopes were occasionally rooted in a more ambiguous future, one that was beyond death, a concept that would later develop into an anticipation of a condition similar to what we mean by speaking of heaven.

The Hebrew people and their religious leaders would turn to their past and to their scriptures which recorded their past in narrative form to find grounds for their hope. They would be told and read about the covenant promise with Abraham; they would repeat again and again the account of Moses and the exodus from slavery in Egypt; they would speak in their religious services about the story of the conquest of Canaan; and they would glory in the days of empire with King David. They would review their mixed history following David, including the Babylonian exile, and their great prophets that spoke of judgment, but also of hope and a new era. They would hear and read 2 Isaiah about a Servant who will faithfully guide and lead all people to a time when there will be justice on earth.[34] Christians saw in the description of the Suffering Servant who suffers and is judged and executed a prophetic description of Jesus, the Christ, and it was easy to identify the Suffering Servant as Jesus the Messiah.[35]

At the heart of the Messianic question is whether Jesus thought of himself as Messiah, and if so, whether he gave the term his own definition. His life and teaching did not perfectly fit any of the views held by people in his time, although his life and teaching epitomized certain characteristics

34. Isa 42–53.
35. Isa 53:1–13.

of these several views. As before, there are competent scholars and church leaders who strongly assert that the notion of a messiah that would deliver the people from their troubles was central to the self-understanding of Jesus. It is and was an integral part of what we mean by the Jesus of history. Equally competent scholars say that there simply is not enough information to speak of Jesus as the expected messiah or as one who understood himself in that role. They maintain that it would be more accurate to speak about how Jesus as Messiah came to be part of the Christ of faith in a succeeding generation, not the Jesus of history.

To some extent, on religious questions such as these, even the most objective scholars often arrive where they start and find confirming evidence for their assertions and convictions. A good case can be made for both positions. I find sufficient evidence to suggest that it is likely that Jesus was aware of his contemporaries' understanding of the place of a messiah in reference to their hope. It is likely that he felt anointed and called to proclaim the kingdom of God as the reign of God, a vocation well within the framework of messianic expectations.[36] It was not the same as claiming to be divine, or even the Son of God as this term implied a special connection with God. It was rather a human role, not unlike that of a prophet, who is anointed to proclaim the kingdom of God.

At this point, it may be wise to summarize the various views about the kingdom of God as the way to speak about the vocation of Jesus and about the term "messiah" as a way of speaking about his identity. These terms are fundamental to understanding the teachings of Jesus. At the risk of possible over-simplification, let me mention three major patterns, although there is diversity within these groupings.[37]

The first is to accept *a direct reading of the text*, that Jesus did understand the kingdom of God as both present and future, and that he had the primary role in bringing in the kingdom of God, a calling that was messianic in character. Often accompanying this view is that Jesus did expect his death, and the turn to go to Jerusalem toward the end of his public ministry of proclaiming the kingdom would be the culmination of his God-given purpose in life. He also believed, although he appears to have been unsure about the time of the coming of the full kingdom that the full realization of the kingdom might occur in the immediate future.[38] Some have suggested

---

36. But my position may be challenged by arguing that I, too, end up where I started, within the Christian position.

37. Theissen and Merz, *Historical Jesus*, 277–78.

38. Luke 21:1–28.

that Jesus was wrong about the timing,[39] although he was right about the divine design. This position accepts the view that the sequence would not change, even if the end did not come within his generation or the generations immediately following. After his death and resurrection, there would be an intermediate stage, often called the age of the church, and that the church should work to implement the values of the kingdom and wait expectantly for the second coming and the full arrival of the kingdom.[40] This view is often framed within the general rubric of salvation-history as a description of the patterned way for God to work to achieve human salvation and the end of history. Critics of this view have pointed out the obvious, that the second coming of Christ and the full expression of the kingdom of God have simply not occurred, and it may have been an expectation of apocalyptic hope of first-century Judaism, but now it should be viewed as only an appreciation of their way of expressing hope in the future in language and concepts that are no longer relevant. The intention of the language is to give hope, and we wait in faith on a providential God.

A second view attempts to stay well within the Christian understanding of the world and the role of Jesus in salvation history. But it puts the *emphasis on the primary purpose of the apocalyptic language about hope* and understands this expression of hope as a symbolic way of speaking. It uses premodern and obsolete categories that can now be discarded, but in setting them aside, we should not lose the hope about which they speak which is expressive of a Christian truth. One highly respected New Testament scholar of a previous generation, C. H. Dodd, spoke about a "realized eschatology," that the kingdom came, as far as history is concerned, fully in the person and work of Jesus as the messiah.[41] The kingdom of God is primarily a present experience, and references to unknown future, while still a part of Christian hope, point to a consummation beyond history.[42] Another well-known New Testament scholar of the mid-twentieth century, Rudolf Bultmann, maintained that the gospel or good news proclaimed by Jesus in the category of the kingdom of God is and can be a current reality.[43] It is a call to accept

---

39. See Schweitzer, *Quest of the Historical Jesus*, 356–58.

40. The dispensational movement, originating in England in the nineteenth century, and active within the evangelical tradition through the last century and into the present, speaks about "dispensations" or periods of time for these phases and attempts to discern the future by a careful reading of Scripture.

41. Dodd, *Founder of Christianity*, 114–18.

42. Ibid., 115.

43. He writes about an existential interpretation of the proclaimed kerygma in several books, but a good explanation of his views can be found in his classic two-volume work *Theology of the New Testament*, 1:1–53.

the message of Jesus, or in the language of existentialism, a summons to a life-changing decision in the acceptance of the kerygmatic proclamation. Bultmann speaks about setting aside the mythological assumptions in which the message is encased and affirming the intent of the message.

Still another view, more within the framework of the academic study of religion and its use of sociological and scientific language, speaks about the *evolution of religious perspectives.*[44] Views within this frame of reference maintain that our religious beliefs evolve over time, and that the proclamation of Jesus contains the universal wisdom within the categories of his time and place in history, but that human understanding and the framing of them changes as history, culture, and language evolve. One view, addressing the altruistic teaching of Jesus, maintains that we do live between two worlds, biological and cultural. We are still subject to the biological realities of the survival of the fittest and make decisions and selections in reference to survival. But there is a cultural evolution as well, one influenced by the teaching of Jesus and the continual affirmation of his values in the life of the church that go against the inherent determinism in this "Darwinian worldview." It is not a denial of evolution, but an invitation to lift one's ethical understanding above instinctive survival concerns and to make love and compassion the guiding principles of life. This interaction between the two worlds continues to be with us, and by understanding it, we can make conscious choices about the good life, of loving our neighbor as we love ourselves.[45]

The Christ of Faith

We have maintained that the vocation of Jesus was to proclaim the kingdom of God and that it had arrived in a special way in his life. He urged individuals to change direction and invite God to reign in their lives, and he gave guidance about how to live a spiritual and ethical life reflective of the will and way of God. He went on in his role as a teaching prophet to challenge social structures that were unjust, oppressive, and caused suffering, and he spoke about the full arrival of the kingdom in the apocalyptic language of first-century Judaism. As people encountered him and reflected upon his life and teaching, they found categories used in their religion, history, culture, and language to describe him, one of which was messiah, a term describing one who is anointed to a particular calling. Though not all agree,

---

44. See, e.g., Wright, *Evolution of God*. The classic three-volume work of Eliade, *History of Religious Ideas*, employs a social scientific methodology. Bellah, in his recent book *Religion in Human Evolution*, uses a similar methodology.

45. See Ferguson, *Lovescapes*, 55–56.

it is likely that Jesus thought of himself as Messiah, called by God to bring in the kingdom of God.[46]

We have maintained that the teaching of Jesus can be better understood by focusing on the vocation of Jesus in reference to the kingdom of God and that he did his "kingdom work" as one *anointed* by God, as Messiah, as the Christ. By understanding the vocation and identity of Jesus, we grasp his reference point and are able to understand more fully his teaching. These two dimensions of the life of Jesus become an integral part of our hermeneutic or framework for interpreting his teaching. There were other categories used by his contemporaries and followers to describe the identity and vocation of Jesus that will guide us as well. The majority of them are not in opposition to the description of Jesus who was messianic in his proclamation of the kingdom, but are complementary to these primary categories.

Within a generation, the followers of Jesus moved from understanding the carpenter from Nazareth who was their colleague and friend to the Christ (Messiah) of faith. He was more than a compassionate healer, a charismatic teacher, and a radical prophet, though he was certainly all of these. This movement to understanding Jesus as the Christ of faith would shape the way people would understand their faith in Jesus, and the records we have of his teaching come primarily from this era of reflection. We turn now to a brief description of these emerging patterns toward the Christ of faith and how the content and pattern of his teaching reflected in the Gospels are shaped by these new categories of understanding.

The Son of Man

One of the primary ways of understanding the term "messiah" was in reference to kingly rule. The early kings of Israel were described as anointed by God, and as time went along, the term was used in reference to an ideal king, a descendent of David who would come to deliver Israel from foreign oppression and reign in righteousness.[47] The prophet Zechariah writes: "Lo, your king comes to you; triumphant and victorious is he, humble and riding on an ass, on a colt the foal of an ass . . . and he shall command peace to the nations; his dominion shall be from sea to sea, and from the River to the ends of the earth."[48] This passage is quoted in the Gospels in the account of

46. There is a point of view that I find persuasive, and it is that Jesus developed his self-understanding as Messiah as he began his public ministry.

47. I follow the interpretation of Zeitlen, *Jesus and the Judaism of the His Time*, 121–25.

48. Zech 9:9–10.

Jesus sending two of his disciples to secure a colt on which he can ride into Jerusalem, an incident often called somewhat ironically as "the Triumphal Entry." The incident is understood as the entrance of Messiah into Jerusalem although a different one than expected in that he comes in a humble rather than a kingly way. It is a clear contrast with Pontius Pilate who may have also entered Jerusalem that day, protected by Roman soldiers riding into Jerusalem on their magnificent horses, trumpets blaring, armed, and dressed in military attire.

This event sets the stage for the final week of the life of Jesus, a week filled with assorted, conflicted, and crucial conversations. One of them is with the high priest who questions Jesus. The high priest is recorded as saying: "I put you under oath before the living God, tell us if you are the Messiah, the Son of God. Jesus said to him, 'You have said so. But I tell you, from now on you will see the Son of Man seated at the right hand of Power and coming on the clouds of heaven.'"[49] In this story, two terms are used to describe the identity of Jesus, the Son of God and the Son of Man. We will say more about the title Son of God below, but let's look more closely at the term Son of Man in that it is the phrase Jesus is quoted as using to describe himself.

The phrase (in Hebrew *bar adam*, or the Aramaic *bar nasha*) is often a simple reference to or a synonym for an individual who is saying, "I am just a person of human parents, just like you." The term is used in the third person as a way of implying reserve or modesty. But this particular event suggests a more nuanced meaning, and it is one that the Gospel authors report that he used frequently as he spoke about himself. The phrase is placed on the lips of Jesus in the Synoptic Gospels sixty-nine times and thirteen times in John's Gospel. It is clear that Jesus was familiar with the term, and it may point to the humility of Jesus in his response to the high priest. But it may have also been a response based on the passage in Daniel (7:13–14), which speaks of a kingly figure which will come and rule in great power. In other instances, Jesus uses the term Son of Man in reference to himself in more than a modest reference to himself. For example he is recorded as saying, "the Son of Man has authority on earth to forgive sins"[50] and "the Son of Man is lord of the Sabbath."[51] These passages suggest divine power and authority, and that Jesus is moving from carpenter to Christ in the belief of the early Christian community.

Some scholars have suggested that the term has a communal connotation, which may mean that Jesus is referring also to his disciples. Jesus did

49. Matt 26:63–64.
50. Matt 9:6.
51. Matt 12:8.

have many companions in his ministry, and they shared the ministry of Jesus with him. But the term in several places points more likely to a messianic figure that will bring in the kingdom. Mark's Gospel records Jesus as saying, "But in those days, after that suffering, the sun will be darkened, and the moon will not give its light, and the stars will be falling from heaven, and the powers in the heavens will be shaken. Then they will see 'the Son of Man coming in clouds' with great power and glory."[52] The term Son of Man may be thought of as a transitional term, likely present on the lips of the historical Jesus, but used by the writers of the Gospels at a later time to speak about Jesus the Christ. The term has clearly moved to the Christ of faith when it is used in reference to the dramatic act of God, called the Second Coming of Jesus, in which God does bring in a new era in which there will be deliverance from suffering and oppression and the institution of a just peace.

In summary, one might think of this term as both son of man and Son of Man. It may be a reference in the third person to a human being, a child of parents, a son or a daughter. It may be an attempt to speak humbly about oneself and saying that I was just another human being present in a particular set of circumstances. Jesus likely used the phrase in this way, but he also may have used the phrase in reference to his mission to bring in the kingdom of God and point to the future consummation of history.

The Son of God

The title Son of God also has traces of being a term used during the life of Jesus, but less so by Jesus as an identifying title and more by his followers. The term has roots in the ancient Near East and in the Hebrew Bible. As it was used in the surrounding region in which Jesus lived, it was a term that often described one who was a descendent of a king. But this usage, while in the background, was not the primary point of reference for its use in the New Testament. As it is used as a title for Jesus in the Gospels, it more likely reflects a Jewish understanding from the biblical narratives found in the Hebrew Bible. In several places, the nation of Israel and its inhabitants are called the sons or children of God[53] and there are passages that refer to God as Israel's father.[54] There are also references to the king as God's son[55] and this meaning is present in the description of David and Solomon as kings.[56]

52. Mark 13:24–26.
53. Deut 14:1; Hos 1:10.
54. Jer 31:9; Mal 1:6.
55. Ps 2:7.
56. 2 Sam 7:14.

This use of the term carries over into the intertestamental period in reference to those who honor God and live righteously.

In the New Testament, there are few references of Jesus referring to himself as the Son of God. One passage in John's Gospel is more an exception than the rule. In John 10:36, in which he defends himself against accusations of claiming to be divine, he is quoted as admitting that he said, "I am the Son of God" and then says it is an appropriate title for one who does the will of God. In this passage as elsewhere, he speaks of his filial relationship with God. But the Gospel accounts suggest that he preferred to refer to himself as the Son of Man. The Son of God title does occur more frequently in the writing of Paul and in the Gospel of John than the Synoptic Gospels, but as one reads these accounts, it appears that they represent the growing belief within the new Christian community that Jesus was in some sense divine or filled with the presence of God. Jesus has become the Christ of faith who in some special way is the Son of God. Paul does use the title "Son of God" with the assumption that Jesus is specially related to God, although he is more likely to describe Jesus as Lord, Savior, and Christ. When he does speak of Jesus as the Son of God, it is often in apocalyptic passages in which there is the theme of hope and the expectation that Jesus will return.[57]

During the lifetime of Jesus (the pre-Easter Jesus), the special experience he had with God was described in filial terms. He experienced God as Abba (Father) in a way that described an earthly father with whom he had a close and intimate relationship.[58] Within the Synoptic Gospels, there are two other references to Jesus moving beyond the more intimate familial use of God as father (Mark 13:32; Matt 11:27), but the authenticity of these passages is often questioned. It is more appropriate to separate the filial reference to God as an earthly father from the more Christological title of Son of God.[59] This title is consistently used in reference to the post-Easter Jesus and is based on the belief in the resurrection. The Apostle Paul writes in his letter to the Romans that Jesus "declared to be the Son of God with power according to the spirit of holiness by resurrection from the dead, Jesus Christ our Lord."[60] Other passages in the synoptic tradition push this appointment or declaration of Jesus as the Son of God back to the baptism[61]

---

57. Gal 2:20; 1 Thess 1:10. I will say more about Paul's view below.

58. Mark 14:36.

59. See the article by Fuller on the Son of God in the *Harper's Bible Dictionary*, 979–81.

60. Rom 1:4.

61. Mark 1:11.

and the transfiguration. These references reflect the point of view of the authors and are integral to the development of their coordinate themes.[62]

The Gospel of John, our latest Gospel, has developed the theology of the post-Easter Jesus in a different frame of reference than Paul or the Synoptic Gospels. John points to the preexistence of Jesus and speaks of him as divine wisdom (logos), which takes expression as the eternal Son of God.[63] With the title "Son of God" we see a clear movement from a description of the Jesus of history to the Christ of faith.

Other Images of Jesus in the Gospels and Paul

While the Synoptic Gospels are different in tone and style than the Gospel of John, it would nevertheless be accurate to say that this same movement is present in them as well. By the time these Gospels were written, Jesus had become one in whom the early generations of Christians have put their faith. There are incidents in the life of Jesus that are described and lessons learned from these descriptions, but the more fundamental goal of these Gospels is to invite faith in Jesus the Christ and to guide Christians in their new found faith.[64]

The Gospel of Mark, commonly accepted as the first of the canonical Gospels, has historically been characterized as being the Gospel that describes the Jesus of history. Mark is very focused on events in the life of Jesus and moves quickly from one event to another, often with the transitional word "immediately." Jesus does appear to being moving quickly from healing to exorcism to teaching and doing so with great authority. Mark captures much in the life of Jesus that might be categorized as historical description, and the other two synoptic Gospels, Matthew and Luke use Mark as a very important resource in the writing of their gospel accounts. But a careful reading of Mark indicates that his account is held together and given coherence by the theme that Jesus is the Messiah, a Messiah who may be identified as the Son of Man as well.[65] This critical and informative observation about the Gospel of Mark, articulated clearly by Johannes Weiss in the late nineteenth century, was soon accepted by many New Testament scholars and is often referred to the "Messianic Secret." From the start in Mark's Gospel, *there is*

---

62. Mark 9:7.

63. John 1:14–18.

64. See Fredriksen's fine discussion of this development in *From Jesus to Christ*, 18–64.

65. The classic work that identifies Mark's theme is Weiss, *Jesus' Proclamation of the Kingdom of God*.

an affirmation of faith in the Messiah: "The beginning of the good news of Jesus Christ, the Son of God.[66]" At the finish of the Gospel of Mark, although there may be a section that has been lost, there is an expression of faith in the resurrection: "Do not be alarmed; you are looking for Jesus of Nazareth, who was crucified. He has been raised; he is not here. Look, there is the place they laid him."[67] Jesus is the Messiah, the risen Christ.

The author of *Matthew* begins with the same set of assumptions and beliefs as Mark about Jesus, but has a slightly different theme that gives order to his Gospel. Matthew's Gospel describes *Jesus as the expected Messiah prophesied in the Hebrew Scriptures*. Matthew begins with the genealogy of Jesus and immediately makes it clear that he is placing Jesus within the framework of biblical history. He gives to Jesus his messianic roots; Jesus is the expected Jewish messiah. As he moves through his description of the life and teachings of Jesus, he references his descriptions with the phrase, "This took place to fulfill what the Lord has spoken through the prophet."[68] He quotes directly from the Hebrew Bible sixty times in the course of his Gospel, and once this foundation has been established, he goes on to develop other themes, ones that are at the heart of the teaching of Jesus. In Matthew's Gospel, we have many passages that are commonly known: a detailed and colorful birth account with the star and the visit of the wise men, the profound Sermon on the Mount which contains the Lord's Prayer, the feeding of the five thousand, a listing of miracles and parables, and a dramatic description of the last week of the life of Jesus. We will return to Matthew's Gospel as we describe the teaching of Jesus in section 2.

The Gospel of Luke, also dependent on Mark's Gospel, gives us still another perspective on Jesus, but does not move away from the affirmation that Jesus is the expected Messiah. The change is that *Jesus came as Messiah not exclusively for the Jewish community, but also for Gentiles*. The Gospel opens with the intended purpose, "to compile a narrative of the things which have been accomplished among us . . . so, most excellent Theophilus, that you may know the truth concerning the things of which you have been informed."[69] Luke intends to write as a historian and inform all those who want a researched narrative. He has read other accounts, and wants to write an "orderly one" for his Greek friend, Theophilus. He carefully sets the stage by framing his account in the context of Herod and Caesar Augustus.[70]

---

66. Mark 1:1.

67. Mark 16:6.

68. See Matt 5:17: "Do not think that I have come to abolish the law or the prophets; I have come not to abolish but to fulfill."

69. Luke 1:1–4.

70. Fredriksen, *From Jesus to Christ*, 27–36.

He proceeds to describe how God's Spirit entered into human history in the person of Jesus and how the message of this Risen Christ has relevance for the Gentile church. He provides a detailed and beautifully written account of how it all happened. He speaks of the birth of Jesus and places it in the context of what has gone before, placing the birth and the surrounding events within the large frame of biblical history. In these early chapters, Luke uses several identifying titles for Jesus—Savior, Lord, Christ, Son of David (another way of saying messiah), and Son of God. His account contains several well-known passages, which depict Jesus as a compassionate healer, a charismatic teacher and a radical prophet, but holding it altogether is the theme of Jesus coming as a universal "messiah" for humankind. There is the birth account and the visit of the shepherds, his presentation in the temple, the precocious child in the temple, the baptism by John the Baptist, and the time in the wilderness. He calls his disciples and proceeds to heal and teach. He encounters those who ask questions and challenge his authority. He continues to teach that his followers should love their enemies, and that God loves even those who fall away, as a father receives his prodigal son with joy and acceptance. There is a large section in Luke that is not repeated in the other Synoptic Gospels in which he travels with his disciples to Jerusalem. He enters Jerusalem, has many conversations, is arrested, tried, convicted, and crucified. Through this story, marvelously told, we encounter a loving Jesus, one who teaches with great wisdom, manages complex and challenging conversations and situations, and who faithfully follows his anointed role as a loving Messiah to all people. Historical events are mentioned and conversations and teachings are recorded, but as with the other Gospels, we see the movement from the Jesus of history to the Christ of faith.

With *Paul*, we have writings that are earlier than the Gospels, but for reasons related to his understanding of his mission, he is less concerned about the historical Jesus. *What he is concerned about is the meaning of Jesus*, and Paul articulates a comprehensive theology that places Jesus at the center of God's redemptive plan for humankind. Paul was a contemporary of Jesus and did have some contact with those who were in the immediate circle of followers of Jesus, but he was independent of this original circle. Initially, as a faithful Jew, he resisted the new Christian movement and saw it as a threat to his Pharisaic Judaism. The book of Acts speaks of his persecution of the new Christian movement, but then records his conversion to the Christian faith[71] and his subsequent mission to proclaim the Christian faith. It is a fascinating story and one of great importance for the early development of Christianity. But it does not take us directly into our subject, the teaching of Jesus. There are references by Paul to the ethical principles of Jesus, but he is primarily concerned to say that Jesus the Messiah, the Son of God, was

71. Acts 9.

the Savior of humankind, and indeed all of creation. Paul's ethical teaching is generally consistent with the teaching of Jesus, and his way of identifying Jesus is in comparable to the ways the Gospel writers identify Jesus. But we are not introduced as we read his writings to an account of the historical Jesus, but an affirmation of Jesus as Savior and Lord who redeems the human family and calls them into a relationship with God through Jesus the Savior and a way of life which honors God, empowered by God's Spirit. Paul is squarely focused on the Christ of faith, and his views had and continued to have influence on the way the teaching of Jesus was understood.

Access to the Identity of Jesus

Our purpose is to find the best possible access to the life and teachings of Jesus. We have maintained that this access is not as easy as one might expect; the access is a trek across a demanding terrain. We are separated from the life and teachings of Jesus by nearly two thousand years, and to find our way back to his time and place requires knowledge and thoughtful strategies. We are fortunate to have records of his life and teaching, but they come to us as accounts written many years after his life, and they have been copied and altered over the centuries. But they tell us a great deal as we learn how to read them wisely, and as we learn from those who have read them and interpreted them across the centuries. We also said that we could learn much about the life and teaching of Jesus by studying the world in which he lived. He was a first-century Jew who lived in the region of Galilee and saw the world through his history, his culture, his language, and especially his religion of first-century Judaism. We have trekked across this rocky terrain and arrived at a third challenge of access. With care, we read the accounts (primarily the Gospels) and we paid attention to his historical setting. We then added a third perspective or viewpoint to observe his life and teaching, that of his vocation and identity. We explored the way he may have understood himself and his mission and how others described him and gave him identifying titles.

With a sense of the complexity and importance of our task and with some caution we said the Jesus understood his vocation as the proclamation of the kingdom of God and to invite his listeners to embrace the reign of God in their lives and in the social structures of their society. We said that the most common term used both by Jesus and by his immediate followers was messiah, an expected and anointed one who would come to deliver the people form their oppression and suffering and bring in a more just and peaceful setting for the welfare of all. We then spoke about the other terms used to identity Jesus and gave special attention to the terms of Son of Man and Son of God.

The question of the identity of Jesus continues to be a complex question, especially as one begins to identify Jesus as more than an extraordinary human being and in some sense divine or filled with the divine presence. Even during and immediately following the culminating events of the life of Jesus, good and gifted people struggled with how best to describe him. He was a compassionate healer, a charismatic teacher, and a radical prophet, but was it wise, given the evidence, to go beyond these identifying qualities and speak of him in terms that implied transcendence. The believing community of followers began to move in this direction, and soon they were speaking not just about the Jesus of history but the Christ of faith. It may have been easier then, prior to the development of rationalism, science, and historical-critical study. In this premodern world, natural and supernatural existed side by side in easy relationship. But the contemporary world has more difficulty going back to the discussions and theological categories at Nicaea and Chalcedon.

Over time, these ecumenical formulations about the identity and divinity of Jesus were continued. The discussions through the Middle Ages continued to reflect on the meaning of the atonement, and there was more refinement in the Reformation. In time, beginning with the Enlightenment, and across the modern period were various quests to understand Jesus, many questioned the categories of an earlier time. This fascinating story will be in our minds.[72] We know that we must take these historical patterns of understanding into account as we attempt to understand the teaching of Jesus. I have traveled these roads, but we will not map them in any detail in our study of the teaching of Jesus. But they inevitably shape the way we read the record, and we will try to be self-aware of prior understanding as we begin the study of the teaching of Jesus to which we now turn.

Study Resources

Discussion Questions

1. What was the vocation of Jesus? How do you think he understood the meaning of his life?

---

72. Several thoughtful books trace this development. Among them are Neill, *Jesus through Many Eyes*, a book that focuses on the early period of development. Pelikan, in *Jesus through the Centuries*, traces the ways that different cultures framed their understanding of Jesus. Duling, in *Jesus Christ through History*, provides a fine textbook for understanding the patterns of interpretation of Jesus.

2. In what ways, as Jesus spoke about the kingdom of God, did he describe it as present and as future?

3. Do you think you can get a trustworthy understanding of Jesus by reading the New Testament? What should you keep in mind as you read?

4. What title do you use when you talk about Jesus and why?

5. Do you identify more with the Jesus of history or the Christ of faith?

Terms and Concepts

1. The Jesus of History and the Christ of Faith: The first of these terms is used to describe the life of Jesus in Palestine in the first century; the second term is used to describe how Jesus was understood by those who believed that he was the Messiah, the Son of God.

2. Kingdom of God: A way of speaking about the power and presence of God in the world for good, transforming human lives, social structures, and pointing to a future time of deliverance and hope.

3. Messiah: A word meaning an anointed one, a person chosen for a particular task in life. Jesus was and is thought to be the Messiah by many people who believe he was sent by God to save humankind.

4. Son of Man: A term in some cases merely referring to an individual as a child of human parents, but also used as a term pointing to one who comes as Messiah; a term used to identify Jesus.

5. Son of God: A term referring to Jesus ascribing to him a special relationship with God and defining Jesus as in some sense divine.

Suggestions for Reading and Reference

Allison, Dale C., Jr. *Constructing Jesus: Memory, Imagination, and History*. Grand Rapids: Baker Academic, 2010.

Dodd, C. H. *The Founder of Christianity*. London: Collins, 1971.

Fredriksen, Paula. *From Jesus to Christ*. New Haven: Yale University Press, 1988.

Pelikan, Jaroslav. *Jesus through the Centuries: His Place in the History of Culture*. New Haven: Yale University Press, 1985.

Schweitzer, Albert. *The Quest of the Historical Jesus*. New York: Macmillan, 1948. Translated by W. Montgomery from the 1st German ed., *Von Reimarus zu Wrede*, 1906.

SECTION 2 _____

The Teaching

Ways of Understanding

SECTION 2 WILL BUILD upon our successful navigation of the terrain that must be crossed to gain access to the teaching of Jesus. We have now arrived and stand in front this profound body of teaching. As we look at it, we must still be wise in our effort to understand it; its meaning is not immediately apparent. In the three chapters of this section, we will explore ways of reading it and maximizing our ability to understand it. Chapter 4 will describe methods Jesus used to communicate his message. Once again we will be reminded that the teaching of Jesus does not come to us as systematic lectures or philosophical essays. It comes to us in the context of Jesus speaking to his contemporaries in several different settings; and it comes in a rich variety of forms and techniques of communication, ranging from rich metaphors to aphorisms to parables. It also comes to us, having been written down several years after Jesus spoke, from the memory and tradition of the believing community. As we learn more about these ways of communicating to his audience, we will move in chapter 5 to the content of his teaching. There are many parts of the content of Jesus that are easy to grasp, even by those who are separated from it by two thousand years and different languages and cultures. When he says, "Love your neighbor," we understand it even though we may find ways not to do it. But there are other parts of his teaching which are integral to his context, not ours, and reading these aspects of his teaching will ask us to be conscious of our assumptions about what he taught, and in some cases to set them aside and venture into an unfamiliar world. We will move in chapter 6 to our continuing study of his teaching and observe that almost all of his teaching was transformational in character. His topics were not abstractions, but engaging and insightful invitations to become a better human being. There were challenges as well, calling many of his listeners and the leaders of the religious community into account. In addition, we discover that he taught as much in deed as he did in word.

"Teacher, which is the greatest commandment in the Law?" Jesus replied: "Love the Lord your God will all of your heart and with all of your soul and with all of your mind. This is the first and greatest commandment. And the second is like it: Love your neighbor as yourself. All the Law and the Prophets hang on these two commandments."

—MATTHEW 22:36–40

4

The Method of Jesus' Teaching

Charting a Path

OUR ENDEAVOR TO ACCESS the teaching of Jesus has led us to the study of history. Chapter 1 was an exploration of the ways that we might go back two thousand years to a different time, culture, language, and way of life. We reflected on the "constraints of history" and observed that the records we have of the past must be examined with great care. We were especially conscious of the constraints of history in reference to our task of accessing the teaching of Jesus and noted that the documents which we have to get back to Jesus are primarily the Gospels and the Synoptic Gospels in particular, and "Q." We noted other books of the New Testament, especially those written by Paul, give some historical information, but it is limited in that Paul is more concerned with the interpretation and meaning of the life and death of Jesus than he is with historical information. The other historical documents that mention Jesus, such as the histories (e.g. Tacitus, Josephus) and gnostic writing (e.g. the *Gospel of Thomas*), are modestly helpful.[1] The Gospels, as are nearly all documents used to recover the past, were written with a point of view, and the goal of the authors was to inform and guide the new Christian community. History provided a frame for the Gospels, but they were written many years after the events that they record, and the careful recording

---

1. Biblical scholar Elaine Pagels suggest that the gnostic literature and particularly the *Gospel of Thomas* may add vital information to the quest for the historical Jesus and his teaching. See *Beyond Belief*.

of the events in the life of Jesus was not the central objective.[2] Even if it were, these authors lived prior to the development of critical-historical study and utilized the concepts and views of reality of the premodern world. There are some additional complications including the ways that the documents are interdependent, have been translated and changed over the centuries, and come to us in Koine Greek instead of Aramaic, the first language of Jesus.[3]

We described our access to the teaching of Jesus as a trek across a demanding terrain and noted that the trek was well worth taking. It provided and continues to provide a great deal of information about Jesus, although we must use the best approaches of historical scholarship to access information and accept the reality that there is not a sufficient amount of factual information to write a full biography.

In chapter 2 we continued our use of history as the primary means of gaining access to the life and teaching of Jesus. Our thesis was (and is) that Jesus lived in a historical setting that influenced his pattern of life, his sense of vocation, and what he taught. Jesus spent the majority of his life in the region of Galilee. This region was some distance from the center of Jewish life and thought in Jerusalem, and it was a context in which Hellenistic ideas were present alongside of first-century Judaism. He grew up in the small village of Nazareth, followed his father into the craft of carpentry, and was likely exposed because of his trade to the larger cosmopolitan city of Sepphoris that was being rebuilt. He was born into a common class, not a family of wealth and connections with the Jewish center of power and influence.[4] At about the age of thirty, sensing the guiding of God's Spirit, he left his carpenter's tools in Nazareth and traveled south to the desert region of Judea and acquainted himself with the ministry of John the Baptist, perhaps his cousin. He listened to John proclaim his prophetic message, that the time had come to repent and seek a true spiritual way. There was fire and judgment in the prophetic proclamation of John. Jesus was baptized by John,

---

2. Luke does say, "Since many have undertaken to set down an orderly account of the events that have been fulfilled among us, just as they were handed on to us by those who from the beginning were eyewitnesses and servants of the word, I too decided, after investigating everything carefully from the very first, to write an orderly account for you most excellent Theophilus, so that you may know the truth concerning the things about which you have been instructed" (Luke 1:1–4).

3. Manson's book *Teaching of Jesus*, though dated, provides a good introduction to the sources for the teaching of Jesus; see esp. ch. 1, "The Sources," 3–44.

4. Crossan, in *Historical Jesus*, uses the phrase Mediterranean Jewish peasant and provides a clear anthropological-sociological definition of peasant, although few scholars have followed him in this usage.

felt the affirmation and calling of God, prepared himself for his vocation with a retreat in the wilderness, and went back to Capernaum to begin his ministry. He gathered a small group of apostles to join him and soon had many others who became his disciples. He became and was recognized as a compassionate healer, a charismatic teacher, and a radical prophet. In time, sensing the need to proclaim his message in Jerusalem, he traveled south with his followers, stopping from to time to time to continue his ministry with those whom he encountered. For example, along the way he met the tax collector Zacchaeus in Jericho, a city in the region now called the West Bank. He then traveled up the dusty roads to Jerusalem and spent his last days on earth engaged in a dramatic challenge and confrontation.

As he engaged in his ministry, his immediate circle of apostles and his many followers began to ask about his identity. Our thesis in chapter 3 is that all great teachers teach from the perspective of their identity and their deepest values. We introduced the subject of the identity of Jesus, a complex one, to our concern in order to gain better access to his teaching. We observed that as Jesus became well known because of his extraordinary and marvelous ways, there were those who asked if he might be the promised Messiah. In time, his immediate circle of apostles probably began to think of him as the long-expected Messiah, the one who was at the center of the hope of the Jewish people. It was a common hope among the Jewish people that an anointed one, a descendent of David, would come and deliver an oppressed people from their suffering. As Jesus was observed by his disciples and by the crowds who came to him for healing, comfort, and guidance, it would have been natural for them to ask if Jesus might be the Messiah. Was his teaching about the coming kingdom of God the proclamation of the Messiah? Many thought so, and the biblical record, while fully aware of how carefully we must read it, suggests that Jesus began to own the title of Messiah, although he never used this claim to gain power and often cautioned others not to use it in order to keep the focus clearly on God. The Gospel record also has Jesus referencing the passage from the book of Daniel and identifying with the one described as a son of man who will come and deliver the people from their bondage.[5]

Hermeneutical Considerations

In our study, we have traveled with Jesus in our minds and imaginations across the years of his life in Galilee and his public ministry. We understand how the record of the events of his life and his teaching were shaped by years

5. Dan 7:13–14.

of development into the genre of gospel. We walked with him in Galilee and followed him to Jerusalem, sensing that his historical setting influenced his personal vocation and sense of mission. We asked, as did his followers, about his identity and why he taught with life-changing insight. We now stand in front of his teaching as it comes to us, eager to learn and understand. Across the centuries, others have been there, and they have found good ways to approach the material and interpret it. We can be grateful and learn from them, although of course they do not always agree in their historical judgments and interpretations. It is the case that one part of their efforts became an integral part of the study of the Bible, almost a separate discipline called hermeneutics.[6] Hermeneutics may be understood as the disciplined effort to find the best approaches to study and interpret ancient literature.[7] It is a central subject in the field of literature as an effort is made to grasp the writing's intent and meaning. Hermeneutics is the study of how this is done. Hermeneutics has been important in the study of law as well. For example, legal scholars and practitioners often speak about a precedent-setting decision, one that has become paradigmatic and guides other comparable decisions. One reads the past with the goal of understanding a complex legal issue and being guided in the present when making a judgment about a similar case. As I have studied the field of hermeneutics, especially in reference to biblical interpretation, I have begun to think of the discipline as addressing three major components of understanding and interpreting the Bible, and a review of these components will be helpful as we begin to describe the teaching of Jesus.

The first and primary work of interpretation is to be conscientious and disciplined *in doing the basic work of studying the language and history of the document to be interpreted.* In previous chapters, we have pointed to many aspects of this work, but perhaps a list of five central tasks will be a good reminder. The list could be expanded well beyond five, but these five might be suggestive and point to others:

1. As one approaches the literature to be interpreted and especially the biblical documents, it is important to understand the *structure and idioms of the language* that are used. This task takes a special form in the study of the Gospels in that they have taken shape from an oral

6. I have approximately twenty-five books in my personal library in the field of biblical hermeneutics, a small illustration of its importance in biblical scholarship. Among this collection are three short introductions to the field: Jasper, *Short Introduction to Hermeneutics*; Grant (with Tracy), *Short History of the Interpretation of the Bible*; and Dunnett, *Interpretation of Holy Scripture*.

7. See Ferguson, *Biblical Hermeneutics*, 4–5.

tradition and are to some extent dependent upon earlier documents. Further, the Gospel documents attempt to capture the teaching of Jesus whose first language was Aramaic and express it in Greek. We must ask: how close are the Gospels in discerning the way that Jesus used language and the idioms of his native language and culture? As we read these documents in English or another first language, we ask also if the translations communicate the subtlety and complexity of Jesus' language and thought. The task at this stage of interpretation is not an easy one.

2. Another hermeneutical task in interpreting the Gospels, and one made challenging because of the richness of the forms of language used by Jesus, is to assess *the types* of *literature and the figures of speech* that are used. Is the body of literature we are trying to interpret prose or poetry, history or allegory, proverb or riddle, or perhaps a form more unique to the Bible, such as apocalyptic? Is he expressing himself in a literal or symbolic way? Is Jesus teaching with the use of a narrative parable or is it an account of an actual event? If he is describing his understanding of an ethical principle in the form of a metaphor or analogy, is it possible to fully grasp the subtlety of his meaning? Is he using hyperbole or riddle to challenge his listeners to think deeply? How does Jesus use irony and humor to communicate his message?

3. Still another basic task, an obvious though very important one, is to *understand the historical background and context of the passage* to be interpreted. In the case of the Gospels, we must ask in what sense his teaching is tied to the theological frame of reference of first-century Judaism. How does it reflect the way he shapes his alternative views over against the mainline and majority views of the religious establishment in Jerusalem? How do the Roman occupation and the presence of Hellenistic thought enter into his way of speaking about the kingdom of God? In what sense does his humble upbringing close to poverty and marginalized people shape his understanding of love and compassion?

4. While not always central in the teaching of Jesus, it may still be important *to think in terms of the geographical setting of his teaching*. In what sense is his teaching shaped by his early life in Nazareth? How much does the rural and desert context in Judea impact his exposure to the simple, stoical, and disciplined life of John the Baptist? How important is self-sacrifice and lack of comfort to the message of repentance and the coming of the kingdom of God, especially as one lives in solidarity

with the poor? How do the natural surroundings of Palestine provide useful illustrations of the truths Jesus is expressing?

5. I mention as well the importance of *knowing the audience to whom the literature is addressed and the life situation (Sitz im Leben)* of those who hear his message. As we read the Gospels and ponder the message of Jesus, we know that he is not talking in general, but to a specific group of people. Are the people being addressed rural farmers or religious leaders in Jerusalem? As this question about audience and life situation is asked, one is also assessing the purpose of the Jesus in proclaiming a message, a fundamental key to understanding and interpreting the passage.

A second major dimension of hermeneutics germane to our study of the Gospels is *to be self-aware about the assumptions we bring to the task of interpreting an ancient document.* Often there are presuppositions that are below the surface, hidden in our history, culture, and language that we bring to interpretation. If we are able to surface these, we will be better able to do justice to the text rather than imposing our buried agenda onto a text. But there are also carefully chosen assumptions which become very important in reading and interpreting the Gospels. These assumptions or starting points are often called a hermeneutic in the sense that one begins the task of interpreting a section of the Gospels in order to integrate it into a larger frame of reference and use it in reference to a particular reading public. Let me once again suggest how five different carefully chosen starting points or assumptions might shape the interpretation of a passage.

1. At the very top of the list, as one deals with the Bible and in particular the teaching of Jesus as recorded in the Gospels, there is an *assumption about the nature of the Bible* and of the New Testament in particular. There are those in the more orthodox and conservative traditions of the Christian church that would strongly affirm that the Bible in some sense *is* the Word of God. This tradition argues that the Spirit of God inspired the authors of the Bible, and in turn gave to the Jewish and Christian community Scripture that is a trustworthy guide for faith and practice.[8] In some cases, the point of view even maintains that the original manuscripts were inerrant. Others in the Christian family maintain that the Bible and the New Testament in particular, is a trustworthy guide for faith and practice, but still a human book subject

---

8. It is important to acknowledge that Islam holds that the Qur'an is the inspired Word of God (in Arabic) and has a high view of the Hebrew and Christian Bibles, as well.

to human frailty. It is a book that developed over the years and gives the Christian community the narrative of the way God has interacted with the human family. But it is not free from error and yet remains our most trustworthy source and is therefore normative. Still others, perhaps outside the Christian context, view the Bible as telling an important story and containing wisdom and descriptions of important people and events, but nevertheless just a human product with mistakes and contradictions. One's interpretation of the teaching of Jesus, coming to us primarily in the Gospels, will be interpreted in various ways depending upon one's assumption about the nature of the Bible.

2. Early in Christian history, before the rise of critical-historical study, there were thoughtful and learned people who developed ways of understanding and interpreting the Bible that they hoped would do justice to its diversity and complexity. One example might illustrate this much larger tendency. As the church developed and reflected upon the faith that was handed down to them, theological movements emerged reflecting the context in which the theology developed. One of great importance was the Alexandrian School in Egypt that inherited a great intellectual tradition. In particular, the thought of Clement (ca. 150–ca. 215) became central to the ongoing theological life of the church.[9] Clement gave himself to the study of Scripture and articulated the *influential allegorical method of interpretation of the Bible*, an approach that would continue for centuries in the Christian church.[10] He assumed that every syllable of Scripture has meaning, but since the Bible comes to us in such a complex form, full of metaphors and symbols, some of the meanings of the Bible are not immediately apparent.[11] There are at least five different senses in which Clement sought to interpret the texts which he addressed: (1) First there is the historical sense, understanding what happened and the flow of activity that is described; (2) There is the doctrinal sense, attempting to express the theological meaning and application of the text; (3) In addition, there is the prophetic sense of the passage, and Clement found this sense in parts of the Old Testament which he believed pointed to the story of Jesus; (4) There is the philosophical sense in which one finds cosmic and universal truths describing the nature of the world; and (5) There

9. Origen (ca. 185–ca. 254), an extraordinary scholar and theologian, was also a part of the Alexandrian School.

10. Augustine made use of the allegorical method of interpretation.

11. Grant and Tracy, *Short Interpretation of the Bible*, 55–56.

is the mystical sense in which one hears the voice of God and it draws one closer to the divine.

3. Still another hermeneutical *starting point is present in the ecclesiastical and theological traditions of the branches and denominations of the Christian church.* For example, as church historians attempt to find broad categories for the diversity of the church, they often speak about the Catholic, Orthodox, Protestant, and Free Church traditions. Each of these grand traditions has distinctive beliefs and practices, ones that set them apart, although one can hope, not out of communion with other branches of the church. For example, the great Roman Catholic traditions would want to affirm that human beings were created in the image of God, and while humans are limited, they can use their intelligence to understand and their will to seek to be and live in harmony with God. They read the Gospel accounts in a way that assumes that Catholic Christians have the inner resources to follow in the way of Jesus. Orthodox Christians, while affirming a Catholic and Protestant emphasis on the Easter events and the doctrine of redemption would tend to read the Gospel accounts more from the perspective of the Incarnation, that God came in the person of Jesus to inform, guide, and inspire us to follow his ways. Protestant Christians, especially those in the Lutheran and Reformed traditions, are likely to introduce the subject of human sin and the need for God's Spirit to save and empower a believer to follow the way of Jesus. Many denominations within the Free Church tradition would have a particular distinctive emphasis such as the need to seek peace in all aspects of life and to listen for the will of God in quiet meditation. As the Gospels are read from these traditions, the teachings of Jesus, as broad as they are, will tend to be read from the distinctive outlook of the tradition: A Catholic scholar might say of Jesus, "He is our Lord and we should follow his example and teachings"; the Orthodox priest might say, "He is the Incarnate One, the light of the world and we should bow in humility before him"; the Protestant pastor might say, "He is our Savior, and he saves us from our sin and will empower us by the Spirit to follow the will and way of God"; and the devout Quaker might say, "He is the great advocate of peace and we should use our ability to pursue the ways of peace."

4. Still another hermeneutic or starting point often *emerges out of the time, culture, and history of the circumstances of the interpreter or the body of believers.* This may be a kind of accurate description of all interpretation and certainly the great creeds of the Christian church reflect the history and circumstances in which they were written. The

well-known and often-used Nicene Creed reflects the historical and political circumstances in which it was crafted. Let me illustrate this hermeneutical reality from the perspective of the modern world. With the Enlightenment, the rise of science, and into the nineteenth century with the evolution of critical history and other social sciences, there was a movement away from understanding the Bible and Gospels from traditional orthodox and literal perspectives. There was a clear movement toward reading the Bible from the circumstances of the present, with the worldview and presuppositions of the present sculpting the hermeneutical starting point.[12] We have called attention to the ways that the historical-critical method has influenced the reading of the Gospels and suggested that there has been a movement toward focusing on the Jesus of history, to some extent a countermovement from the church's tendency to speak about the Christ of faith. This tendency may be illustrated from one distinguished New Testament scholar of the twentieth century, Rudolf Bultmann. His point of view to some extent grew out of his German Lutheran heritage, although it is more the product of a modern worldview. An extraordinary and influential scholar, he argued for two principles in guiding interpreters of the Gospels. The first of these principles was his call for demythologizing the Gospels and removing the premodern understanding of the world that used categories of miracle and supernatural intervention. Bultmann maintained that it is the life-giving truths of the stories, which should be preserved for the Christian community, rather than the literal reading of the narratives. For example, the virgin birth and even the resurrection should be understood in modern categories. The meaning of these stories should be emphasized rather than attempting to find a way to view them as historical events. The virgin birth calls attention to the birth of a remarkable human being in a metaphorical way and this great truth must be affirmed in the Christian church. The resurrection calls attention to the reality that he "lives on" in the memories and imaginations of Christian believers.[13] Further, he said that it is quite difficult, even with the best historical strategies, to access the life and teachings of Jesus. We simply cannot know a great deal about these subjects, but we do know that "Jesus happened" and transformed human life. This transformation took place in response to the proclamation of the message of Jesus (the kerygma), and we

12. This subject is book length, and there are excellent studies of this trend. See, e.g., Reventlow, *Authority of the Bible.*

13. His views need amplification, and a good place to start is his book *Jesus and the Word.*

can enter fully into the Christian life and community by responding with an "existential" decision to endorse the kerygma and follow the Christian way.

5. I mention one last example of a type of hermeneutical starting point. It comes not so much from a branch of the church as it does *from the perspective of the needs and outlook of a marginalized segment of the population or group that has been discriminated against in society.* These movements and points of view draw upon the themes in the interpretation of Jesus that speak of him as a second Moses, liberating the people from misery and suffering and from slavery and oppression. In the early sixties, there was a movement now called liberation theology which had its roots in Latin America but which spread across the continents.[14] In this movement, the life and teaching of Jesus was seen as containing both the model and the way of liberation. Jesus incarnated the quest for liberation by his actions and his nonviolent approach became a fundamental strategy. The quest for liberation spoke to oppressed people of every kind, from indigenous people to those caught in poverty, from those who remained victims of colonial and post-colonial actions of powerful nations, and to those who are victims of political and religious persecution. The same motivation was also present in the rise of feminist theology. This movement called attention to the ways that women have been discriminated against and were victims of being forced to stay in arbitrary and confining roles, often a product of patriarchy. These demeaning and limiting roles, often defended with reference to biblical texts, exist not just in the third world but also in the first world. Once again, there was a turn to the Gospels, the example of Jesus, and the larger teaching of the Bible to find a ground, inspiration, and guidance in women's liberation.[15]

There is still one other dimension or emphasis within the field of hermeneutics that is especially germane to the interpretation of the Bible and of the Gospels in particular. We have implied its presence in our earlier discussion, but because of its importance it needs to be stated in a direct way. It is a way of defining hermeneutics *that says the interpreters of the Bible are called upon to bring forward the great truths of Bible and interpret them in*

14. Gutierrez, *Theology of Liberation*, provided the guidance and inspiration for the movement of liberation theology. In the United States, the work of King in liberating African American people from oppressive laws and practices became a global cause.

15. There is body of great literature that articulates the motive and method for the liberation of women. In the Christian community, and in reference to biblical guidance, there is a rich variety. See Schüssler Fiorenza, *In Memory of Her.*

way that brings guidance in the present and hope for the future. One biblical scholar, Carl Braaten, defines hermeneutics as "the science of reflection on how a word or an event in a past time and culture may be understood and become existentially meaningful in our present situation."[16] Again, let me suggest five ways this may be done with the teaching of Jesus, especially within the church community:

1. The first and very common way this is done is *through the sermon or homily* presented in Christian churches around the world every Sunday.[17] It is the priest's or pastor's responsibility to select a passage or a text, study it with care, and then amplify and apply it to the lives of the people in the congregation. For example, the clergyperson might take a text such as "You shall love your neighbor as yourself"[18] and speak about the context in which Jesus spoke this. There would then be an effort to define love with attention to the way the word *agape* is understood and translated from the Greek. The sermon or homily could provide examples of the ways that congregants might love all those whom they encounter in their lives—in the family, in schools, in places of work, and in all of their associations. There might be illustrations from the Gospels of how Jesus practiced *agape* in his encounters.

2. A second way that the teaching of Jesus may we brought forward into the contemporary situation in the parish context is to *offer a class on the disciplines of developing the spiritual life, ones which have the capacity to empower one to follow the Christian way.* If people are told that they are encouraged to love those whom they encounter, they might say that they simply do not have the skill, motivation, and experience to love those whom they meet daily, and especially those who are difficult in a variety of ways. The leader of the class might draw upon the teaching of Jesus about the kingdom of God and turn directly to the Lord's Prayer and illustrate from the phrase "Your kingdom come."[19] There could be a lesson on being open to the power and presence of God (reign of God) in one's life and how God's Spirit transforms and enables us to be more loving. There could be guidance in the cultivation of openness and receptivity to the empowering presence of God

16. Braaten, *History and Hermeneutics*, 131, quoted by Ferguson, *Biblical Hermeneutics*, 5.

17. The same case might be made for the celebration of communion or the Eucharist, although there is less spontaneous interpretation and more adherence to traditional formulations.

18. Matt 22:39.

19. Matt 6:10.

through prayer. The point could be stressed that Jesus speaks about the transformation of a person, giving them a new sense of purpose in life, the grace of empowerment, and a commitment to follow the Christian way.

3. Still another possible way that the teaching of Jesus could be brought into the present is to provide guidance in *applying the teaching of Jesus to corporate structures and the laws of society*. One brings the teaching into the present by providing an *increased understanding of the way that social structures can be unjust and discriminate against certain people*. In this case, the application of the teaching of Jesus seen by most people as the heart of his teaching might be introduced. He says, "In everything do to others as you would have them do to you; for this is the law and the prophets."[20] This verse might be applied in a personal way, treating another individual in a caring and understanding way, sensing that if we were in that person's situation, we would want someone to care and help us. This is the most common way the verse is brought forward into the present. But an equally important application of this teaching is for us to examine our own situation and sense the ways that we may have been discriminated against and kept from pursuing our dreams because of not having access to the best schools and other opportunities. There are many ways we might apply the Golden Rule, but certainly one is to be willing to enter into the political process and give time, energy, and wisdom to ensuring that regional laws and social structures ensure that our "neighbor" has every opportunity to grow and develop into a competent and fulfilled human being. This is a central way to do to another, as we would have them do to and for us.

4. One of the more difficult teachings of Jesus is *to love our enemy*, and in the Christian community, the command also needs to be brought forward into the present. Jesus says, "You have heard it was said, 'You shall love your neighbor and hate your enemy.' But I say to you, Love your enemies and pray for those who persecute you."[21] I personally find it very difficult to love those who do not like me or treat and judge me unfairly. It brings out my deepest fears of being rejected and feeling unlovable. It can evoke hurt and anger, and I am sure that I am not alone with these feelings. How then might this teaching be brought into the present and become a value we own and practice in our lives? In this case, we have the teaching of Jesus that implies that there are no

20. Matt 7:12.
21. Matt 5:43–44.

exceptions in the life of love, even though we may fail daily. We might begin then with an honest appraisal of the situation, determine what we may have done to threaten or offend another, and then approach the person with humility and a request for forgiveness. One could make a clear statement of the truth and say, "I am sorry for what I have done to offend you." And after a pause, say "and I am hurt by your rejection of me and I hope we can clear this up." To love is to speak the truth and attempt to change those conditions and circumstances that harm and hurt others as well as us. In the midst of this demanding challenge, we may have to remind ourselves that if we are attacked or misjudged that Jesus also says: "But I say unto you, do not resist an evildoer but if any one strikes you on the right cheek, turn the other also."[22] I find this commandment of Jesus the most difficult, but I also see ways of making it a part of my life by observing how Jesus dealt with those who were his enemies—with courage, congruence, honesty, and respect. I find the conversations during the last week of the life of Jesus especially informative about how one relates to an "enemy."

5. I will mention one further way that the teachings of Jesus might be brought forward into the present and provide guidance and hope for the future. It has to do *with facing the final weeks, months, and days of our lives and accepting our mortality.* There are many passages in the Gospels that describe how Jesus cared for those who were at the end of life. There is also the description of the circumstances and his own behavior as he faced the end of his life. There is, for example, the story of the delicate and sensitive way that he handled the death of Lazarus with the sisters, Mary and Martha. It is not the time or place to "unpack" the issue of the resuscitation of Lazarus, but only to call attention in this narrative to the way Jesus helped with the grief described in this situation.[23] It is also informative for me to read the accounts of the end of the life of Jesus, and without going into the authenticity of each of the texts, let me say that the impact of the texts as they stand provide guidance about how to face and yield to death. The phrases "It is finished" and "Father, into your hands I commend my spirit" give us a glimpse of how Jesus dealt with death.[24] To be able to say, "It is finished" and "Father, into your hands, I commend my spirit" becomes my goal as I reach the end of life. It reflects the peace of one with unshakable faith, even though earlier in the accounts, there were

22. Matt 5:39.
23. John 11.
24. Luke 23:46.

moments of fear, doubt, and desolation. The hermeneutical challenge for the pastor or priest in a parish is to use these and other passages to guide people at the end of their lives.

The Use of Language in the Teaching of Jesus

With an awareness of the place of hermeneutics in our reading of the Gospels, we are better equipped to interpret the teaching of Jesus. We know that he was the teacher *par excellence*, thought so by his contemporaries and by those who have been exposed to his teaching across the centuries. There are many titles used to describe Jesus, with some lists having more than forty names.[25] Teacher is one of the most common along with the title Messiah (Christ in Greek) that in time morphed into a last name. The title of teacher is used forty-five times, most frequently as a title of address, but at times used by Jesus as a self-designation.[26] The title of Rabbi, a distinctive role in the Jewish culture of Jesus' time, is applied to Jesus fourteen times. And while Jesus had not gone through the normal prescribed course of training to be a rabbi, his wisdom and insight regarding the Law were equal to the skill of other rabbis. He had the remarkable ability to speak and respond wisely and well in nearly every situation.

Part of his ability to respond so well was rooted in his ability to use the language of those with whom he spoke. Noted British New Testament scholar T.W. Manson suggests that the majority of the teaching of Jesus was in his first language of Aramaic as he engaged in his itinerant ministry in the Galilee. Jesus had a sense of identity with and belonging to the large crowds of people in the Galilee; they were his people and he communicated effectively with them. But Manson also notes that he was comfortable with the Hebrew of the rabbinical schools and the language of learned Jews. He does engage in debate with the scribes of the temple, a common form of interaction, and his knowledge of the Hebrew Scriptures is extensive and profound.[27] In addition, he teaches in the synagogues with the knowledge of the liturgical methods and applying the lessons from the Hebrew text of the Bible. There is also the story of Jesus at the age of twelve sitting among the teachers in Jerusalem, and "all were amazed at his understanding and

---

25. See Barclay, *Jesus as They Saw Him.*

26. Stein, *Method and Message of Jesus' Teachings.* I will draw from Stein's description of Jesus as a teacher.

27. Manson, *Teaching of Jesus,* 47–48.

wisdom."[28] Jesus may have had some capability in Greek as well in that it was the language of commerce and trade, but it is unlikely that Jesus had sufficient fluency or even the occasion to teach in Greek. Latin, too, was in the mix in that it was the language of the Roman government, and it may be that Pontius Pilate addressed Jesus in his trial in Latin.

Jesus was often practical and on point as he spoke with his contemporaries, but as he moved into the role as teacher, he expresses insights and wisdom characteristic of the *sage*. The forms of language he used, such as the parable and the proverb, caused his listeners to ponder and think more deeply about a subject or an answer to a question. He often drew upon the wisdom literature that was present in his culture and of course the wisdom literature in the Hebrew Bible such as the Proverbs and the book of Job. Not infrequently, those who were out to catch him in a mistake or a saying that could be used against him were quieted by the wisdom of his responses. There is the account of a scribe who listened in on the conversation about which commandment should have the highest priority. Jesus replies from the Shema and adds the additional commandment of loving one's neighbor.[29] His answer was sufficiently profound that it is said, "After that no one dared to ask him any question."[30] Jesus also moves with agility into the role of a teaching *prophet*. Without fear or intimidation, Jesus spoke boldly about hypocrisy and the need to change direction.[31] He spoke with conviction to those in power who allowed injustice to continue and who presided over religious customs and practices which did not meet the spiritual needs of the people. He would use the strategy of saying: "You have heard it said . . . but I say unto you." For example, he says, "Your have heard that it was said of those of ancient times, 'You shall not murder'; and 'whoever murders shall be liable to judgment.' But I say to you that if you are angry with a brother or sister, you will be liable to judgment."[32] Again and again, he focuses in the inner attitude and targets the façade of hiding behind behavior which may appear in keeping with religious custom but which is hypocritical in character.

The Forms and Figures of Speech in the Teaching of Jesus

The content of the teaching of Jesus was immediately engaging and relevant to the lives of those who came to him for healing and guidance. He spoke

28. Luke 2:46–47.
29. Lev 19:18.
30. Mark 12:28–34.
31. Matt 23.
32. Matt 5:21–22.

with an inner authority and authenticity, which caused people to stop and listen, and what he said gave insight and wisdom about the most important concerns of life. We will soon say a good deal more about the content of his teaching, but at this point it is important to understand the manner of his teaching because the manner and content are complementary, and in many ways with Jesus, the medium, while not fully the message, certainly embodies and carries the message and makes it exciting and compelling.

The best-known form of the teaching of Jesus is the parable. A parable may be defined as a short narrative that teaches a moral lesson or provides religious insight. In Sunday school, children are often told that a parable is "an earthly story with a heavenly meaning." Jesus often used a parable to communicate an important point about life and its meaning, inviting by the use of the parable a new way of seeing an issue or an ethical principle. The parable is way of asking people to reflect, use their imagination, and ask important questions. Upon hearing a parable, his listeners not only used their mind to reflect on its meaning, but the parable also reaches into the heart and challenges the will; both the left side and the right side of the brain are in play. His listeners would likely say things such as: "I have never thought of it that way" or "Now I get it." It is the way of a great communicator to use narrative, not just rational argument or the statement of information, most of which will stay "north of the neck."

What makes the parable so effective in the teaching of Jesus is that it compares a subtle truth with a situation in life that would be familiar and important to his listeners. In order to make the comparison, Jesus would use figures of speech such as a metaphor or a simile, and the entire parable would take the form of an analogy. A *metaphor* is a comparison in which a word or a phrase literally denotes how one kind of object or idea is used in place of another to suggest a likeness between them. The likeness between the subject and the content in the narrative are immediately apparent in the telling of the story. Jesus says, "The kingdom of heaven is like a treasure hidden in a field, which someone found and hid; then in his joy he goes and sells all that he has and buys the field."[33] Or he says, "Again, the kingdom of heaven is like a merchant in search of fine pearls; on finding one pearl of great value, he went and sold all he had and bought it."[34] In both cases, the kingdom is infinitely valuable as are the treasure and the pearl. A *simile* is not altogether different, but it is a comparison of two unlike things and there is the statement that they are alike in the way they exist and function. For example, Jesus says, "The kingdom of heaven is like yeast that a woman

33. Matt 13:44.
34. Matt 13:45–46.

took and mixed in with three measure of flour until all of it leavened."[35] There are times when it may be difficult to clearly see the difference between a metaphor and a simile, although in the case of these three short parables, it is relatively easy to see how the kingdom of heaven is valuable like a treasure and a pearl. But it is a bit harder to see in what way the kingdom of heaven is like yeast in three measures of flour until all of it is leavened. One listening to Jesus might want to ask, "What is the yeast?" and "Will the kingdom grow and expand like loaves of leavened bread?" The listener is invited to ponder. Often the figure of speech called an *analogy* may be used more generally and be similar to either a metaphor or a simile. There may be times when an analogy may be used as a comparison between two or more things that will function and be like one another in some respects but different in other respects. The metaphor and simile, and the more generic term analogy stir the imagination and take us to a deeper level of understanding.

One of the best-known parables of Jesus is the parable of the prodigal son and the elder brother.[36] Jesus tells the story of a younger son who approaches his father and asks for his inheritance, not wanting to wait until the father's death. The father grants the younger son's wishes, and the son travels to a distant country and there he squanders his property in dissolute living. With no financial resources in a land that is in a state of famine, he comes to his senses and decides to return home and ask the father's forgiveness. The father welcomes him home and there is celebration of his return. Meanwhile, the elder brother who has been dutiful all along raises the question why the younger son should be welcomed with a party, and he is reassured by the father that he has had and will continue to have all the benefits of the family. But now is the time to rejoice because your brother who has been lost has now been found. In this parable, as with parables in general, the wisdom of biblical scholars suggests the focus should be on the great truth that God welcomes all that come to him with gracious love, both the one who has lost his way and the one who feels hurt and in his pain, he is self-righteous and harshly judges. The feast is for all, and the kingdom of God is like this story, inviting all to receive forgiveness and embrace the power and presence of God.

Still another form of the teaching of Jesus, similar in many ways to the parable is the *allegory*. The difference between the two is that the parable as a general rule teaches one primary lesson or spiritual truth whereas the allegory often assigns meaning to all the characters and details of the story. For example, Jesus teaches the narrative of the sower and when asked by his

35. Matt 13:33.
36. Luke 15:11–32.

disciples to explain it, he gives meaning to each dimension of the story. He says that a sower began to sow and some seeds fell on the path and birds came along and ate them; the sower also sowed seeds that fell on rocky ground, and because there was little fertile soil, the plants sprung up quickly, but soon withered. Other seeds fell among thorns, and the thorns soon crowded out the good crop. But other seeds fell on good soil and brought forth an abundance of grain. In response to his disciples' questions, Jesus explains that the sower (a reference to himself teaching about the kingdom of God) does plant the seeds but that the evil one comes along and snatches away what is sown on the path. That which is sown on rocky soil describes the one who hears the message and receives it initially with joy, but there is no depth of understanding and the truth does not endure. The seed that is sown among thorns describes the one who hears the message, but is drawn away from the truth by the cares of the world and the lure of wealth. But there is the one who receives the truth and understands it and such a person will bear great fruit.

Jesus, in order to emphasize a point, would often use *overstatement* and *hyperbole* (exaggeration). It was an effective way of gaining the attention of his listeners and a practice common in Semitic speech.[37] A few examples from the Gospels will illustrate this form of language. Jesus is recorded as saying, "Whoever comes to me and does not hate father and mother, wife and children, brothers and sisters, yes, even life itself cannot be my disciple."[38] The truth of this passage is that the follower of Jesus must give the highest priority to being a faithful disciple. It is not that one must, in a literal sense, hate one's family, but must arrange the demands of life in such a way that the claims of the kingdom of God come first, and other responsibilities in life can then fall into place. A similar use of overstatement is found in the Sermon on the Mount. Jesus says, "If your right eye causes you to sin, tear it out and throw it away; it is better for you to lose one of your members than for your whole body to be thrown into hell."[39] Here again, we find Jesus emphasizing the need to be pure in one's outlook and perspective and to avoid looking at another in terms of lust or exploitation. We should not understand this passage in a literal way, but as a form of speech that enhances communication.

The same is true with the use of hyperbole in the teaching of Jesus. It is a slightly different form of speech than overstatement although both use exaggeration. With hyperbole, the statement is sufficiently exaggerated to

---

37. Stein, *Method and Message*, 8–33.

38. Luke 14:26.

39. Matt 5:29.

make the literal sense of the passage impossible to apply. Jesus, for example, says: "Why do you see the speck in your neighbor's eye, but do not notice the log in your own eye? Or how can you say to your neighbor, 'Let me take the speck out of your eye' while the log is in your own eye? You hypocrite, first take the log out of your own eye, and then you will see clearly to take the speck out of your neighbor's eye."[40] Clearly, it is not possible to have a log in one's eye, but it is a way of focusing the attention of the hearer on the hypocrisy of judging another when you have the same flaw or sin in your own life. Another example deals directly with our entrance into the kingdom of God. Jesus says, "Then Jesus looked around and said to his disciples, 'How hard it will be for those who have wealth to enter the kingdom of God.' And the disciples were perplexed at these words. Jesus said to them again, 'Children, how hard it is to enter the kingdom of God! It is easier for a camel to go through the eye of a needle than for someone who is rich to enter the kingdom of God."[41] The message of course is that wealth can become our primary value and preoccupation, and when it does, we move away from the reign of God in our lives.

On occasion, Jesus would use a *pun* in which two words may sound alike but have different meanings or the same word may have two different meanings. There is the dramatic account of the very important conversation between Jesus and Peter about taking the mission to Jerusalem. Jesus asks his disciples who people think he is, and indirectly whom the disciples think he is. Several answers are given, but Peter's answer, however, is on target when he says, "You are the Messiah, the Son of the Living God." In turn Jesus responds to Peter with the affirmation, "And I tell you, you are Peter, and on this rock I will build my church."[42] We see in this passage where the similar terms *petros* and *petra* are used for "Peter" and "rock" and in Aramaic, they have an exact same spelling. The force of the passage is increased because of the use of the pun. Once again, it catches the attention of the listener and underlines the importance of the statement.

Another very characteristic form of language used by Jesus and also common in the languages of the Middle East is the *proverb* or aphorism. Jesus could easily turn to this form because of his familiarity with the literature used in first-century Judaism, often called intertestamental because it was written between the writing of the final book of the Old Testament and before the writing of the New Testament. This literature contained the proverb as a form of expression, and it was also present in the Hebrew Bible,

40. Matt 7:3–5.

41. Mark 10:23–25.

42. Matt 16:13–20.

especially in the wisdom literature such as Proverbs and the book of Job. Many of the proverbs spoken by Jesus, filled as they are with wisdom, have become part of current language. For example, we have the following maxims from Jesus that are now used in contemporary English. In some cases it is only the first part of the sentence that has become a common idiom or it may be a paraphrase. For example:

"Love your neighbor as you love yourself." (Matt 22:39)

"Love your enemies and pray for those who persecute you." (Matt 5:44)

"Give us this day our daily bread." (Matt 6:11)

"For where your treasure it, there your heart will be also." (Matt 6:21)

"In everything do to others as you would have them do to you . . ." (Matt 7:12)

"If a kingdom is divided against itself, that kingdom cannot stand." (Mark 3:24)

"For all who take the sword will perish by the sword." (Matt 26:52)

"One does not live by bread alone." (Luke 4:4)

Even those unfamiliar with the Bible often have their favorite sayings of Jesus, and frequently they are in the form of a proverb.

The rabbis and sage teachers in the Middle East in the time of Jesus would also use the *riddle* and *paradox* as a way to stimulate and provoke thinking and questions among their listeners. While it is not the primary form of language Jesus used, it nevertheless is present, and these forms have caused even the best of New Testament scholars to struggle to find an accurate reading of Jesus' meaning. For example, the Gospel of Mark, at the trial of Jesus before the Jewish Council, has a witness say that he heard Jesus say, "I will destroy this temple that is made with hands, and in three days I will build another, not made with hands."[43] The witness may have been hostile, but Jesus had spoken about the temple being torn down, but likely it was reference to the system of religion in the temple being changed rather than a physical destruction of the temple.[44] It is also the case that the Gospels recording these discussions were written after the Roman destruction of the temple, and it may be the way the Gospel author is demonstrating the truth of Jesus' comment. But taken at face value, this statement is confusing,

43. Mark 14:58.
44. Matt 24:2.

a genuine riddle for his listeners to ponder. It does become in the Gospel records a critical issue in the trial of Jesus. In another case, Jesus confounds his listeners with the statement about the time for fasting. He says, "The wedding guests cannot fast while the bridegroom is with them, can they? As long as they have the bridegroom with them, they cannot fast."[45] Here Jesus is responding to the Pharisees who had been fasting, but wondered why Jesus and his disciples were not fasting. Jesus may be saying in this form that he will only be present for a time, and it is a special time for celebration while Jesus is still with them rather than a time for fasting.

On occasion, we read in the Gospels that Jesus occasionally used what is close to a *paradox*, a statement that is seemingly contradictory or opposed to common sense and yet it has the ring of truth. For example, Jesus spoke about contributing money for the common good in the temple, and the account says, "He sat down opposite the treasury, and watched the crowd putting money into the treasury. Many rich people put in large sums. A poor widow came and put in two small copper coins, which are worth a penny. Then he called his disciples and said to them: 'Truly I tell you, this poor widow has put in more than all those who are contributing to the treasury. For all of them have contributed out of their abundance; but she out of her poverty has put in everything she had, all she had to live on.'"[46] On another subject, Jesus is recorded as saying about the Pharisees: "Woe to you, scribes and Pharisees, hypocrites! For you are like whitewashed tombs, which on the outside look beautiful, but on the inside are full of bones of the dead and all kinds of filth. So you also on the outside look righteous to others, but inside you are full of hypocrisy and lawlessness."[47] In these two cases and many others, Jesus uses the paradox as a way to stress a fundamental truth, and by expressing it in the form of a paradox, he captures the listener's imagination and enables the listener to reflect on the truth in terms of personal behavior.

Jesus, as his words are recorded in the Gospels, was also fond of using *irony* and *questions* in his conversations and his teaching. Irony is a way of making a statement expressing something other than and especially the opposite of the literal meaning. It might have the tone of humor, and it is way of wryly suggesting another way to look at a situation or truth. For example, Luke records the parable of Jesus about the lost sheep, a narrative that in itself is ironic, but the particular verse in the parable is especially ironic: "Just so, I tell you, there will be more joy in heaven over one sinner who repents

45. Mark 2:19.
46. Mark 12:41–44.
47. Matt 23:27–28.

than over ninety-nine righteous persons who need no repentance."[48] Jesus also would ask a question in response to a question as a way of inviting the questioner to test the integrity of the question and be sure that the question was a question not a statement in an attempt to test Jesus. He would also use questions to invite his listeners to think more deeply about an issue or a concern, not unlike the questions of Socrates. In one encounter, Jesus was asked about paying taxes to Caesar. It is an attempt to catch Jesus with a lack of loyalty to the Jewish concern over an alien government, or conversely to get him to break a Roman law. He is asked: "Tell us, then, what you think. Is it lawful to pay taxes to the emperor, or not? But Jesus aware of their malice, said, 'Why are you putting me to the test, you hypocrites? Show me the coin used for the tax.' And they brought him a denarius. Then he said to them, 'Whose head is this, and whose title?' They answered, 'The emperor's.' Then he said to them, 'Give therefore to the emperor the things that are the emperor's and to God the things that are God's.' When they heard this, they were amazed; and they left him and went away."[49]

The language of Jesus has much that might be considered *poetry*. One scholarly treatment of the teaching of Jesus directly calls Jesus a poet and sees in the parables an expression of a poet's imagination.[50] Often the poetry will take the form of climactic parallelism where there is a correspondence between the various lines, usually four, and the point is underlined by its different expression in each line that leads to the climax.[51] For example, the Gospels record Jesus as saying the following:

> Ask, and it will be given to you; search, and you will find;
> knock, and the door will be opened to you.
> For everyone who asks receives, and everyone who searches finds,
> and for everyone who knocks, the door will be opened.[52]

Again, we read:

> But I say unto you that listen,
> Love your enemies,
> do good to those who hate you,
> pray for those who abuse you.[53]

48. Luke 15:7.
49. Matt 22:17–22.
50. Theissen and Merz, *Historical Jesus*, 316–46.
51. Stein, *Method and Message*, 27–32.
52. Matt 7:7–8.
53. Luke 6:27–28.

Certainly the Beatitudes and the Lord's Prayer fall into the category of poetry. Even with all of the scholarly questions about the authenticity of the many of texts, it is still possible to say that Jesus spoke profound truth in remarkable and beautiful ways.

What we haven't said as directly yet is that Jesus also spoke through his actions. In many cases, his encounters with people of all kinds carry a figurative meaning beyond well beyond the action itself. His compassionate healing carried the message of selfless love, and his actions in the temple with the moneychangers spoke prophetically about the using the temple for prayer. As we turn now to content of his teaching, we will focus on both his words and his actions as an expression of the radical teaching of Jesus.

Study Resources

Study Questions

1. How does the field of hermeneutics help one to read and understand the Bible?

2. What are the various components of hermeneutics?

3. How does one's assumptions about the Bible influence one's interpretation of the Bible?

4. How does Jesus' use of language increase his effectiveness as a teacher?

5. Which of the various forms of language that Jesus used do you think made his teaching the most effective?

Terms and Concepts

1. Hermeneutics: The discipline that guides those who seek to understand and find the best approaches to interpret literature, and especially literature of the past such as the Bible.

2. Allegorical Interpretation: A way of interpreting literature, and especially the Bible, to discern symbolic meanings that go beyond the literal meaning.

3. Parable: A short narrative that teaches a moral lesson or insight about life, a form of teaching used frequently by Jesus.

4. Metaphor: A comparison in which a word or a phrase denotes how one kind of object or idea is used in place of another to suggest a likeness between them.

5. Hyperbole: An exaggeration designed to engage the reader or listener that is sufficiently exaggerated to make the literal sense of the passage impossible.

Suggestions for Reading and Reference

Dunnett, Walter M. *The Interpretation of Holy Scripture*. Nashville: Nelson, 1984.

Grant, Robert M., and David Tracy. *A Short History of the Interpretation of the Bible*. 2nd ed. Philadelphia: Fortress, 1984.

Jasper, David. *A Short Introduction to Hermeneutics*. Louisville: Westminster John Knox, 2004.

Reventlow, Henning Graf. *The Authority of the Bible and the Rise of the Modern World*. Translated by John Bowden. Philadelphia: Fortress, 1984.

Stein, Robert H. *The Method and Message of Jesus' Teaching*. Philadelphia: Westminster, 1978.

5

The Message of Jesus' Teaching

Starting Points

WE GAVE ATTENTION IN chapter 4 to the field of hermeneutics and explored the ways that the life and teaching of Jesus have been interpreted. Our observation was that the cultural, philosophical, and theological assumptions that we hold, whether in the background and below the surface or used intentionally, become very important in shaping the results of our interpretation. We said that having an awareness of and carefully choosing our hermeneutical approach would enable us to better discern the meaning of the teaching of Jesus and improve our capacity to help others to understand his message. Without self-awareness, we run the risk of imposing our assumptions and biases onto our interpretation, although admittedly, this risk is present for all who step on this holy ground.

We also reviewed the creative forms of language and the rich variety of figures of speech Jesus used to communicate his message. As the Gospels record his teaching, we view him moving easily from parable to proverb, from hyperbole to poetry, and to fill his teaching with engaging metaphors, provocative riddles and paradoxes, perplexing questions, disconcerting irony, and wry humor. He was a charismatic teacher, capturing the attention of his listeners, stimulating their imaginations, questioning their assumptions, and challenging them to be and act in new and loving ways.

While pointing to universal truths and being profoundly insightful, Jesus nevertheless taught within the framework of his Jewish faith in a Roman imperial world. He used the categories of first-century Judaism and the language of the people who were his people, those who shared his childhood, knew him as a child of Mary and Joseph, as a carpenter in the village of Nazareth, and sought him out for healing, guidance, and understanding. The first part of his public ministry was spent in the region of Galilee, addressing the concerns of poverty and powerlessness, the rule of a foreign government, and the debilitating presence of hunger and disease. He spoke to his people about the presence of God and asked them to embrace it, and he demonstrated the power of God by healing their diseases. He became for these people the meeting point of hope and history.

Our goal is to understand what he said and what he did with an open and positive spirit and with an awareness and use of rigorous historical methods that give us the best possible access. History is our starting point, although others would prefer to start with the presuppositions of a God-inspired scriptural account and the divinely guided traditional, ecclesiastical, and orthodox understandings. These views will be partially present in my understanding; it is difficult not to be influenced by one's history. But they do not necessarily trump trustworthy historical knowledge. As we turn to the content of Jesus' teaching, I want to suggest some very preliminary starting points, taking into account the insight and wisdom of the traditional views held within the Christian church. The hermeneutical starting points I am suggesting have already been implied in what has been said, but they need to be clearly identified as a part of my hermeneutical strategy. Initially they are five in number with more to be articulated as we move along in our effort to understand the life and teaching of Jesus.

1. The first is that I *come to the task of interpretation from within the Christian family, a position that gives me a positive outlook and eagerness to learn.* I have no desire to discount or set aside the message of Jesus. Neither am I angry at traditional views or any views that may be different from my own. I just want to understand the message, and an integral part of this understanding requires a critical-historical inquiry. Over the last several decades, it has become permissible to have suspicion about traditional and orthodox views. It is now possible and even expected that we bring to our reading of the Gospels the understanding that they are more extended sermons than historical accounts. In fact there was a kind of crossroads in the last half of the twentieth century about how we understand Jesus, one that invited some questioning and the affirmation of the Jesus of history as the starting point of Christology.[1]

---

1. See, e.g., Sobrino, *Christology at the Crossroads*, for an account that comes out of the Latin American context.

2. While always respectful and ever learning, I move toward a *radical historicity in reference to divine revelation*, although I am keenly aware that our connection with the divine is through faith, not through the limited perspective of history.[2] It follows that the second hermeneutical principle is that I continue to believe that our *best access to the life and teaching of Jesus is to let history be the primary teacher*, although valuing the diligence, scholarship, and wisdom of the saints and sages of the past and the present. As far as possible I want to know what happened and what he said, not merely to accept the literal reading of the Gospels or to endorse a particular tradition of the church. We know that our Gospels are the best resource we have and provide us with a normative understanding of Jesus and his teaching. We also know that good and wise people, seeking the guidance of God's Spirit, sought to understand Jesus across the history of the church and their views have much to teach us. But we know as well that authors of the Gospels wrote with a premodern worldview and a desire to guide the new Christian community, not necessarily to provide historical information.

3. A third hermeneutical starting point is that I am open to and will often suggest and use the more progressive approach to express the teaching of Jesus.[3] *I affirm the strategy of speaking about the universal truths, expressed by Jesus in the language and concepts of his time, in a contemporary way.* I know there is resistance to this strategy, and I do understand the argument that such an approach carries the risk of distorting the teaching of Jesus. But all attempts to pass on the teaching of Jesus carry this risk. I would maintain that it has been done all through history, even in the creedal statements, and that the best way for us to grasp and internalize the teaching of Jesus is to put the teaching within the framework of our contemporary understanding of reality. I am suggesting that we recognize that the biblical authors use the premodern view of the world with its concepts and language to articulate their understanding of the life and teachings of Jesus. It is possible to translate his radical teaching into the language and concepts of our time, knowing that another generation must do that with our articulation of what Jesus did and said.

---

2. I do not discount the more philosophical and experiential ways of discerning divine revelation. Here I speak in reference to Jesus.

3. Often this perspective is called "liberal" which has both a positive and negative connotation. I am encouraged by the way that Ottati uses the term liberal in *Theology for Liberal Protestants*.

4. My positive spirit in this endeavor is nurtured by my deep appreciation of the Jesus who "comes through" in the Gospel accounts and who is characterized in the Gospel of John as a person *"full of grace and truth."*[4] *He was a person full of love and integrity who articulated a way to make a life-giving connection with transcendence.* This passage, however, has generally been interpreted as saying that Jesus *is* divine and came to "dwell among us" from a preexistent state in the form of *logos* or the Word. I believe he was the Word but that the Word came as the human Jesus, open to the full presence of God. The historical Jesus came as the presence of the *logos* or the Word, full of grace and truth.[5]

5. His love and integrity were the result of his deep faith in God; *the divine presence filled his life.* As nineteenth-century theologians such as Friedrich Schleiermacher and Albrecht Ritschl described him, Jesus was a person with a fully developed God-consciousness. God's presence and the divine will and way were at the center of the person of Jesus, a historical person who lived in the region of Galilee about two thousand years ago. His contemporaries understood him variously, but one category noticeably missing even by his detractors is that of hypocrite. He was a free and authentic person. *His message came not only in word, but also in deed.* He practiced what he preached. He lived his convictions, was authentic, and he displayed extraordinary courage.

I will say more about cultural assumptions, historical strategies, and theological and ecclesiastical traditions as we go along, but wanted my hermeneutical starting points to be up front in that they are present in contemporary Jesus studies and, in my view, reflect a more credible way of understanding the Christian faith. I want to use the last starting point that Jesus taught in both word and deed as our guide for the next two chapters on the teaching of Jesus. He did teach in word and deed (*praxis*), with profound and visionary insights and a life filled with grace and integrity. We turn then to his message as it came to us in word and deed as he lived and spoke as a compassionate healer, charismatic teacher, and a radical prophet.

---

4. John 1:14.

5. Those engaged in interfaith literacy and understanding often assume that no exceptionalist claims can be justified in our interconnected and pluralistic world. I am conscious of this principle in reference to my comments about Jesus. While not making an exceptionalist claim, I am saying that transcendence flowed through him.

The Understanding of God and the Faith of Jesus

Throughout his life, Jesus was motivated by his faith in the personal God of his Jewish heritage. When he speaks about God, he uses the language of Judaism and the Hebrew Bible, which provided spiritual and ethical guidance to the Jewish people. There are times when this language about God is anthropomorphic in character, as language about God often becomes when we speak about that which cannot be contained within the limits of our thought and language.[6] So Jesus uses metaphors and analogies to speak about God, ones that reflect his observations about the history of the Hebrew people, the time and place in which he lived, and the challenges of the human drama. There was a movement, introduced in the nineteenth century, which called into question the reality of the God described within the framework of the human experience. It maintained the view that our language about God is merely a superstitious projection onto a cosmic screen, not unlike the gods within the Greek pantheon. Ludwig Feuerbach was cogent and persuasive with this point of view, and such noted people as Friedrich Nietzsche, Karl Marx, and Sigmund Freud followed him in this position.[7] Perhaps we do have a tendency to create God in our own image, but just because we do does not necessarily prove that there is no divine reality. It is rather to suggest that what is meant by God is beyond the human language which forces us to speak of God by using analogy, metaphor, and negative descriptions such as "God is not limited."

Theologians and clergy within the Abrahamic religions have often spoken about the divine in terms of the divine presence and *the imminence of God*. Frequently, the language of the Spirit of God is used to express the divine presence. God is not just the rational order of the cosmos, nor is the divine like the description within deism, which affirms that God created the cosmos but now lets it function on its own. Rather the divine is personal and intersects with human history and experience. Those who speak about the imminence of God are careful not to imply pantheism, that God is nothing more than the rhythms of the universe. However there is a religious point of view that speaks of panentheism, a thoughtful articulation of the divine presence that sees the divine in the flow of human life and of the

---

6. There is the risk of understanding God as another being, one wiser, more powerful, and yet with very human emotions, whether they are positive with the description of love, or as judge, and sometimes with anger. Another credible understanding of God in the biblical tradition is to understand the divine as the ground of being. See Hart, *Experience of God*.

7. Feuerbach, *Essence of Christianity*.

cosmos but does not equate divinity as the flow and avoids the less subtle anthropomorphisms.[8]

Jesus speaks of the presence of a personal God in terms of a loving parent, *God as Father*. The use of metaphoric language was common to the time and religious culture of Jesus, and the notion of divine parentage for nations, clans, or even individuals was common in the ancient world. Other nations and tribes would trace their heritage back to a divine ancestor and various narratives and myths became a part of the religious life of ancient people. At times, the parental ancestor was even thought of as the progenitor or literal parent, but within the context of the Hebrew people, the notion of the fatherhood of God had moved to understanding God as creator of human life, the Father with whom love and worship are possible, and one who cares for humankind as a loving parent.[9]

Jesus would have heard and reflected upon the teaching in the Hebrew Bible that God is the Father of Israel.[10] As a general rule, these references to God as Father would be connected to a specific historical event such as the deliverance of the people from Egypt. In addition, God is often described as creator of all people and nations, but Israel is given a unique place as a special child.[11] The constant care of God over Israel is like the care and nurture a child will receive from one's parent.[12] At times, when Israel does not live up to the expectations of the covenant, there may be discipline and even the belief that God will focus the divine love on the righteous within Israel, a remnant that will preserve and practice the true faith.

It was a common practice to address God in prayer as Father, and the phrase "Our Father who is in heaven" found its way into the Lord's Prayer as Jesus teaches about prayer. So when Jesus spoke of God as Father, he was drawing upon his heritage and upbringing, not suggesting a whole new way of understanding God. But what Jesus did express was a new appreciation of God understood in terms of parental love.[13] To speak of God in this way was not an abstract creedal statement, but an invitation to an intimate relationship, one that is expressed and taught by Jesus again and again. It is

8. See the work of Fox, e.g., *Coming of the Cosmic Christ*.

9. Manson, *Teaching of Jesus*, 89–115.

10. Deut 32:6; Isa 63:16; Mal 2:10.

11. Hos 11:1.

12. Deut 1:31.

13. Schüssler Fiorenza and other feminist theologians do raise questions about the use of the masculine term of Father and the patriarchalism inherent in this practice. This point is persuasive, and attempts to speak about God in terms of parental love should speak as well about God's love being similar to a mother's love. See Schüssler Fiorenza, *In Memory of Her*, 76–80.

present in not just one of the gospels, but present across the range of sources, Mark, Q, Matthew, M (only in Matthew), Luke, and L (only in Luke), and John.[14] A review of these references underlines what we have said, that the loving God, as intimate as a Father, is the center of the life of Jesus, and his experience of *Abba* is so moving that it can only be expressed to those that can grasp it.[15] *For Jesus, God was an experiential reality that shines through in all that he says and does.* His disciples and followers saw the presence of God in Jesus and sought him out for guidance and healing. Even the Roman centurion at the time of Jesus' death says, "Truly this man was God's Son."[16]

It would be accurate to say that the Jewish religion did have a profound concern about how to receive forgiveness for their sins. Long sections of Exodus, Leviticus, and Deuteronomy provide guidance and list ways of atonement, often in the form of sacrificing an animal. While Jesus respected the Law, he was primarily concerned about the spirit of the Law not its cultic practices, especially in reference to atonement. An integral part of the ministry and teaching of Jesus is to help his followers and listeners find a sense of forgiveness and being in harmony with God.[17] It is evident at the beginning of the public ministry of Jesus. We observe the calling of Levi, a tax collector who had been ostracized from the Jewish community, yet Jesus invites him to be part of his inner circle. We read, "He went out again beside the sea; the whole crowd gathered around him, and he taught them. As he was walking along, he saw Levi, son of Alphaeus sitting at the tax booth, and he said to him. 'Follow me.' And he got up and followed him."[18] The story goes on to say that at dinner in the evening, there were Pharisees and scribes who questioned Jesus about eating with sinners and tax collectors to which Jesus replies, "Those who are well have no need of a physician, but those that are sick: I have come to call not the righteous but sinners." In this incident, Levi is experiencing forgiveness and being offered a place in the beloved community. He receives and experiences the parental love.

14. Manson, *Teaching of Jesus*, 94–98, lists the references and identifies them in reference to their usage.

15. *Abba* is the Aramaic word for father, a word that suggests familial intimacy. See the use in Mark 14:36, in which Jesus addressed God as *Abba* in the garden of Gethsemane.

16. Matt 27:54. This passage does describe an earthquake, as well, likely interpreted by the Roman centurion as a sign from God.

17. I will say more about forgiveness in the next chapter, but there are clear sections in the Gospels in which Jesus teaches about forgiveness by *word* as there will be in the next chapter as he teaches in *deed*.

18. Mark 2:13–17.

There is another incident which points to the way that Jesus offered forgiveness. It is a story about a woman who comes to Jesus during a meal in the home of a Pharisee. She comes with a deep need to make contact with Jesus and to find forgiveness and acceptance. She does what is possible in the setting and what she judges to be a point of contact; she uses her tears to clean his tired and dusty feet, dries them with her hair, and then rubs them with ointment.[19] Jesus, in violation of protocol, accepts her gracious and very personal action, and replies to the Pharisee, "Therefore, I tell you, her sins, which were many, have been forgiven; she has shown great love. But the one to whom little is forgiven, loves little. Then he said to her, 'Your sins are forgiven.'" In this case and the previous one, we observe that Jesus offers "Messianic forgiveness," indirectly claiming authority for what in the Jewish system is reserved exclusively for God. But if Jesus is bringing in the kingdom of God, the power and presence of God, then he brings with this remarkable gift the redemptive power of forgiveness; forgiveness is the pearl of great price.

Jesus also teaches about forgiveness in the powerful and sensitive parable of the Prodigal Son, with the loving father forgiving the wayward son and celebrating his return.[20] In this case, it is the Father who offers forgiveness, but it is freely and graciously given, not earned by acts of atonement. We observe in these cases the radical teaching of Jesus.

The teaching of Jesus about the nature of God as loving Parent may be summarized in the categories of the Lord's Prayer. The first part of the prayer deals with the larger world and God's care for the world. The second part of the prayer has to do with each individual, and taken together, it is a succinct expression of Jesus's teaching about his loving Father.[21]

God as caring for the world:

1. "Our Father in heaven, hallowed be your name." All who live in the world should honor the one and only universal God who can be known as a loving Parent.

2. "Your kingdom come." May this God of all that exists come and reign in our world and bring peace and justice.

3. "Your will be done on earth as it is in heaven." May God's will and way be done on the whole earth.

God as caring for individuals:

19. Luke 7:36–50.

20. Luke 15:11–32. Abernathy, *Understanding the Teaching of Jesus*, 62–68, uses these three illustrations.

21. Manson, *Teaching of Jesus*, 113–14.

1. "Give us this day our daily bread." It is the prayer that asks God to take care of us as parents take care of their children.

2. "And forgive us our debts, as we also have forgiven our debtors."[22] May God forgive all that we have done and haven't done in mistreating others, even as we should forgive those who have mistreated us.

3. "And do not bring us to the time of trial, but rescue us from evil." Truly, we need God's protection and deliverance.

There is yet another metaphor that Jesus and his contemporaries often use for God, also drawn from their historical context. It is the deep conviction that *God is like a king*, one who has power and rules over all. God is as intimate as a loving parent, but also as powerful as a king. In many ways this draws on another concept often used to describe God. God *is transcendent*, above us, and has power over us and over history. It is at this point that we begin a discussion of parts of the teaching of Jesus that have been difficult to understand. In the first place the image of king is not altogether attractive to us and those who live in and value a democracy; it is also a masculine term. The kings we have learned about have not always been just. But even more difficult to fully understand is the point at which Jesus speaks about the transcendent God in eschatological language which points to the final consummation of history. It is not our language nor do we easily grasp or always literally believe the notion that there will be a Second Coming with the end of an old order and the arrival of a new order, possibly governed by a Messianic King.

To speak about the metaphor of king that is used by Jesus for God requires that we go back to the notion of the kingdom of God.[23] We spoke of the kingdom of God as the reign of God and we amplified this brief definition by saying that it is the power and presence of God. There have been those who emphasized the social and political nature of the kingdom of

---

22. Some translations use trespasses for debts, and others say sin. The two versions, one in Matthew 6:9–13 and one in Luke 11:2–4, suggest that we ask forgiveness for both our active misdeeds and for our passive neglect of our responsibilities.

23. As we mentioned earlier, this topic is full of complexities, and there are differences of opinion by the finest scholars. There are also differences in the Gospels. It requires a book-length treatment, but given our purposes, we can only be brief and try to provide a summary of the teaching of Jesus about the kingdom of God, and the implication that God is like a king. Allison, *Constructing Jesus*, provides a recent and extremely helpful treatment of the kingdom of God. I have been helped by many classic works and remain grateful for Manson's *Teaching of Jesus* even though it was published several decades ago. Vol. 2 of Meier's *Marginal Jew* is thorough and clear on the subject, typical of his patient care for the multitude of details and thoughtful integration of the material.

God and suggested that it sets an ideal of a just and peaceful social order that we should try to establish. The risk of this view is that it is too driven by an earlier liberalism which saw it as an expression of the inevitable progress of history and the gradual trend to a more just and humane society and world.[24] Others have understood it as a term pointing to the end of the present world order and have attempted to find biblical clues that allow them to anticipate, and in some cases even predict, an apocalyptic ending. Both views have an element of what is meant by the kingdom of God, but represent two extreme opposites and miss the mark by stressing just one aspect of the meaning of the kingdom of God. It would be more accurate to say, judging from the teaching of Jesus found in the Synoptic Gospels and Q, and weighing the authenticity of the passages, that Jesus taught that the kingdom was both a present reality and the future culmination of God's sovereign rule.

We begin with the observation that Jesus speaks about both the present and future of the kingdom of God and integrates the two metaphors he uses for God, the loving Father and the just and sovereign king. We should not lose track of the loving parent with whom we can have a relationship as we explore what Jesus meant as he spoke of God as like a king. Jesus begins his ministry with the proclamation: "Repent, for the kingdom of heaven has come near."[25] Mark records the same proclamation: "The time is fulfilled, and the kingdom of God has come near; repent, and believe in the good news."[26] Jesus is implying that the kingdom is coming in his presence and that it is good news. He is also saying that his hearers should embrace the message, repent or change directions, and accept the reign of God in their lives. What might his hearers have understood by this proclamation? For one, they would have heard God as king inviting them into a relationship, and that the relationship would be one of king and subject. They would have also understood that the relationship would be characterized by allegiance, personal loyalty, trust, and obedience. In turn, one would receive the loving care of God for protection, guidance, and a new way of life based on the will and way of God.

They would have also heard that it is not only individual believers who will sense the power and presence of God in their lives, but there is also a corporate implication, that one will belong to a larger domain, the people of God and a beloved community. It will be characterized by mutual love

---

24. Rauschenbusch, *Social Principles of Jesus*, provides a persuasive view of this perspective, but he is perhaps too optimistic in his outlook.

25. Matt 4:17. Kingdom and king also carry patriarchal overtones.

26. Mark 1:15.

and respect, a common commitment to justice, and a quest to build a commonwealth of peace.[27] But these realities would not come easily; there will be resistance.[28] Evil will not disappear nor will the other challenges of life such as poverty, illness, and grief over the loss of life. There are two "kingdoms," one ruled by the sovereign and loving God and the other by evil. Humans stand between them and must choose under which rule they are to live. And there is no doubt about which kingdom will prevail; the sovereign God will establish the lasting kingdom. As they would listen to Jesus, they sense his intensity and passion about this new order. He teaches them to pray, "Your will be done on earth as it is in heaven."[29] To the questions and uncertainty that he encountered by those seeking his counsel, Jesus would reply by telling parables and inviting a firm commitment. He said to those worried about their future, "But strive first for the kingdom of God and his righteousness, and all these things will be given to you as well. So do not worry about tomorrow, for tomorrow will bring worries of its own. Today's trouble is enough for today."[30]

Jesus spoke to individuals about the way they should live together, but he also spoke about the kingdom of God in reference to the future. The people with whom Jesus associated in his public ministry were concerned about the future and found hope in the coming of a promised Messiah who would bring in a reign of justice and peace. They saw in Jesus, both in his extraordinary life and his words, a ray of hope. They asked, "Could this be the Messiah and will our situation change because of him?" At the root of their sense of despair was a governmental and social system that kept them in poverty and the feeling of powerlessness. Two New Testament scholars who have often collaborated in their work have called the unjust structures present in the time of Jesus a domination system.[31] It had the following features:

1. Rome ruled the region and had co-opted the elite class of the Jewish population. Rome had also given regional authority to the Herodians, and both the Jerusalem aristocracy under the high priest appointed by Rome and Herod Antipas were expected to preserve order and meet the tax levy of the Romans. There was both religious and political legitimation for the oppressive practices.

27. Some see in the Sermon on the Mount (Matt 5–7) and the Sermon on the Plain (Luke 6:20–49) the spirit and the ethical norms for the kingdom. The word commonwealth is often suggested as an alternative to kingdom.

28. Luke 11:14–23.

29. Matt 6:10.

30. Matt 6:33–34.

31. See Borg, *Jesus*, 225–29, and Crossan, *Jesus: A Revolutionary Biography*, 104–5.

2. In this preindustrial agrarian society, the powerful and wealthy maneuvered to serve their own financial interests that kept the vast majority of the people in an economically oppressive condition. They were dominated and kept in poverty by the rich and powerful.

3. It is likely that in the time of Jesus these conditions were quite oppressive, and the working class people saw the lavish life of the rulers and could barely if at all sustain their way of life.

Jesus was not blind to these conditions, had experienced them in Nazareth, and saw and heard the pleas of his people. A small group of Jewish people formed a resistance movement called "Zealots" and actively resisted the government structures. Jesus did not form a political and military movement, but chose nonviolent resistance and provided emotional and spiritual support for those who suffered from poverty. He was a radical prophet, calling for justice and speaking about a spiritual kingdom (commonwealth) in which these conditions would change. In the last week of his life, he specifically challenged the religious establishment in Jerusalem and said, "Is it not written, 'My house shall be called a house of prayer for all the nations?' But you have made it a den of robbers."[32]

Jesus placed his faith and hopes in the promise of God and spoke about how the day will come when justice and peace will prevail with the coming of the kingdom of God. There are many, and I am in sympathy with them, who interpret his sayings about the coming kingdom as having been fulfilled in the "Jesus event." This point of view is often called "realized eschatology" and maintains that we continue to partner with God in creating a just peace in the world, but that the final consummation is beyond history. It is difficult not to read several of the authentic sayings of Jesus pointing to a new order within history. A summary of these sayings may help us as we try to discern the meaning of the apocalyptic sayings of Jesus.

1. Jesus, from his exposure to Hebrew Scripture and his interaction with those who gave the prevailing interpretation of it, did have a sense that God would enter into human history to form a righteous people and would also judge the unrighteous.[33] Often this pattern of ideas was connected to the arrival of a Messiah, an anointed ruler, not unlike and in the lineage of David.

32. Mark 11:15–17.
33. Jer 31:31–33; Isa 65–66.

2. This coming Messiah was often identified as the Son of Man, a term that Jesus often used as a title.[34] Jesus sensed the call of God to bring these events to fruition. The new age is dawning in the person of Jesus.

3. But he was reluctant to say when and how. For example, it could come at any time;[35] the exact date was unknown;[36] and it will come like a thief in the night.[37] So setting a date is impossible, but be prepared.[38]

4. There will be some disturbance when it comes such as the destruction of the temple.[39]

5. There will be great celebration such as banquet.[40]

Many have read these and other passages in a quite literal way, and others have maintained that Jesus was using metaphorical language such as the banquet to give hope to a despairing people and saying that in the end, God will settle all scores. I admit that it is a hard for me to take all of the eschatological language literally. It seems more credible to understand Jesus using the language and ideas of his religion and culture to speak about despair and hope. I am more inclined, though respectful of others who disagree, to see Jesus placing his hope in God who empowers us to seek relief from poverty and powerlessness, to guide us in our quest for a good life and a just peace in the world, and ultimately to fairly judge us all with mercy beyond history. In this vision, the gracious God who loves us like a parent and the sovereign God who is like beneficent sovereign will bring us into eternity in ways we cannot understand but can trust.

Love as the Foundational Value in the Kingdom of God

Jesus' teaching about the kingdom of God has to do with his understanding of God as a loving parent and as sovereign ruler. He integrates the two metaphors for God and invites all who listen to his teaching to place their faith in God in order to be nurtured by a loving parent and be given hope because it is God's kingdom that will prevail. It is within this frame of reference that

34. Dan 7:9–14.

35. Mark13:28–33.

36. Mark 13:32.

37. Luke 12:39.

38. Matt 25:1–13. The first generation of Christians did understand that the end might be near, and the Apostle Paul expresses this view in his writing. See 1 Thess 4:13–18.

39. Mark 13.

40. Luke 22:16–18.

Jesus speaks about how one lives as a subject in the kingdom of God. The values, which are to fill the life of the one who is a citizen in the kingdom of God, revolve around his understanding of the double-love commandment—to love God "with all your heart, with all your soul, and with all your mind, and with all your strength"; and the second is "you shall love your neighbor as yourself."[41] Even the scribe who had asked the question about which commandment is the first or has the highest priority had to agree and replied, "You are right, Teacher."

The ethical teaching of Jesus flows from the double commandment of love and is interwoven with the Law.[42] Jesus does not discount the Law; he remains a faithful Jewish believer. In fact for Jesus it is the expression of his understanding of God as kingly, that is, powerful, fair and just. The Law is the way that love is worked out in the complexities of human life and social structures. What he resists is the way that the Law, intended to guide and be a means of living in a fair and ordered way, is made into an end in itself. It becomes an absolute end rather than the means to the end of creating a way of living together that is fair and compassionate. We see Jesus pointing to the intention of the Law and underlining the spirit of the Law that is to insure the well-being of the people. For example, there is the story of Jesus healing the man with a withered hand on the Sabbath and then being asked if he should heal on the Sabbath. Jesus points out that the intention of the Sabbath is not to prevent doing good to others but to provide for rest and worship. He points out that even his detractors would take a sheep out of a pit on the Sabbath.[43] He teaches, "The Sabbath was made for humankind, and not humankind for the Sabbath."[44] He argues for an alternative way of seeing, being, and living in reference to the Law.

When Jesus speaks about love, he speaks about a particular kind of love that is translated from his Aramaic into the Greek as *agape*, a word that means unlimited love.[45] "It is a form of love that extends beyond the normal limits of human interaction and selflessly reaches out to all of humanity . . . and goes to the point of need with a caring and healing response."[46] One way of clarifying the meaning of *agape* is to distinguish between love based

41. Mark 12:30–31.

42. Meier, *Marginal Jew*, vol. 4.

43. Matt 12:9–14.

44. Mark 2:27.

45. A classic work on the meaning of *agape* is Nygren, *Agape and Eros*.

46. The Latin word *caritas* and the Greek word *charis* have a similar meaning to *agape*, but with shades of difference. See Ferguson, *Lovescapes*, 43–50.

on appraisal and love grounded in bestowal.[47] It is common to appraise a setting, an object, or a person and affirm that they are worthy of love. We may say, "I loved that beautiful sunset last evening." Love is evoked by the presence of beauty, truth, and goodness when it is encountered. It is easy for us to be attracted to a beautiful painting, a profound book, or a kind person. In a more profound way, we express our love for God as the divine fills our lives with peace and joy. Love flows from us because we appraise and experience God as inspiring our love.[48] In other cases, we bestow love on those who are not necessarily attractive and loveable, but nevertheless in need of love. Jesus often speaks about extending love to our neighbor regardless of the attractiveness of our neighbor. The character of *agape* is that it is bestowed without the conditions of the attractiveness of the person; it is done for the sake of others in order to increase their well-being. Jesus is quoted as saying, "You have heard it said, 'You shall love your neighbor and hate your enemy.' But I say unto you, Love your enemies and pray for those who persecute you.'"[49] In the same section, we read, "You have heard it was said, 'An eye for an eye and a tooth for a tooth.' But I say unto you, do not resist an evildoer. But if anyone strikes you in the right cheek, turn the other also; and if anyone wants to sue you and take your coat, give your cloak as well; and if anyone forces you to go one mile, go also the second mile."[50]

Love of this sort has many life-giving and nurturing features, ones displayed again and again in the interactions of Jesus with those with whom he lived and met in his itinerant ministry. There is some risk in using contemporary categories in describing these interactions, but as one reads descriptions of these encounters, certain qualities seem to be present. His fundamental commitment to loving God with his whole being, and loving his neighbor without qualification are apparent. The following characteristics of love (*agape*) appear to be present in both word and deed:

1. For the most part, his recorded encounters go beyond casual politeness and move toward *intensive* caring.[51] They are focused and concentrated, even if the meeting is not over a long duration. He heals a leper, but engages him in conversation that will be helpful and beneficial to Jesus as well.[52] There is love in word and deed.

47. Singer, *Nature of Love*, 1:3–22.

48. *Eros* is often used to describe this kind of love.

49. Matt 5:43–44.

50. Matt 5:38–41.

51. See the work of Post, *Unlimited Love*, 15–35. Post's categories are somewhat dependent upon Sorokin's book *Ways and Powers of Love*.

52. Mark 1:40–45.

2. As a general rule, Jesus extends love to nearly all who come his way, although some of the encounters with those seeking to undermine his ministry have the component of tough love. But his love is *extensive*, valuing all as his kindred.[53] He says, "Who are my mother and my brothers? And looking around him, he said, 'Here are my mother and my brothers.'"[54] He takes the opportunity to teach about all people being his kindred when his family members come to him and seek to talk with him.

3. It is also the case that Jesus' love does not end but has *duration*. Jesus does not reject Peter although Peter can at times be difficult. He even denies his affiliation with Jesus at the critical moment in Jesus' life but there is no indication that Peter ever received more than a correction.[55]

4. The love of Jesus is *pure* in the sense that it does not have ulterior and hidden motives but is focused on the one in his presence. Jesus, as he is described in these encounters, is remarkably free from his own needs and can extend himself into the lives of those whom he meets. He is present with Blind Bartimaeus, acknowledges him, heals him, and speaks a kind and encouraging word.[56]

5. The love of Jesus is *appropriate* for the occasion. It focuses on the need and provides the answer of the cure. The woman who was ill for twelve years got his attention and she was cured.[57] He says, "Daughter, your faith has made you well; go in peace, and be healed of your disease."

We might summarize the understanding of love in the teaching and actions of Jesus by saying that it is love in word and deed, a tangible response to an individual in need. It is freely given, not a saying or an action expressed for his own needs for attention and affirmation. It focuses on the illness or the suffering of the other, even if it is costly. In many cases Jesus takes care of the individual, but also expresses concern about the deeper cause whether it is unjust law, an empty religious custom, or neglect by those with responsibility. And his love shows no partiality; it is available to all regardless of wealth, social class, or cultural norm.[58]

---

53. Mark 3:31–35.

54. Mark 3:33–34.

55. Mark 14:66–72. See also Matt 16:21–23, in which Jesus scolds Peter.

56. Mark 10:46–52.

57. Mark 5:25–34.

58. See Williams, *Spirit and the Forms of Love*.

Love as the Guiding Principle in Shaping Ethical Norms

Jesus spoke with a variety of people about a range of specific ethical concerns as he moved across the region of Galilee in his itinerant ministry and then to Judea toward the end of his ministry.[59] In addressing these issues, he was providing guidance for people who had received and embraced the power and presence of God. To repent or to change directions meant to live in a new way that honored the double-love commandment and the Law. In some cases, his ethical teaching has been collected and categorized, as for example in the Sermon on the Mount, and in other cases it comes to us in a particular action, as parable or perhaps another form of communication. But as a rule, Jesus does not give us a systematic ethical system, but vivid examples in teaching and actions that occur as he travels and encounters others.[60]

Jesus thought about ethical behavior in terms of the Torah, a term that has a range of meanings including instruction, teaching, direction, and law. Often, these directives would have roots in the Hebrew Bible, but would come to the people in oral form. Parents, religious leaders, elders, and judges would guide the people with these teachings. At times when there was a king, these directives would come with the authority of the monarchy. This guidance would include both secular and religious issues, although there was no division between sacred and secular or church and state in the culture. So there would be laws related to financial transactions and purity rules for offering a sacrifice. As the law developed, it was associated with God and became known as the Law of Yahweh and took written form in the Pentateuch. There was a special emphasis on the Law of Moses that was seen as an expression of God's will. In that not all issues in human relationships and social systems were covered, there was often a consensus reached on the basis of wisdom and common sense.[61] Jesus inherited an understanding of the Law that had both authority and some flexibility.

Jesus valued the Law, but the way of understanding the Law was somewhat fluid for three primary reasons: (1) the corpus of the Hebrew Bible was still being formed; (2) different groups had competing views; (3) and

59. I am aware that there are fine New Testament scholars who say that Jesus may have spent time in Judea and Jerusalem in the early or middle part of his ministry. John's Gospel places the conflict with the moneychangers in the temple early in the ministry of Jesus. I am choosing the more traditional view that this conflict came at the end of his ministry.

60. There are a number of excellent studies of the ethics of Jesus, although often in the larger context of Christian ethics. See, e.g., Gustafson, *Ethics from a Theocentric Perspective*; Maguire, *Ethics*; Ramsey, *Basic Christian Ethics*; and Spohn, *Go and Do Likewise*.

61. Meier, *Marginal Jew*, 4:26–37.

the more definitive interpretation and history of the interpretation of the Law such as now exists in the Talmud did not exist. In addition, as we try to understand the ways in which the Law influenced Jesus, we discover that each of the authors of the Gospels have varying views of the Law and place their views within the teaching of Jesus. In fact, the material selected for inclusion in the Gospel accounts may have been filtered depending on the point of view and editorial goal of the Gospel authors. Matthew's Gospel, for example has Jesus saying, "Do not think that I have come to abolish the Law or the prophets. I have come not to abolish but to fulfill."[62] Just how Jesus was destined to fulfill the Law has been variously interpreted. Many have argued that the Easter events fulfilled the Law and became the "new testament" or account of how God relates to humankind. Others have argued that Jesus fulfilled the expectations of the Law by lifting up the ethical and moral concerns and downplaying the ritualistic practices and purity rules. Such a distinction would not have existed in the time of Jesus, although the point of view does have some merit as we try to discern what is universal and what is only germane to the particular time and situation in the teaching of Jesus. Within this context and this very brief introduction, we go to several specific issues that were as complex in the time of Jesus as they are now.

Our goal will be to discern how Jesus makes ethical judgments and provides ethical guidance on the basis of his respect for the Law and his clear statement that the double-love commandment is foundational. It is the Law and love that guide him. It is clear that Jesus calls for radical obedience to the will of God, as partially expressed in the Law, but goes beyond a mere avoidance of breaking the Law to a new relationship with God, one resulting in the transformation of the person of faith. This transformation changes the person and focuses on internal motivation that has love as its goal. Let us look at several ethical issues and see how it is that Jesus guides his followers:

1. There is the issue of *murder*, often placed in the context of retribution. In Matthew 5:21–22 we read: "You have heard that it was said to those of ancient times, 'You shall not murder; and whoever murders shall be liable to judgment.' But I say to you that if you are angry with a brother or sister, you will be liable to judgment and if you insult a brother or sister, you will be liable to the council." In this saying, we see both the compassionate teacher and the radical prophet at work, not only confirming that you shall not kill, but that you shall not even be angry with your brother or sister. There is clear movement from the act of

62. Matt 5:17.

killing to the attitude of being angry and insulting one close to you. Jesus places the emphasis on the internal motivation and the spirit of the exchange based on the new relationship with God that has been and is transforming; it makes radical obedience possible.[63]

2. The same spirit of internal motivation is present with the issue of *adultery*. Matthew 5:27–28 quotes Jesus as saying: "You have heard that it was said, 'You shall not commit adultery.' But I say to you that everyone who looks at a woman with lust has already committed adultery with her in his heart." What is present here is another command for radical obedience, and it has to do with the attitude of exploitation of another, violating the commandment to love one's neighbor. In this case, as with the case of murder, Jesus uses some harsh language about judgment if these negative attitudes are present.

3. We might illustrate this teaching of Jesus by mentioning still another issue, called *lex talionis* in Latin that teaches reciprocity, that the norm is "an eye for an eye and a tooth for a tooth." Jesus, again using the construct of past precedent, says, "You have heard that it was said, 'An eye for an eye and a tooth for a tooth.' But I say to you. Do not resist an evildoer. But if anyone strikes you on the right cheek, turn the other also; and if anyone wants to sue you and take your coat, give your cloak as well; and if anyone forces you to go one mile, go also the second mile."[64] In this case, Jesus calls into question this issue of vengeance and asks those in the kingdom to return evil with good and love for hate, and to be willing to help the other who is in need even if it means walking an extra mile.[65] In another teaching, Jesus illustrates the way that love is expressed by the Good Samaritan (Luke 10:25–37), a parable that contrasts the behavior of the Samaritan with that of the priest and the Levite, who were within their legal rights to bypass the man who was beaten and left for dead on the Jericho road. The Samaritan answers the radical call of God to show love, the higher priority, and the implication is that the priest and the Levite should have seen that love was far more important than adhering to religious customs which kept them distant from those who are different, perhaps unclean.

4. Still another issue, easily as complicated then as now is *divorce*. There is multiple attestation (Mark, Q, Matthew/Luke, and Paul) regarding the prohibition of divorce, yet the issue invites questions, especially in

63. Abernathy, *Understanding the Teaching of Jesus*, 113–14.

64. Matt 5:38–41.

65. Abernathy, *Understanding the Teaching of Jesus*, 115–16.

our culture in which divorce is a common practice.[66] However, many of the questions arise from the context in which Jesus spoke. First, the practice of divorce was common in Israel and across the ancient Near East, nearly as common as it is in the present day. In Israel, there were rules on how it was to be handled, and Jesus knew these rules. Second, in that it was quite common, there are few specific statements of prohibition given in the Hebrew Bible; it was accepted as a necessary norm. The goal was to manage it in an orderly way. Third, the response of Jesus to the issue should not be viewed primarily from our time, but from the conditions of his time, although what he says is relevant to our current situation. In that regard, fourth, we need to exercise some caution about how we attempt to discern Jesus' point of view. The questions of history and hermeneutics enter into the conversation, especially as we try to bring the teaching of Jesus into relevance for our time. This issue does get more attention than other practices and sayings of Jesus. We do focus a great deal more on this issue than some others that were also present in the law and practiced by Jesus. For example, we are more inclined to need his guidance on the issue of divorce than we are to follow his custom, common in his culture, to wash one's hands before eating.

Jesus would have known about the teaching in Deuteronomy (24:1–4) that provides a system of divorce. There is some mention of divorce in the prophets (Isa 60:1 and Jer 3:1–2, 8) but these references are a metaphorical way to speak of Yahweh's connection with Israel in which "divorce" was often an issue. It is mentioned as well in Malachi 2:10–16 with special emphasis on the final line which reads, "For I hate divorce, says the Lord, the God of Israel." Here, the clear emphasis is on the people being faithless in their relationship with Yahweh. These passages in the Hebrew Bible, taken with the multiple references in the Synoptic Gospels, would argue for understanding the view of Jesus as being opposed to divorce. While we have no direct evidence for it, we might conjecture that the single and celibate lifestyle which he chose would incline him to argue that the single life is preferred "in these times" in order to concentrate on the coming kingdom. So a separation, if there is conflict in a marriage, might be possible, although not divorce and remarriage.

There is one other passage, Mark 10:2–12, in which Jesus is described as dealing with this challenging question from a group of Pharisees. Jesus is asked whether divorce is allowed as taught by Moses.

66. Meier, *Marginal Jew*, 4:74–181.

Jesus replies that Moses granted the certificate of divorce because of "hardness of heart." Here, the implication is that divorce happens because two people are unable to always live together in a harmonious way, or to say it another way, unable to live together according to the will of God, that is, to love one another as one loves oneself in the marriage relationship. Jesus stays with the ideal in his answer, an answer we often hear in the marriage vows, "But from the beginning of creation, God made them male and female. For this reason, a man shall leave his father and mother and be joined to his wife, and the two shall become one flesh. So they are no longer two, but one flesh. Therefore what God has joined together, let no one separate." As Jesus encounters those with this difficulty, he demonstrates understanding and compassion. In the case of the Samaritan woman, he offers "living water," even though she has had five husbands and is living with a man who is not her husband.[67] The woman's life is transformed by her encounter and conversation with Jesus. There is compassion, forgiveness, and guidance.

5. Still another ethical concern that Jesus addresses is the practice of swearing an *oath*, a statement by which people in the time of Jesus gave assurance that they had spoken the truth or by which they obligate themselves to perform certain actions. The teaching appears in Matthew (5:34–37), and interestingly, it is present in the book of James (5:12) as well. It is not altogether easy to determine the dependency relationship between the two passages, but it is clear that this teaching was integral to the body of teaching for the first generation of Christians. Inevitably, the question arises whether this is an authentic teaching of Jesus, and I will follow John Meier in maintaining that it is.[68] What is being called for in both passages, although there may be some differences of emphasis, is direct and honest speech. This command would have been difficult for his listeners in that swearing oaths was such a common practice, especially in a culture that was oral and not dependent on legal papers that express promises and obligations. The practice was sanctioned in the Law, which means that once again Jesus was exercising some authority over the Law. But for Jesus, the practice often meant a trivial recital of an oath to "get things done" and led to hypocrisy and a fundamental lack of integrity. For Jesus, speaking the truth was essential and integrity was the higher value.

67. Luke 4:7–26.
68. Meier, *Marginal Jew*, 4:198–206.

6. Still another concern that Jesus faced in his encounters with the religious leaders of his time, perhaps less of an ethical issue than other
issues that deal directly with morality, *was adherence to the Sabbath.*
Regarding this issue, as we have already implied, Jesus was not so
much challenging Sabbath observance as he was the way it was practiced. Jesus was clearly in favor of Sabbath observance, but did not
want legalism to control the issue of how one observed Sabbath regulations. Essentially, Jesus had a common sense and humane approach
to the Sabbath and spoke about a proper sense of priorities.[69] His view
is often summed up in the Mark 2:27–28 in which Jesus is quoted as
saying, "The Sabbath was made for humankind, and not humankind
for the Sabbath." This principle is evident in several instances. There
are the miracles of exorcism and healing that took place on the Sabbath, some of which are disputed by the religious leaders and others
that seem to provoke no resistance. In nearly every case, Jesus shows
acceptance of the sacred institution of the Sabbath which is present in
the Torah, but acts in opposition to a sectarian legalism and replaces it
with common sense and compassion. There is the case in which Jesus
allows his disciples to pluck heads of grain and to eat them on the Sabbath because they were hungry. When challenged by the Pharisees,
Jesus answers with the precedent of David who got "dedicated" food
from the temple for his companions, and then Jesus points out that the
priests do it as well. Mercy rather than sacrifice has priority in the case
of human need.[70] Immediately following this incident is the one in
which Jesus heals the man with the withered hand on the Sabbath, and
when challenged, he once again argues for compassion.[71]

7. We might summarize the ethical teaching of Jesus with the observation
that he expands the application of the love commandments, applying
them to a wide range of situations. Jesus is clearly teaching that love,
mercy, and forgiveness are the highest standards of human behavior.
We can illustrate this widening of the application of love with his clear
command to love one's enemies.[72] Once again, he contrasts his teaching with what is the accepted norm in the culture. The Gospel of Matthew has Jesus saying, "You have heard it was said, 'You shall love your
neighbor and hate your enemy.' But I say to you, Love your enemies

69. Ibid., 296–97.

70. Matt 12:1–8.

71. Matt 12:9–14.

72. Meier, *Marginal Jew*, 4:478–576. This particular section in Meier's masterful
work is especially poignant and illustrates the title of his book *Marginal Jew*.

and pray for those who persecute you, so that you may be children of your Father in heaven; for he makes his sun rise on the evil and on the good, and sends rain on the righteous and on the unrighteous. For if you love those who love you, what reward do you have? Do not even the tax collectors do the same? And if you greet only your brothers and sisters, what more are you doing than others? Do not even the Gentiles do the same? Be perfect, therefore, as your heavenly Father is perfect." I want to underline three themes from this passage:

- The first is that Jesus illustrates his teaching about love with contrasts about accepted practices in the culture of his time. It was widely accepted that one should repay mistreatment with an action that would even the score or perhaps raise the winning margin. He illustrates this point with tax collectors who exploited the poor, collecting more than what was required and serving an alien government. Instead, Jesus says we are to love our enemies and pray for those who abuse us. Jesus showed love to tax collectors![73]

- He says that this kind of love is the manifestation of being one who is a child of God. God graciously provides much-needed sunshine and rain for all people, whether they are righteous or unrighteous. One who is in the family of God has the family characteristics, the qualities of God; there is a new relationship with God which is transforming and which empowers one to be like God. Jesus here is teaching about the boundless goodness of God who fills the life of those in the beloved community, and that God's children should also express boundless goodness to those near and far.

- The third point that I want to stress is that we are called to be perfect as our loving Parent is perfect. The translation of the Greek word into "perfect" may be somewhat troublesome in that it might imply a kind of rigid legalism or unattainable goal ("nobody is perfect!"). But the word means wholeness, full-grown, or mature. It implies that those who have received the power and presence of God have been turned toward a commitment to the will and way of God and have taken on the character of God. The Common English Bible translates the verse in the following way: "Therefore, just as your heavenly Father is complete in showing love to everyone, so also you must be complete." We may not be there as yet, but we are on the way in our new relationship with God, one that is changing us into a truly loving person.

73. Luke 19:1–10.

We began our discussion of the ethical teaching of Jesus with the maxim that he taught in both word and deed. As all great teachers, he lived and practiced what he taught. It was not just ethical theory to be learned, but a total commitment to be lived in the daily rounds of life. In this chapter, we have emphasized the way that Jesus taught in word and deed. We will now turn in our next chapter to the question of how it is possible to live in harmony with these ethical norms that set such a high standard. How is it possible for people of faith to practice and speak in a more loving way? In essence we will suggest that it is only possible as we embrace the power and presence of God. Only then will our lives be transformed.

Study Resources

Discussion Questions

1. What are some hermeneutical starting points that you would affirm as you interpret the teachings of Jesus? Would you understand them as conservative or as progressive?

2. How does Jesus integrate his respect for the Law (Torah) and his commitment to the double-love commandment?

3. What primary metaphors does Jesus use in understanding God? What language would you add as a way of speaking about God?

4. The Law of Moses says, "Thou shall not kill." How does Jesus extend and amend the law?

5. How does Jesus amend and extend the meaning of *lex talions*, or "an eye for an eye"?

Terms and Concepts

1. Hermeneutical Starting Points: Carefully selected assumptions upon which to base one's interpretation of Scripture or any piece of ancient or modern literature.

2. *Lex Talionis*: The Latin name for the law governing retaliation. The law states that retaliation for personal injury cannot exceed the injury done.

3. The Double-Love Commandment: The teaching of Jesus that says we are to love God with our whole being and our neighbor as ourselves.

4. Torah: Specifically it is the name for the Law of Moses, but it is also used more generally to speak about the Jewish Law.

5. *Praxis:* The understanding of religious thought and guidance that integrates principle and practice.

Suggestions for Reading and Reference

Abernathy, David. *Understanding the Teaching of Jesus.* New York: Seabury, 1983.

Hart, David Bentley. *The Experience of God: Being, Consciousness, Bliss.* New Haven: Yale University Press, 2013.

Meier, John B. *A Marginal Jew: Rethinking the Historical Jesus.* Vol. 4, *Law and Love.* New Haven: Yale University Press, 2009.

Ottati, Douglas F. *Theology for Liberal Protestants: God the Creator.* Grand Rapids: Eerdmans, 2013.

Spohn, William C. *Go and Do Likewise: Jesus and Christian Ethics.* New York: Continuum, 2000.

6

The Mission of Jesus' Teaching

The Demanding Challenge

JESUS WAS A PERSUASIVE and charismatic teacher who called his hearers to a new way of life. His teaching was transformational in character, inviting all who heard the message to change directions and follow the will and way of God. The word he used for change, translated into Greek as *metanoia* (noun) and *metanoeo* (verb), has the overtone of regret for following one way of life and the challenge to pursue of new way of life. Jesus begins his teaching mission with the proclamation of good news; God is present and now is the time to make this decision to embrace the kingdom or reign of God. While his listeners may not have fully grasped the implication of such a decision, they did know it would be a major change in their way of life. Jesus was asking them to receive the power and presence of God and integrate and pattern their lives around this new relationship.

The early mission of Jesus was characterized by his teaching about this new way of life. He did it in several ways that might be summarized in five categories. First, he spoke about God's *gracious invitation to forgive and transform* those who opened their hearts and minds to God's power and presence. Second, he said that this new relationship and way of life are filled with *demands and expectations and will require a profound commitment*. Third, he demonstrated the divine power and presence in the ways that *he showed compassion for those who were physically, emotionally, and spiritually ill*. Fourth, *he spoke and acted in a prophetic way as he challenged the domination system* that kept people in poverty and oppression leaving them marginalized and powerless. Fifth, he asked them to *join with others in a life-giving community* which would sustain their new faith, carry the good news to others, and be the agency of God in seeking a more just and humane world.

In these early weeks and months of the public ministry of Jesus, there was a sense of urgency about this mission, and Jesus had a large following because of what he said and what he did. As Jesus moved across the region of Galilee, and likely into Judea, his message had the tone of one who antici-pated that the kingdom of God would come, not just in terms of the good news about the gracious power and presence of God for individual lives but also in corporate terms linked to messianic expectations. He gave people immediate insight and comfort, but also the hope that life's circumstances could be better. The coming kingdom of God gave hope for a divine interven-tion into history that would bring in a new era of peace and justice. Across the centuries, interpreters of the teaching of Jesus have offered a variety of views on how to understand these sayings of Jesus that have apocalyptic and eschatological connotations. But while differing in these interpretations of what might happen at the end of history, nearly all have agreed that Jesus was also focused on the present and current life situation of those whom he encountered. He was a compassionate healer who cared about ill people, a charismatic teacher who provided life-giving insight, and a radical prophet who spoke truth to power and challenged unjust social conditions.

But these components of the teaching of Jesus about the present and the future have raised questions about how to understand his ethical teaching and how best to respond to his message. There is the complexity of the pres-ent and future in his proclamation of the kingdom of God. Were his ethical teachings meant for an interim period prior the coming of the kingdom? When might this happen and how should we prepare for it? How is it pos-sible to live up to the standards that you have set for those who are "subjects" in the kingdom of God? The demanding challenge to live a God-centered and ethical life seemed almost beyond the reach of those who had chosen to be followers of Jesus. Once again, competent scholars and faithful interpret-ers of the radical teaching of Jesus have differed in their answers to these questions. A review of the various ways that have been expressed about how to follow the ethical norms, which are prescribed in the teachings of Jesus, may provide context, perspective, and guidance in our quest to understand. I find a measure of truth in nearly all of the interpretations, and I will propose a composite view which will draw from several of them and that will remain open to new perspectives which come from our current situation. Our her-meneutical task is to interpret these teachings of Jesus in a way that brings them across centuries, cultures, and languages into the present for guidance and into the future for mission goals and a hopeful outlook.

Robert H. Stein, as he reviews the range of interpretations, suggests six attempts to find a way to understand and follow the ethical teaching of Jesus.[1] I will follow his outline, offer alternatives and additions, and present a point of view that understands the radical teaching of Jesus to be a profound guide for the Christian community and many others in the human family who are committed to helping our conflicted and threatened world move toward a more compassionate and just world.[2] A small digression: I am aware of the risks of naïve idealism (and may be guilty of taking them) in that it inevitably leads to disappointment and disillusionment and the rise of a cynical outlook. But I am also aware of the risks of being exclusively guided by a hardened realism that has strategies that contain violence and pursue personal and national interests. I am also aware that focusing on the ethical teaching of Jesus may sound narrowly aligned to one religious tradition and focused on the problems of first-century Galilee and Judea. Still another risk is suggesting answers to the problems of others, while failing to understand their history and culture and the complexity of their challenges. Conscious of these risks and narrow perspectives, I will seek to understand the universal character of the ethical teaching of Jesus, to be informed by the presence of the love ethic in nearly every religious tradition of the human family, and to take into account, as far as I am able, the harsh realities of our troubled world.

Professor Stein begins with what he calls the *Catholic* view that he describes as a two-level ethic.[3] At the first level, there is the general guidance for all Christians that means adherence to the Ten Commandments and the most direct ethical teachings of Jesus such as the love commandment and the Golden Rule (Matt 7:12). All Christians should endeavor to make these principles central to the ethical decisions and way of life. But, emerging as early as the second century, another standard of Christian behavior developed, one that involved giving up all of one's personal possessions, leaving family responsibilities, and devoting one's life to a higher calling. There was the beginning of a clear division between clergy and laity, and for those deeply committed, the possibility of entering a monastic order and living as a cenobite. There is an enticing attraction to follow a more intentional spiritual life, but there is no clear distinction made between the two levels of discipleship in the teachings of Jesus. All Christians must be guided by such

---

1. Stein, *Method and Message*, 89–96.

2. See Rifkin, *Empathic Civilization*, in which he argues that there is a gradual shift in the global consciousness toward compassion.

3. Stein, *Method and Message*, 90–91.

verses as found in Mark 8:34–35: "If any want to become my followers, let them deny themselves and take up their cross and follow me. For those who want to save their life will lose it, and those who lose their life for my sake, and for the sake of the gospel, will save it." It is important to note that this teaching does say "anyone" and does not suggest two levels of commitment. In fact, there may be a whole spectrum of levels of commitment.[4]

Dr. Stein calls a second view the *Utopian* interpretation.[5] He references groups from the Free Church or left wing of the Reformation and Roman Catholic orders such the Franciscan movement, each with their emphasis on pietism and holiness. Many of these groups sought to create a new society of love and peace on earth. The Sermon on the Mount was seen as providing a way to live together without benefit of social infrastructure such as the police and an army, judicial systems, and basic government; and in some cases there was no marriage. Possessions and money would often be held in common and all would help raise children. The society would seek to build a common life characterized by the presence of love, peace, and justice. One has to admire those who endeavored to live together in this way, and there continues to be some separate groups who join together to live intentionally by the teachings of Jesus. However, it would be difficult to say that Jesus was proposing such separate societies, and he did acknowledge the presence and function of government structures.[6] The teaching of Jesus about compassion and the quest for peace and justice applies all across society and is not limited to a small group, although such groups can have a nurturing and prophetic ministry.

Dr. Stein proposes a third interpretation rooted in the *Lutheran tradition*, one that maintains that the values inherent in the teaching of Jesus are intended for all people.[7] The Lutheran view would go on to maintain that humans are unable to meet the level of righteousness in these ethical norms or the level of righteousness outlined in the Hebrew Bible. What they contain are God's high expectations for human behavior. They do guide the faithful, but they also serve the primary purpose of revealing human sinfulness and the need for redemption. We learn that "all have sinned and fall

---

4. I would also briefly mention that it might be helpful in speaking about the Catholic view to deal with the thought of Augustine and the ethics of the two cities, the city of God and the city of the world. His teaching on this subject speaks of two levels or worlds. Augustine's view is quite profound and persuasive, but a full review of his understanding of the two cities would lead us away from our current discussion.

5. Stein, *Method and Message*, 91–92.

6. See Mark 12:13–17, in which Jesus speaks about Caesar and taxes.

7. Stein, *Method and Message*, 92–93.

short of the glory of God."[8] If they are viewed as expectations that must be met in order to be accepted by God, then they become a kind of legalism or "works righteousness" often leading to unhealthy guilt or conversely the attitude of self-righteousness if one believes these expectations have been met. What they do is call attention to the human need for grace in order to be justified before God.[9] The redemptive work of Jesus is the expression of grace and atonement, and by faith humans can be justified before God. There is certainly a valid point to be made about grace in the Lutheran (and Reformed) view, but it may be overly reliant upon the teaching of Paul and tends to overlook the clear statement in the Gospels about how one should live in accord with the teaching of Jesus. There is no indication in the Gospel record that they are exclusively intended to point out human sin and failure.

A fourth method of interpreting the ethical teaching of Jesus, which is listed by Professor Stein, is what he calls the *liberal* interpretation.[10] He has in mind a theological understanding that was present in the late nineteenth century and which continued well into the twentieth century, particularly in Europe and North America. Its present manifestation is often called "progressive." This view emphasized that the essence of the ethical teaching of Jesus must be internalized within the individual, altering one's disposition and attitude and then transforming those who have committed themselves to the spiritual life into persons who seek to express these values in personal behavior and expand them to social systems. The ethical teachings of Jesus are not a set of legal prescriptions that must be followed in a formal and rigid way, but an invitation to make the disposition of love central to one's life and to express this love in every circumstance. The goals of the Christian church should be to extend these ethical principles and make them applicable across society and, in so doing, help build the kingdom of God. The emphasis is on both the transformation of the person and the application of the teaching of Jesus to society. The intentions of the liberal tradition within the larger Christian community were noble and persuasive in many ways, but there were critics of the movement who maintained that "liberals" were naively optimistic about changing society, failed to recognize the nature of sin in individuals and evil in society and the world, and too easily placed their own values, not necessarily those of Jesus, in the context of the ethics of Jesus.

Still another mode of understanding the ethical teaching of Jesus, listed by Dr. Stein, is the *interim ethic* interpretation. It is associated with

8. Rom 3:23.

9. This point of view would also characterize the evangelical tradition within the larger Christian family.

10. Stein, *Method and Message*, 93–94. The word "liberal" is a somewhat loaded word, and often the word "progressive" is substituted.

the writing of Albert Schweitzer, who maintained that the kingdom of God was an anticipated future apocalyptic event in the teaching of Jesus, one that would bring history, as we know it, to an end.[11] Jesus, during his lifetime, really did expect an eschatological ending to come, perhaps in the very near future, and that what his followers needed was ethical guidance for how to live in the interim period prior to the full arrival of the kingdom of God. The radical nature of the ethical teachings of Jesus is intended then, not for guidance across history, but for just a brief period, and in this brief period, it would be possible to live in accordance with the challenging demands of the teaching. Schweitzer went on to say that Jesus was mistaken in his view about the apocalyptic arrival of the kingdom of God and was disillusioned at the end of his life. Schweitzer then added that the radical demands are in some cases impractical and impossible to fulfill, although Dr. Schweitzer in his remarkable way gave his life to their fulfillment by serving as a medical doctor in Africa. One can only admire his brilliance and dedication and affirm that the ethical demands of the teaching of Jesus are radical. It is also true that the ethics were integral to the teaching of Jesus about the kingdom of God, but there is little support among New Testament scholars for relegating the ethical teachings of Jesus to an interim period.

Dr. Stein does propose one other school of thought about the ethical teachings of Jesus that he calls the *existentialist* interpretation.[12] In this view, often associated with the writing of Rudolf Bultmann and with roots in the writing of Søren Kierkegaard, the ethical teaching of Jesus is not a new set of rules or laws displacing those laws that are present in the Hebrew Bible. Rather they are an invitation, based on the call of Jesus to make an "existential decision," to commit to the will and way of God. In fact, we cannot even confirm that many of the sayings of Jesus are authentic, although several may have their historical origins in the life of Jesus. But the authors of the Gospels to guide the new Christian community have redacted many of the sayings. So the emphasis is more on the radical nature of this call for a life-changing decision; it is more important than understanding a comprehensive ethical system, not that what we have in the Gospel accounts does not provide guidance. But the issue is the decision to follow the will of God, a way discerned by the examples and guidance that Jesus provides. These examples are not so much to be imitated as they are to be followed, as

11. Ibid., 94–95.

12. Ibid., 95–96. In that Dr. Stein's book was published in 1978, he does end his analysis with the existentialist point of view, but if he were to edit and rewrite the book, he might add two or three additional views such as the view of liberation theology and the view of those who have been engaged in more recent stages of the quest for the historical Jesus. I will discuss these views in my analysis.

one applies the principles to the contemporary life situation. It is possible to see these principles in the Gospel accounts even though we may see them described by the categories of a premodern understanding of the world. We may also observe that these ethical teachings had specific relevance for the particular setting which is described but it is also possible to discern the underlying intention and then *decide* to follow the will of God as faithfully as it can be known. Again, there is much in the existentialist view that has merit, but critics have pointed out that there may be too much of the teaching of Jesus that is not seen as authentic or germane, and a point of view that is too individualistic and not sufficiently concerned with social systems.

Still another way of understanding and responding to the ethical teaching of Jesus is present in the movement of *liberation theology*, one that was yet developing as Dr. Stein proposed his six views. This movement was an integral part of a tidal wave of justice that flooded the globe following the events of the 1960s. There was the ministry of Martin Luther King Jr. and many others who sought a fundamental change in the status of minority people; there was the worldwide quest for a change in the status of women; and there was an increasing awareness of the oppressive control and exploitation by the wealthy nations of the poor of the world. Prophetic voices created and sustained the world's passion for justice, and a new movement for justice emerged in Latin America, drawing upon the life and teachings of Jesus.

The voice was heard around the world, but its early and clear expression came from people in Latin America, such as Gustavo Gutierrez,[13] Jon Sobrino,[14] and Leonardo Boff,[15] to name just three among many. They saw in the historical Jesus an ideal expression of compassion and practice that framed a theological response to injustice. They argued that we must view Jesus and his teaching within the social, political, economic, and cultural structures in which he lived. As one examines the social structures in the age of Jesus, it is possible to see conditions that kept the vast majority of the people oppressed and marginalized. Such a study reveals a radical prophet whose message addressed the suffering of the people of his region. First-century Palestine was under Roman occupation and was subject to the rule of Herod and his successors. The vast majority of the people in both the region of Galilee and in Judea were poor. The ethical teaching of Jesus is aimed at those practices that kept the people in poverty. There was the Roman demand for taxes and even the temple's charge for the practices of worship

---

13. Gutierrez, *Theology of Liberation.*

14. Sobrino, *Christology at the Crossroads.*

15. Boff, *Jesus Christ Liberator.*

became Jerusalem's most important source of revenue.[16] There were a series of regulations assigning different places for those with less power. Jesus lived in this political climate of unrest under the presence of Roman occupation and economic exploitation legitimized by the religious establishment. Jesus as a compassionate healer, charismatic teacher, and radical prophet carried out his vocation within this field of clashing forces that kept the poor in poverty and a privileged minority in power. The healing practices, the direct and insightful teaching, and the prophetic proclamation of Jesus become the context for interpreting the ethical teachings of Jesus.

It is a bit hard to find one word that characterizes the understanding and response to the teachings of Jesus of the past several decades. It is the intellectual and to some extend the spiritual world in which I have lived and been influenced. I have understood it as a time in which scholars and religious leaders from around the world have attempted to use the refined tools of the historical-critical method and hermeneutical theory to find the *Jesus of history* and suggest a credible interpretation of his life and teachings. The new quest with its different chapters and with many yet to be written has not had nor does it currently have a single voice. It has generated a variety of interpretations, many of them helpful and illuminating, and some fanciful and unpersuasive. There are profound interpretations that acknowledge the new perspectives on Jesus provided by careful historical study, but remain with the more orthodox view of Christian understanding.[17] There are others that find in this new Jesus of history a frame of reference for living in a postmodern world with all of it overwhelming challenges.[18] There are those, some which are written by people who have been wounded by a narrow and exclusive fundamentalism or seen others wounded, who are eager to point out the dangers and inconsistencies of traditional belief and practice.[19]

As I review these trends in Jesus studies, I find myself drawn to four major developments, ones that many of the contemporary scholars and religious leaders share. The first is that it is possible, with careful and sophisticated historical study, *to know a substantial amount about the historical Jesus.*[20] Major differences exist on what and how much we can know, but there is a sense that the burst of historical study that began in the second half of the twentieth century and continues into the present has given us

16. Echegary, *Practice of Jesus*, 32–35.

17. See, e.g., Johnson, *Real Jesus*; Wright, *Original Jesus*.

18. See, e.g., Borg, *Jesus*; Crossan, *Historical Jesus*.

19. See, e.g., Bawer, *Stealing Jesus*; Meyers, *Saving Jesus from the Church*.

20. In the mid-twentieth century, in part because of the influence of Rudolf Bultmann, there was a consensus that we could know (for sure) very little about the historical Jesus.

access to the historical Jesus. A second major trend is that this access has shifted the *Christian understanding of Jesus toward his historical roots and away from the classical creeds that give us the Christ of faith.* For example, few would deny and most would welcome the historical studies which place Jesus in the context of first-century Judaism and understand him more from this frame of reference than from the older view which saw him as the intentional founder of a new religion. A third change, as much in attitude as in outlook, is the way that *these historical studies of Jesus have both threatened and liberated members and ecclesial bodies within the Christian community.* For some, they pose as a threat because there are inherent tendencies in these studies that put more emphasis on the human Jesus than the Christ of faith and tendencies which challenge what some see as essential belief in order to be Christian. Others have felt liberated in that they can now use other language in their liturgies and adopt alternative views on such issues as the substitutionary atonement. A fourth view (and one might list several others) that I want to suggest is that there is gradual and in some cases partial shift toward *rooting one's understanding of Jesus (Christology) in his history more than the classical creeds of Nicaea and Chalcedon.* One may still speak of the Trinity, but find persuasive ways of articulating the presence of God in the human Jesus that gave to the human family a new way of perceiving the loving and gracious character of God.[21] It has become possible to be comfortable staying in the Christian community and being open to and accepting of the historical realities of Christian origins. It is also possible to find ways of moving from a non-defensive and appreciative understanding of the history of Jesus to the Christ of faith, possibly with new language or with a more metaphorical understanding of earlier ways of articulating the Christian faith. It is acceptable to understand these earlier expressions of Trinitarian Christianity as using the language and concepts which were a part of the worldview of the time and the way which the people of that time put the world together and made sense out of it. We do the same and have the same limitations as we attempt to express our faith in God who is not just another being among beings, but the very ground of all being and reality. We cannot fully capture the reality of the divine with our language, limited as it is by our understanding and our ability to use it. But it is our way and can point to the Way; we do walk by faith and not fully by sight, although sight is an important ingredient in our walk.

---

21. See, e.g., Parini *Jesus: The Human Face of God.*

The Response to the Teaching of Jesus

We are now ready to propose a way of understanding and responding to the life and teachings of Jesus. We will be informed by the biblical record, primarily the Gospels and Q, but learn as well by other writing in the New Testament and from the early centuries of Christianity.[22] We will also draw upon a wide range of scholars and church leaders across the centuries that have prayerfully and carefully recorded their understanding of Jesus and his teaching. In addition, we are eager to be taught by the extraordinary scholars and teachers who are currently engaged in Jesus studies. It is a vast treasure from which to draw. We will use the five categories expressed in the introduction to this chapter and frame our understanding of the mission of Jesus as a charismatic teacher, a compassionate healer, and a radical prophet. The five categories are:

1. Jesus offers the good news of God's gracious invitation to forgive and transform those who embrace the kingdom of God;

2. Acceptance of this invitation leads to a new life in the kingdom that will have demands and expectations and will require a profound commitment;

3. He demonstrates the reign of God in compassionate healing of those who were physically, emotionally, and spiritually ill;

4. He spoke and acted in a prophetic way as he challenged the domination system; and

5. He invited his followers to join with others in forming a life-giving community that would share the message of good news and seek to shape a more just and humane world.

The Gracious Invitation to Forgive and Transform

Jesus began his public ministry by announcing the *good news* that God was present and inviting all to repent, change directions, be forgiven, and transformed. We turn first to the good news that Jesus brought and announced to his listeners.[23] The Greek term *evangelion* is the way this announcement is translated from the Aramaic of Jesus and the Hebrew of the Bible. It was not just general good news about an event that may have occurred in in the com-

---

22. We will, e.g., take seriously the Gnostic Gospels, unearthed by an Egyptian peasant in 1945. See the thoughtful account of their value in Pagels, *Gnostic Gospels*.

23. Mark 1:14–15; Matt 4:17.

munity where Jesus was speaking, but an announcement that the kingdom of God was at hand. The contemporaries of Jesus would have appreciated good news of any kind in that so many of them were leading lives filled with the struggle to overcome poverty and find adequate shelter and food for their families. Jesus was not unconcerned with the challenges of dealing with poverty, hunger, and illness but he chooses to place these concerns and the many others that they would bring to him in the context of God's power and presence. It is in the context of the reign of God that he will address their struggle. He wants them to understand that God is present with them and they need to open their hearts and minds to the divine presence.

To comprehensively hear and receive the power and presence of God, they will need to repent, change directions, and discover a new orientation in life. Jesus says that to receive the good news of the gospel, one needs to sense that a life apart from God is unwise and self-destructive, but a life filled with the presence of God, while not problem free, will bring guidance, perspective, and hope. Jesus says that this is the message of good news that he is bringing. He is teaching that the gracious God of all is forgiving and will receive those who turn in the direction of the kingdom of God. Not only will the endorsement of the kingdom of God give one the liberating sense of being forgiven, but also it will be transforming in the sense of giving one a new way of thinking about life and its challenges. To have the presence of God is to know that one is not alone and that God will enable and empower the person in the kingdom of God to live with meaning, courage, and compassion.

As Jesus speaks to his contemporaries, he applies this good news to tangible situations and offers healing and life-giving solutions. His announcement of the good news is more than a pious platitude, but a tangible response in a particular situation or conversation. For example in language which is alive in the circumstances of the conversation, Jesus speaks to a group about how God provided their wandering ancestors bread (manna) from heaven, and that this same "bread" "which comes down from heaven . . . gives life to the world. They said to him, 'Sir, give us this bread also.'"[24] The author of John's Gospel goes on to quote Jesus as saying, "I am the bread of life. Whoever comes to me will never be hungry, and whoever believes in me will never be thirsty." One's life will be centered in understanding and practicing the will and way of God. This is the bread of life.

The Gospel of Mark records a conversation with a scribe who asks Jesus which of the commandments is first and should have the highest priority. They agree that the double-love commandment, to love God with

24. John 6:31–36. John's Gospel draws less upon kingdom language and uses other metaphors to enlighten. The Gospel of John is written well after the time of Jesus and does have a theological orientation.

one's whole being and one's neighbor as oneself, is the heart of the law and no commandment is greater than these. The scribe adds that these commandments are much superior to burnt offerings and sacrifices. At the end of the conversation, Jesus saw that the scribe answered wisely, and Jesus says to him, "You are not far from the kingdom of God." In this passage, Jesus is saying that to be a person in the kingdom is to have an orientation in life and behavior that are focused on God's presence and the practice of selfless love. To invite God to reign in one's life is to be transformed and have a divine perspective and practices that follow the will of God.

The New Life in the Kingdom: Demands, Expectations, and Commitment

There are many personal needs and social causes that ask for our attention, time, and loyalty. Daily, we are required to think about food and shelter for our family and ourselves. As we engage in our professions, we are asked to give time and talent to the demanding work of a career. Our lives are full and our activities require our attention almost around the clock. Living this way may mean that we can easily lose track of our values and purpose in life and be led in a harmful direction. For example, our culture entices us with the false promise of happiness if we seek wealth and accumulate possessions. Jesus counsels his listeners about this risk saying, "Be on your guard against all kinds of greed; for one's life does not consist in the abundance of possessions" (Luke 12:15). With just a bit more subtlety, we are enticed, often because of our own insecurity and anxiety, with the illusion that if we seek power and prestige, we will be thought of as successful and important. It is not uncommon for people to pursue a way of life that is self-centered and which ignores the needs of others, rejecting the value that we are our sister's and brother's keeper.[25] The biblical account of the temptations of Jesus articulates the risks of misplacing our loyalties and priorities. The story places Jesus in the wilderness of Judea as he prepares for his life's vocation.[26] The story unfolds with the devil offering Jesus a range of options that would derail him from his calling. The first has to do with our physical needs. Jesus, on a fasting retreat, is hungry, and the devil says, "If you are the Son of God, command this stone to become a loaf of bread." Jesus answers him with the sentence that echoes across the centuries, "One does not live by bread alone." The devil also leads him to a high and prominent viewing

25. Luke 12:32–34: "Sell your possessions and give alms." The term alms inherently means "to the poor."

26. Luke 4:1–13.

point where it is possible to see towns and cities and says: "To you I will give their glory and all this authority . . . If you, then will worship me, it will all be yours." Jesus, his priorities firm, replies: "It is written, 'Worship the Lord your God, and serve only him.'" And in the last attempt to lead Jesus astray, the devil takes Jesus to Jerusalem and places him on a pinnacle says: "If you are the Son of God, throw yourself down from here" because God will protect you. Jesus answers, 'It is said, Do not put the Lord your God to the test.'" This story in Luke's Gospel makes it clear that the priority of the one who embraces the kingdom of God must seek the will and way of God.

The story also hints at the legitimacy of having one's basic needs met, a concern that can easily become our highest priority. Jesus, within the Sermon on the Mount, addresses this issue.[27] He does acknowledge that we may be concerned about what we will eat and drink, although the birds of nature do not worry and yet have what they need. We might also be concerned about having adequate and stylish clothing, and he says that the lilies of the field are more elegant and beautiful than even Solomon in all of his glory. God will provide the necessities of life; do not make them, as important as they are the highest priority in life. Jesus is then recorded as saying: "But strive first for the kingdom of God and his righteousness, and all these things will be given to you as well." The highest priority is to seek the will and reign of God in one's life.

To give the reign of God the highest priority in life is also to take on responsibilities, accept demands, and make commitments. In a conversation with his disciples, Jesus says to them that if they want to be his followers, they must be willing "to deny themselves and take up their cross . . ."[28] Jesus makes it clear that his followers will need to deny themselves in the sense of being preoccupied with self-centered behavior, interests, and goals. In fact, it is likely that they will have to take up their cross, make sacrifices, and endure some suffering in order to be a true disciple. Jesus is clear that there is a transcendent purpose that is higher than one's personal goals for comfort and security. But Jesus also explains in this passage the blessed irony of placing God's will as the highest priority in life. If is easy to think of this priority as denying happiness and a good life because of the sacrifices that must be made. Instead, he explains: "For those who want to save their life will lose it, and those who lose their life for my sake will find it. For what will it profit them if they gain the whole world and forfeit their life?" In fact, to place one's life in the hands of God is to find *life* and its true purpose, a

27. Matt 6:25–34.
28. Matt 16:24–26.

freeing release of control which brings profound fulfillment and a deep and abiding peace.

Jesus: The Compassionate Healer

Again and again, the biblical account maintains that Jesus went well beyond the words he spoke and demonstrated the truth and realities of what he was saying in tangible actions. There is a remarkable kind of harmony and integrity between his words and actions, even in the face of opposition and the prospect of suffering and rejection. Few would question the compassion of Jesus in his healing ministry, but many wonder about how he did it. It does raise the question of miracles that are not easy for most modern people, standing on this side of the scientific revolution, to accept. It is not possible in the current study for us to have an extended conversation about miracles, but perhaps a few observations will move us forward. John Meier suggests a definition of miracle in three categories:[29] (1) an extraordinary event that is perceivable by a fair-minded observer; (2) an event that offers no reasonable explanation in terms of our understanding of the way forces operate in our world of time and space; and (3) an event that is the result of a special act of God, doing what no human power can do.

Some of the miracles of Jesus do invite explanations that go beyond our normal understanding of how things work and point to the third part of Meier's definition. However, there are some of the healing miracles of Jesus that might be explained as unpredictable occurrences, but still be understood as the result of the various ways that the mind and emotions, in the right setting, contribute to physical healing. But it is the others that do fit into the category of natural causes that create questions. Given what we know from these stories, there is no easy way to explain these events by using scientific categories. There is the tendency to simply deny that they occurred, and then assume they were added to the legend of the activities of Jesus in a time when a healing miracle was an accepted way to describe what happened.

It is very legitimate to raise historical and philosophical questions about the healing miracles of Jesus, and of course the so-called nature miracles and it needs to be done in a thoughtful and scholarly way.[30] I will

29. Meier, *Marginal Jew*, 2:512.

30. There many fine books that address the issue of miracles in the life of Jesus. Although dated and aimed at a popular reading public, Lewis' small book, *Miracles*, addresses some of the issues. In a series entitled Theology and the Sciences, Peters and Bennett, *Bridging Science and Religion*, speak to some of the critical questions and

leave these questions for another day, but add two observations. The first is that *there may be explanations of these events that make more sense to the modern mind*. To find these explanations is important, but a full review of these explanations is beyond the scope of our current study. But there is little doubt that Jesus demonstrated extraordinary compassion for the sick people whom he encountered, whether the illness was categorized as physical (leper) or spiritual (exorcism), and his compassion may have been a part of the healing. The second is that there is a credible historical record that these people, as they encountered Jesus went away with a change in their condition. It is possible to say that no modern person truly believes in miracles, but it *is also the case that many healings which occur in our time need explanations which are not exclusively empirical*. Jesus did change those whom he encountered, but we are left to wonder just how he did it, apart from the flow of divine love. At the risk of being accused of a cop-out, I will focus on the expression of love and compassion in the life of Jesus rather than on the philosophical question of the notion of miracle.[31]

It is important to underline that the healing miracles of Jesus had several characteristics that separate them from the practice of magic that was not uncommon in the time of Jesus. For example:[32]

1. The miracles were in the context of a relationship of faith and love, not a magic show in which the hand moves faster than the eye.

2. The person has a genuine need or illness and has no ulterior motive apart from the need for healing. There is no exchange of money, for example.

3. There is, in most cases, openness to healing and the faith that it can happen. The people are eager and ready.

4. With few exceptions, Jesus calls upon the power of God, and attributes the healing to the grace of God. Jesus does not assume he can "force the hand of God" but understands the action as the will and action of God.

5. Jesus' miracles do not directly punish or hurt anyone, and the emphasis is on the well-being of the patient, or in the case of the other miracles, an improved condition (calming the storm).

---

issues. I have been helped by the classic work of Barbour, *Religion and Science*, and a useful textbook by Barnes, *Understanding Religion and Science*.

31. Martin, *Jesus: A Pilgrimage*, 289–330, makes a strong case for seeing the miracles of Jesus as "miracles" and resists explaining them away.

32. Ibid., 548.

A review of some of the miracles will underscore these several characteristics. One type of healing present in the ministry of Jesus was the exorcism, a type of healing that on occasion lends itself to the category of therapeutic healing or overcoming what might be a fit or an expression of epilepsy. In the first chapter of the Gospel of Mark, Jesus is described as removing an unclean spirit from a man whom he met in the synagogue of Capernaum.[33] The author of Mark has placed this event early in the public ministry of Jesus, and it represents a challenge by Jesus who has begun a ministry to resist and eliminate harmful influences on the welfare of his contemporaries. The unclean spirit cries out, "What have you to do with us, Jesus of Nazareth? Have you come to destroy us? I know who you are, the Holy One of God. But Jesus rebuked him, saying, 'Be silent, and come out of him.' And the unclean spirit, convulsing him and crying with a loud voice, came out of him." In this example, we do have to take into account the clear editorial goals of the author of Mark's Gospel, but we also observe the way Jesus is understood as one who is intent on healing the ills of those whom he encounters. "At once his fame began to spread throughout the surrounding region of Galilee." This sort of miracle is repeated in the case of the Gerasene Demoniac (Mark 5:1–10), the Possessed Boy (Mark 9:14–29), the Mute and Demoniac (Matthew 9:32–33), and possibly with Mary Magdalene (Luke 8:2) and the Syrophoenician Woman (Mark 7:24–30).

The more common healing ministry of Jesus concerned those with illness or conditions impacting the normal functions of an able-bodied person. For example, again in an early section of the Gospel of Mark, we have Jesus healing a person who is paralyzed and crippled.[34] The story begins with the setting of Jesus in Capernaum, after being away in his ministry across the region of Galilee. In this story, there is a large crowd of people seeking to access Jesus, so many in fact that the people who had brought the paralytic man to Jesus had to remove part of the roof of the house and lower him into the presence of Jesus. Jesus first addresses the man's spiritual condition and assures him that his sins are forgiven, an action that caused some disturbance because it was believed that only God could forgive sins. Jesus, in response to this concern, heals the man and says to him, "Stand up and take your mat and go to your home." Jesus uses the healing to demonstrate that he has been given the authority by God to forgive sins as well as to heal. There is spiritual and physical healing. The crowd was amazed "and glorified God, saying 'We have never seen anything like this.'"

33. Mark: 1:23–28.
34. Mark 2:1–12.

Jesus healed those with other ailments including blindness that was common in the region of Galilee (and the ancient world) at that time. Later in the Gospel of Mark, (10:46–52), Jesus was in Jericho, a long walk from his home base in Capernaum, and meets a blind beggar named Bartimaeus, who was sitting beside the road. He hears that Jesus has come near and calls out for help and healing. Jesus asks him to come near, at which time Bartimaeus asks Jesus to let him see again. Jesus replies, "Go; your faith has made you well." He then becomes a follower of Jesus. The importance of this story is that it once again underlines that Jesus is willing to be interrupted in his busy day, and even more important, it indicates that the faith of the one who asks to be healed has an integral part in the healing process. Again, it is the openness of the needy one to the healing power of God, which seems to flow from Jesus.

Jesus also has encounters with those with leprosy, a skin disease that may not have been specifically what is now called Hansen's disease. Other skin diseases were common at that time and leprosy may have been a more generic term. The author of Mark's Gospel, once again, places this kind of healing early in the ministry of Jesus (Mark 1:40–45). A leper was an outcast in large measure because the disease was thought to be contagious. But the leper, violating protocol, boldly approaches Jesus and says, "If you choose, you can make me clean." The passage continues, "Moved with pity, Jesus stretched out his hand and touched him, and said to him, 'I do choose. Be made clean.' Immediately the leprosy left him, and he was made clean." Note that Jesus uses touch in this healing story. This story adds the conclusion that Jesus asks the leper to tell no one and to go immediately to the priest who had the authority to remove his outcast status. But the healed leper could not contain himself and spread the word about the marvel of his healing which made it difficult for Jesus to move easily from one location to another because of the crowds which sought to make contact with him.

There are many other examples of healings in the Gospels, but we will use these incidents to demonstrate the compassionate nature of Jesus' ministry. In addition to these descriptions of healing there are also the stories of Jesus bringing the dead back to life. There is the daughter of Jairus,[35] the raising of the son of the widow of Nain,[36] and the raising of Lazarus.[37] There are many technical historical questions about these accounts, the primary one being whether they do go back to the time of Jesus or whether they are part of the faith of the authors who want to confirm the faith of the new

---

35. Mark 5:21–43; Matt 9:18–26; Luke 8:40–56.

36. Luke 7:11–17.

37. John 11:1–45.

believers. But as one studies them, they appear to at least be an echo of a past reality and they certainly fit the character of Jesus. The raising of Lazarus is especially touching in that it is a situation with very close friends who are in deep grief about the loss of their brother. Jesus tends to the sisters in a sensitive way as well as bringing Lazarus back to life. Once again Jesus is seen as a profoundly compassionate person.

Jesus: The Radical Prophet

The biblical account portrays Jesus as a fearless prophet, calling attention to unjust social systems that kept people in poverty and all of its accompanying consequences. In fact, the stories of Jesus, while distinctly personal are also quite political.[38] Jesus does show compassion to those whom he meets and continually responds to their individual needs. But he appears to be aware that the social systems in which people live can cause untold suffering, and he is persuaded that these domination systems should and can change.

There is the fascinating story in the Gospel of Luke (19:1–10) about a tax collector in Jericho whom Jesus encounters in his trip from Galilee to Jerusalem toward the end of his public ministry. The story vividly illustrates the prophetic challenge of Jesus to the domination system. Jericho is a small town, although a very old one even in the time of Jesus. It continues to exist in the area referred to as the West Bank in the Palestinian Territory. In the time of Jesus, there was much poverty, injustice, crime and the resulting human suffering. Incidentally, as it was in the time of Jesus, so it is now a city of oppression and occasionally violence. As Jesus entered Jericho, a large crowd of people who are eager to see and perhaps hear the compassionate healer and radical prophet from Nazareth meets him. Jesus would observe, as he enters the town, a social system that has been described as a "premodern domination system"[39] with a small class of wealthy and powerful people who rule the city. As he spoke with the people under these conditions, he would have discovered that some of the people had been co-opted in order to sustain the social order. He would have also observed that there was a second class of people, the vast majority, who were peasants and carried out the work that was largely agricultural in nature.

This town and the surrounding agriculture lands would have had the following features:

38. Borg, *Jesus*, 225–29.
39. Ibid., 81–82.

1. It would have been *politically oppressive*, ruled by a monarchy and those from their own ranks who have been recruited into the system. The people would have had no voice or power in shaping the political structures.

2. It would have been an *economically exploitive society*, one in which the wealthy and the powerful acquired a high percentage of the society's annual production of wealth and which secured their lives of privilege and luxury.

3. The *religious leaders legitimized these conditions*. Rulers would have claimed a divine right to rule as they choose, and would have argued that the social order reflected the will of God. This point of view would have been difficult to argue against in that it would so easily be construed as an argument against God.

4. *Police and military forces would have maintained the social order* and resistance would have meant armed conflict.

According to Luke, Jesus is toward the end of his public ministry and understands that he will culminate his life work when he leaves Jericho and begins to hike the steep road up to Jerusalem. He had likely been in Jericho before, and tradition places the temptation of Jesus to rule all the kingdoms of the world from a sight on hills above Jericho. Jesus enters the city with a clear sense of his vocation, knowing that he is called to heal people and to improve their lives; in short to do what he can to transform the people and the society in which the live. So he paused long enough to have a conversation with a Jewish tax collector named Zacchaeus who vividly represented the domination system. Zacchaeus was not popular in Jericho, and when Jesus asks for time with him, the people are disappointed and begin to grumble and wonder why he would spend time with one who had betrayed them. Zacchaeus had sold out and joined forces with the oppressive Roman rulers and the group put in power by the Romans, the Herodians, or by origin, Idumeans. Perhaps because of his own poverty, Zacchaeus may have believed that becoming a tax collector was the only way of escape from poverty. He was assigned to collect a certain amount of money from the people and then was allowed to keep whatever was left over after he paid the rulers. This practice gave Zacchaeus ample motivation to collect more than was required by the government officials.

Jesus did meet with Zacchaeus that day, and the results of the conversation illustrate the ministry of Jesus. It is likely that Jesus spoke with him about his Jewish faith and upbringing, his betrayal and isolation from his family and community, and the unfulfilling quest for money. By choosing

to spend the day with Zacchaeus, Jesus communicated in action his compassion and his willingness to help Zacchaeus with his life and perhaps to
reorient it. They probably shared a meal and spoke about the kingdom of
God, about forgiveness and healing, and about how the power and presence
of God can renew a person and give them courage, meaning, and hope. Zacchaeus may have told Jesus that he did have a sense of failure, diminished
self-esteem because of his chosen work, and about the current unhappiness
in his life. It is likely that the conversation turned to issues of oppression,
poverty, powerlessness, and domination. Those in power might have been
sensitive to Jesus spending time with Zacchaeus and upset with the outcome
of the conversation. The conversation did transform Zacchaeus; he left the
position of tax collector and promised to give half of his possessions to the
poor and pay back anyone whom he had defrauded four times what he took.
There is a clear break with the domination system and those in power would
not have been happy, and while we have no record it, they may have taken
action against Zacchaeus. It was a risky decision for him to make.

On the other hand, the common people in Jericho and the region,
those living in poverty and oppression, and probably his family and network of friends would have been amazed and tremendously pleased to have
Zachaeus return to his community of faith and support. The respect, love,
and forgiveness offered to Zachaeus transformed him, and the people observed the power of God in the compassionate healer and radical prophet
who visited their city.

There are other instances in the Gospel accounts of Jesus challenging
the domination system. Perhaps the most dramatic one comes, according
to the Synoptic Gospels, not long after the conversation in Jericho, and in
John, early in the ministry of Jesus. As he arrives in Jerusalem, Jesus has
conversations with people at the temple, the center of the activities of the
city. Early in these conversations in the last week of his life, the Synoptic
Gospels describe Jesus as challenging those who were buying and selling in
the temple.[40] The target of Jesus' challenge may not have been the normal
business of buying and selling on the outer edges of the temple; it was like a
city square. But the selling of doves to be offered for sacrifice and the money
changing which occurred were the focus of Jesus' anger. Jesus overturns the
tables of the moneychangers and the seats of those who sold the doves to be
used for sacrifice. He says to them, "It is written, 'My house shall be called a
house of prayer (for all nations in Mark); but you are making it a den of robbers." At the heart of Jesus' action is the way in which the religious devotion
of prayer and sacrifice had been taken over by those who collected money,

---

40. Matt 21:12–17; Mark 11:15–19; Luke 19:45–48; John 2:13–15.

often from those with deep piety, but in poverty, in order to support an unjust political order. Perhaps no other action was so pointedly prophetic and ultimately one that would be used against Jesus in his trial, especially as it was joined with the comments of Jesus about the destruction of the temple.[41] Jesus was indeed a radical prophet.

Jesus: The Life-Giving Community

Across the centuries in Christian thought, there has been a lively discussion about whether Jesus intended a new community to be formed around his life and teaching, separate from the believing community of Judaism in which he participated. Occasionally, the discussion has taken the form of whether Jesus "founded" the Christian church, or whether he remained within the community of first-century Judaism and was a prophet of reform. The majority of pastors and scholars in the modern era have tended to maintain that Jesus did stay within his Jewish heritage, valued it, and spoke prophetically to it. The Apostle Paul, while not addressing this topic directly speaks of the redemptive events of Easter as the foundation of a new order and the breaking point with Judaism. He writes with lament about the need for the beginning of the new community, *ekklesia*, a term meaning "assembly" or "gathering." He says, "I have great sorrow and unceasing anguish in my heart" that this new community must be formed.[42] He makes it clear that he continues to be loyal to his Jewish heritage, but sees the coming of Christ and his resurrection as the fulfillment of the messianic expectations. God will continue to honor the covenant with the Jewish people, but now God's grace, expressed in the life, death, and resurrection of Christ is extended to all people. It has become a universal gospel, not a prophetic addition to Judaism. It is frame of reference that has been the Christian church's traditional understanding of how the church was intended to be created and came to be formed. Even the Gospel accounts have Jesus sensing this future reality, although these accounts were written after the Easter events and may not be authentic observations of Jesus.[43]

But it is not likely that the Jesus of history intended to form a new religion, even if it were an outgrowth of Judaism. The counter argument is that Jesus, given the divine in him that was present as well as his humanity, did in fact see beyond his death to the eternal plan of God. This plan did involve a

41. Matt 14:1–2; Mark 13:1–2; Luke 21:5–6.

42. Rom 9:2. Paul develops his thought in Rom 9–11 and in his actions recorded in Acts 10–11.

43. Mark 10:32–34; Luke 17:20–37; 18:31–34; Matt 20:17–19.

new community being formed, the Christian church, which would become the new Israel and the way in which God would extend the message of love and redemption to all of humanity. The Gospel accounts, written well after the death of Jesus, do mix the divine and human in Jesus and attribute a perspective to him that is beyond the eyesight of a normal human being. In part, because we are focusing on the Jesus of history and in part because of our commitment to finding the basis of faith in the human Jesus, we would be more inclined to see in these passages in which Jesus seems to see beyond his circumstances and his death, an interpretation based on faith and with the goal of helping the new Christian community to become informed and more mature in its outlook.

This point of view is not to say that Jesus did not think in terms of a community of faithful followers who would be committed to forming a community of fellowship and support, sharing the message of Jesus about the kingdom of God, and being direct and bold in its prophetic proclamation regarding injustice and the resulting oppression and poverty. *Jesus does assume the reality of the believing Jewish community.* He was acquainted with the history of the Hebrew people. He had heard the stories of the exodus, had great respect for the Torah, and had studied the messages of the prophets. The Gospel of Matthew records Jesus as saying, "Do not think that I have come to abolish the law or the prophets; I have come not to abolish but to fulfill. For truly I tell you, until heaven and earth pass away, not one letter (*iota*) will pass from the law until it is accomplished."[44] Matthew's Gospel continues to say that the teachings of the Torah are foundational for Jesus's teaching. These teachings explain the righteousness about which Jesus speaks, and that has been practiced by the scribes and Pharisees.[45] The narrative of the Hebrew Bible is foundational for the life and teaching of Jesus, a narrative that traces the history of a community of people across hundreds of years.

Jesus begins his life in a synagogue[46] and participates as a boy, in Luke's account, in a thoughtful discussion about the Torah with the scholars of the temple in Jerusalem.[47] He leaves his work as a carpenter and associates with the prophet, John the Baptist, who proclaims that the Jewish community must change or expect divine judgment.[48] He is then baptized by John and

44. Matt 5:17–18.
45. Matt 5:20.
46. Luke 2:22–24.
47. Luke 2:41–52.
48. Matt 3:1–17.

begins his ministry in the synagogues of Galilee and beyond.[49] In fact, Jesus uses the temple and the synagogues as an integral part of his mission strategy, although he was not bound to these settings in that he often met people and ministered to them in the streets of villages and rural regions of Galilee. *Jesus uses and takes full advantage of the Jewish community for his ministry.*

But he does form a life-giving and supportive community for his ministry. He calls his inner group of disciples, mentors them, and asks them to join him in teaching the message of the kingdom of God, the compassionate healing of the ill, and the prophetic call for justice.[50] In addition to his inner circle of disciples, he has many others ("great crowds") who join him to learn and assist in the mission, although adequately warned about the challenges of such an undertaking.[51] The mission of Jesus is not the work of a single individual, although certainly lead by a charismatic individual, but the work of a community of believers who follow the teaching and guidance of Jesus.

In this section of our study, we have focused our attention on the method of Jesus' teaching, the message of Jesus' teaching, and response to the teaching of Jesus' teaching. Our goal in the next section will be to explore ways that illustrate Jesus as a charismatic teacher, a compassionate healer, and a radical prophet. We will explore ways that the life and teaching of Jesus can leap across time and history, be translated from another culture and different languages, and be expressed and applied in a contemporary context. It is to this formidable task that we now turn.

Study Resources

Discussion Questions

1. Do you think it is possible to truly follow the teachings of Jesus? Is it possible to love one's enemy and to do to unto others what you would have them do unto you?

2. How would you interpret those verses in the Gospels that infer that Jesus believed in the full coming of the kingdom of God as an end of history as we know it in his time?

3. What do you think gave Jesus the capacity to heal those who were ill, even though he was not a medical doctor nor did he have access to modern medicine?

49. Matt 4:23.
50. Matt 10:1–15.
51. Matt 8:18–22; Luke 9:57–62.

4. How did Jesus challenge the injustice that he saw in his itinerant ministry?

5. In what ways did the Christian church develop out of the life and teaching of Jesus?

Terms and Concepts

1. Miracle: An extraordinary event that is perceivable by a fair-minded observer; one which offers no reasonable explanation in terms of our scientific understanding of how things work; and one that may be the result of a special act of God, doing what no human power can do.

2. Domination System: A system of injustice that is politically oppressive, economically exploitive, legitimized by authority, and often enforced by police and military forces.

3. Liberation Theology: To view Jesus as an ideal expression of compassion and practice that challenged unjust social, political, economic, and cultural structures and norms.

4. *Metanoia*: A Greek word used in the New Testament which is a translation of Jesus' call to repent or show regret for one way of life and a challenge to pursue a new way of life.

5. Utopian: An ideal vision of a way to life; when a group of people join together to create an ideal society based on the values of love and peace, often with shared wealth and without government structures and security forces.

Suggestions for Reading and Reference

Barbour, Ian G. *Religion and Science: Historical and Contemporary Issues*. San Francisco: HarperSanFrancisco, 1997.

Echegaray, Hugo. *The Practice of Jesus*. Translated by Matthew J. O'Connell. Maryknoll: Orbis, 1984.

McLaren, Brian D. *The Secret Message of Jesus: Uncovering the Truth That Could Change Everything*. Nashville: Nelson, 2006.

Meyers, Robin R. *Saving Jesus from the Church*. New York: HarperOne, 2009.

Sobrino, Jon. *Christology at the Crossroads*. Translated by John Drury. Maryknoll: Orbis, 1978.

SECTION 3 _____

The Translation

Interpreting the Teaching of Jesus
for a Contemporary Setting

In SECTION 3, WE will engage in the hermeneutical challenge of translating and interpreting the life and teachings of Jesus for our time, an effort already begun in the previous chapters. As we have observed, it is a complex task in that it requires explaining a first-century Jewish teacher and prophet to all of us who live in the first half of the twenty-first century. It means translating the language, understanding the culture, and explaining the historical circumstances of Jesus in a way that makes him understandable, credible, and relevant. As we make this "big jump" over the centuries, there are risks, chief among them is that we will misunderstand Jesus and create him in our image and miss the subtleties of his life, times, and teaching.[1] Kenneth E. Bailey, who lived and worked in the Middle East for the greater part of his teaching career, offers wise guidance to those who wish to understand Jesus in his book *Jesus through Middle Easter Eyes: Cultural Studies in the Gospels*. His message is that we are able to understand the subtlety and range of the life and teaching of Jesus if we know his culture and guard against placing Jesus into the categories

---

1. A fine New Testament scholar, Cadbury, in a previous generation spoke of this risk in *Peril of Modernizing Jesus*, 3.

of our own culture. What we do know is that Jesus "happened" and his teaching about love, his life of compassion, and the redemptive character of the Easter events, however we may understand them, created one of the "greatest flowerings of the human spirit" in all of human history.[2] We will attempt to find a way to understand this happening in chapter 7 by examining how Jesus understood the reality of God's power and presence in the world. In chapter 8, we will turn to an exploration of how Jesus taught a way to respond to and incorporate the divine presence into our lives resulting in a measure of peace and guidance. In chapter 9, we will explore how these teachings can be applied to the ethical challenges and the critical social issues of our time.

> The most painstaking historical and geographical study of Jesus' physical environment is not sufficient to prevent the quite careless modernization of his thought.[3]

---

2. The phrase is borrowed from George F. Kennan's diaries and quoted by Buchanan, *Christian Century*, 3.

3. Cadbury, *Peril of Modernizing Jesus*, 8.

7

God in the World

The Radical Teaching of Jesus about God

THE PURPOSE OF THIS chapter is to explain how Jesus understood God
and how it shaped his teaching. We will then explore ways that his understanding of God might be relevant for honest seekers in today's world. It
has been my observation from years of service in the church and experience in higher education that our understanding of the divine and how
we perceive our relationship with God profoundly influences our faith
and spiritual vitality. While I have done no systematic data gathering
about this issue, I have discovered in years of service with people struggling with their faith that it is quite common for people either to neglect
their faith commitments or "lose" their faith because they have rejected a
particular view of God or the divine.[1]

We are often taught a quite simplistic understanding of God in our
early years, a view that may be altogether appropriate for children, but if
this view does not mature it no longer serves us well in our adult years. In
my transition from perceptions of God in my childhood and adolescence to
my university, seminary, and graduate education, those who suggested new
ways of understanding God helped me. Especially helpful to me were the
writings of Paul Tillich and Karl Barth, not always thought of as being on
the same page. Tillich invited me to look beyond anthropomorphic images
of God and spoke in the categories of being and non-being, the ground of

---

1. I have found the work of Fowler on faith development extremely helpful on
this issue. See *Stages of Faith*.

being, and phenomenological descriptions of the divine.[2] I relaxed some and said, "I think I'll stay within my faith commitment for a while." Karl Barth's views, while using more orthodox language, taught me to think about the "wholly other" God who was not a Santa Claus or an ageing parent but a mystery for me to probe and serve in humility.[3] His teaching that Jesus was the human face of God was especially poignant for me.

As a way gaining some clarity on this issue and deepening our own beliefs, we will review alternative views of the divine. Our goal is to see if there is a distinct contrast in these alternative concepts of the divine with the views of Jesus and whether there may be ways that they complement Jesus' understanding of God.[4] I am intrigued by the question of how it might be possible to find some common ground within the plurality of religious traditions and a way of integration within the family of religions that adheres to a philosophical monotheism.[5]

Jesus accepted and then developed a way of understanding God from his Jewish heritage. The home of his childhood was likely filled with the stories from the Hebrew Bible, how God created the world, the beginning of the human story from the early chapters of Genesis, the travels of Abraham and Sarah, the patriarchs and the life of Joseph in Egypt, Moses and the Exodus, and the history of the Hebrew people led by kings and challenged by prophets. The teaching of these stories, at home from his parents Mary and Joseph and likely in the synagogue in Nazareth would have stressed the belief in Yahweh, the Creator of the universe and the Sustainer of human life. He would have learned that God entered into the life of the Hebrew people, made a covenant with them, and asked them to live an ethical and spiritual life.

As we carefully read and attempt to discern the meaning of the teaching of Jesus, we learn that he thought and taught about God in the categories of this rich heritage, a heritage filled with informative and dramatic stories, guidance (often called Law) about individual behavior and social responsibility, and encouragement to lead a spiritual life dedicated to God. When he began his public ministry about the age of thirty, he drew upon his learning and his experience in the community of faith. At the center of his teaching and what motivated him in his move from carpenter to prophet was his deep faith in the God who was not only the sovereign Creator, but also a

2. Tillich, *Systematic Theology*, 1:234–321.

3. Barth, *CD*, vol. 2, *Doctrine of God*.

4. Stella, in *Finding God beyond Religion*, offers more popular suggestions on ways of perceiving the divine that resonate with contemporary honest seekers. Miles, in his Pulitzer Prize–winning book *God: A Biography*, speaks of the evolution of the human family's understanding of God.

5. The John Templeton Foundation has invited scholars to address this question.

loving Father who entered into the life of the Hebrew people. God was the cohering center of his teaching and guided his own life and vocation. In his teaching, there are self-references, but unlike the primary emphasis of the church's teaching in which Jesus is central, he pointed to the God who stands behind all that is, orders it, and calls people to give themselves to the divine will and way. One can hear almost Jesus singing the great hymn of the church, "To God be the glory, great things He has done."

What were the central characteristics of the God about whom Jesus taught and served? How did Jesus understand God, describe God, and teach and act in reference to his understanding? To answer these questions, we are reminded that to access the understanding of Jesus about God requires careful study and that it is all too easy for us to impose our own understanding of God into the mind and words of Jesus. We live with these risks, but the greater risk is not to take a risk at all. There is so much to learn which can transform our lives and make them more fulfilling and responsible. So, with humility and respect before the mystery of God and Jesus' profound understanding of God, we would suggest five categories to describe the radical teaching of Jesus about God: love, presence, truth (or light), just (or justice), and sovereign (sovereignty).[6]

God Is Love

It is interesting and worth noting that the biblical witness makes few "is statements" about God, and Jesus was cautious about describing the essence of God. He did not attempt to prove the existence of God or use philosophical language as he spoke about God. He, like the tradition that he inherited, often told stories and parables about God, which provoked the imagination and stimulated the thought of his listeners. Generally, Jesus used analogies and metaphors as he spoke about God, and on occasion he would help his listeners understand God by saying what God is not like (*via negativa*). For example, in speaking with "a certain ruler" he says that God is not like me, and "no one is good but God alone."[7] God's goodness is not like and well beyond the goodness of human behavior. But from his life and teaching we are able to identify qualities that Jesus says characterize God. *The first of these is that God is love.* The author of the letter 1 John says it very directly

---

6. Here I am deeply indebted to the great teachers of faith, primarily within the Christian tradition, but also from the other Abrahamic traditions, Judaism and Islam, and from other families of faith. I also note that I am adding to the categories for God used by Jesus suggested in ch. 5, that of father and king.

7. Luke. 18:18–20.

with one of the "is statements": God is love.[8] God is not an impersonal force or an abstract principle that gives meaning and order to the universe, although God does give meaning and order to the universe in a loving and personal way. But the intention of Jesus is to engage listeners and guide them in their experience of God.

In order to accomplish this goal, Jesus often spoke about God as love with the analogy of a loving parent. On many occasions, the Gospel record places the Aramaic word for Father, Abba, onto the lips of Jesus. It carries the meaning of familial intimacy and suggests a personal loving relationship with his Father. In an especially trying and poignant moment in Jesus' life, Mark records Jesus using the word Abba in the garden of Gethsemane. Facing arrest and execution, he prays, "Abba, Father, for you all things are possible; remove this cup from me; yet, not what I want, but what you want."[9] Again and again, the Gospels have Jesus using the word "Father" as a way of speaking about God, and this usage has passed into the life of the Christian church as its members pray weekly in worship the prayer which Jesus taught, "Our Father in Heaven, hallowed be your name."[10]

Jesus also used the analogy of father in the well-known story of the prodigal son.[11] The parable speaks about a younger son who asks his father for his inheritance which the father grants. The son squanders his money in "dissolute living" and then repents and returns home, knowing that life with the father is far better than living in a "far country" in a famine and taking care of pigs and eating their food. The father celebrates his return and forgives him as an expression of his love. The father in the parable is a reference to God who gladly receives us as we return from our wandering and ask for forgiveness.

Not only does Jesus teach that God is love in his words and behavior, but those who follow him and later write about the meaning of his life and teaching call attention to his coming as an expression of the love of God. The articulation of this conviction is clearly expressed in the Gospel of John. The well-known statement is: "For God so loved the world that he gave us his only Son, so that everyone who believes in him may not perish but may have eternal life."[12]

---

8. 1 John 1:8.

9. Mark 14:36. I am sensitive to using the masculine word Father to describe God, but in this section, we are describing the language Jesus likely used, drawn from his religious culture.

10. Matt 6:9.

11. Luke 15:11–32.

12. John 3:16.

God as Presence

A second category we might use to describe the way Jesus understood God was rooted in his profound sense of *God's presence. For Jesus, God is an experiential reality and ever present.*[13] Jesus has a profound God-consciousness.[14] The terms Spirit and Holy Spirit carry the meaning of personal presence and are used throughout the Bible and frequently in the Gospels to speak about the omnipresence of God in the world, the community of faith, and in the life of the faithful. God is personal, not just an intellectual concept. The notion of presence is close to the previous category of love or loving but has a shade of difference in that God's presence may be experienced in many ways, one of which is to feel profoundly loved. Again, the references to this dimension of Jesus' sense of God's presence are recorded often in the stories of the Gospels.

Jesus seems to be especially conscious of the presence of God in settings in which he is challenged or threatened. At these moments, Jesus has a direct and dramatic sense of God's presence. For example, toward the end of his public ministry in anticipation of the possible crisis that might occur when he and his disciples go to Jerusalem, Jesus takes three of his disciples, Peter, James, and John, to a high mountain. There he prays and seeks God's empowerment. The experience may be likened to a retreat in preparation for the challenge he anticipates. It is a mysterious event, but as it is recorded, Jesus in a moment of deep meditation is "transfigured before them, and his face shone like the sun, and his clothes became dazzling white."[15] Moses and Elijah in a vision appear before them, and the disciples offer to make camp for them. But "suddenly a bright cloud overshadowed them, and from the cloud a voice said, 'This is my Son the Beloved, with him I am well pleased; listen to him.'" The disciples were overcome with fear, "But Jesus came and touched them saying, 'Get up and do not be afraid.'" It is a bit hard to decipher what occurred on that occasion, but clearly there is in Jesus a deep sense of God's presence and anointing for his mission. A similar experience is also recorded in the Gospels when John at the start of his public ministry baptized Jesus. These stories are a way of describing the immediate presence and experience of God by Jesus.

13. Borg, *Jesus*, 117.

14. The theologians of the early centuries spoke infrequently about the soul of Jesus and his internal life with Origen being the exception. See the account in Grillmeier, *Christ in Christian Tradition*, 138–48. Much later, theologians of the nineteenth century such as Ritschl and Schleiermacher were more willing to speak of Jesus as having a "God-consciousness."

15. Matt 17:1–13.

The immediate presence of God is not the exclusive experience of the religious mystic, but also is available to ordinary people who struggle with life. For example, there is the story of Jesus as he encounters the woman of Samaria.[16] As Jesus speaks with this woman, it is acknowledged as a clear break in the custom that a Jewish man should not ordinarily speak with a woman from Samaria. But Jesus is not bound by this protocol and asks her for a cup of water. As he does, he treats her with loving respect, uses the water as a symbol of life, and invites her to partake of it. He also speaks about her troubled past and the guides her to worship God in "spirit and truth." He says, "God is spirit and those who worship him must worship in spirit and truth." The word spirit in this context speaks about the personal and omnipresent character of God. Like the wind, the presence of God is always with us even though we may not always be conscious of it.[17] In this incident, Jesus expresses loving care for a disconsolate woman and leads her in receiving the loving presence of God. The use of the term spirit also suggests, especially in a premodern context, that God is not a statue or an iconic object, but a personal presence. In a most thoughtful book about the character of God, David Bentley Hart argues for the reality and experience of God in the categories of being, consciousness, and bliss, a point of view to which we will return below.[18] This woman consciously experiences the bliss of God's presence.

God as Truth or Light

Jesus, unlike Plato or Aristotle, does not gather a group of budding philosophers around him to speak and learn about epistemology with the goal of answering the question "What is truth?" It is not that Jesus does not care about making true statements that are descriptions of what is and what has occurred. Rather, his intentions are to teach others about personal truth, to provide insights, ideas, and experiences that are life-giving and can enrich, deepen, and bring focus and meaning to life. The emphasis of this charismatic teacher and radical prophet is to empower people to experience God who is the Truth and who brings light so humans can find their way through the dark maze of life.

---

16. John 4:1–26. In this account the term Spirit appears in 4:24. As one works with material in John's Gospel, it is more difficult to confirm whether the passage comes directly from an event in the life of Jesus (often called authentic) or whether it is a story more in keeping with the growing oral tradition about Jesus.

17. John 3:8.

18. Hart, *Experience of God*, 87–290.

The Gospel of John and 1 John are more inclined to use the category of truth/light in their description of Jesus' understanding of God than the authors in the other writings of the New Testament. It is also the case that these statements in the Gospel of John and 1 John are more reflective and theological in character than they are accounts describing the historical events of the life of Jesus. But at least one account describes an event in which Jesus uses the word "truth" in a conversation; as we have observed, it is with the woman from Samaria.[19] As he speaks with her and she asks what he means by "living water," he explains that the water she is drinking will need to be sought again in order to quench her thirst. But he goes on to explain that there is another kind of "water" that fully satisfies one's thirst and gushes up into eternal life. She asks Jesus for this kind of water. He then speaks with her about her personal life, one of serial marriages (five husbands) and currently living with a man who is not her husband. Jesus sensitively invites her to place her faith in God and to worship in "spirit and *truth*." God need not be worshipped only in Jerusalem or on a sacred mountain; God is not at an exclusive locale, but omnipresent (spirit) and the ultimate Truth which will quench your ever-present thirst for a life free from longing and need. It will give you a life filled with peace, purpose, and joy. To repeat: "God is spirit and those who worship him must worship him in spirit and truth." God is the true answer to her longings.

The concept of God as truth also occurs in an earlier section of John's Gospel where Jesus is described as the one who brings the truth and light of God. "The true light, which enlightens everyone, was coming into the world."[20] In another instance, Jesus speaks to some Jews who had become his followers, and he says to them, "And you will know the truth, and the truth will make you free."[21] He explains to them that the truth about which he speaks will set them free from missing the mark in life (sin) and self-destructive behavior. In a later section in John, Jesus is recorded as saying, "I am the way, the truth, and the life," by which the author of John is saying that he will lead them to the truth of God.[22] With another metaphor, the author of John's Gospel says that Jesus is the *true* vine and God is the vine

---

19. John 4. As mentioned, there are legitimate questions about whether this event can be traced back to an actual conversation between Jesus and the woman from Samaria, but the account is very much in keeping with other accounts of Jesus in conversation with those who seek guidance from him. The same observation needs to be made about the more reflective and theological accounts in the Gospel of John and the 1 John.

20. John 1:9.

21. John 8:32.

22. John 14:6.

grower. As one links to the true vine, one is connected to the true source of life and "farmed" by God.[23]

The author of John's Gospel and John of Patmos in 1 John often use the metaphor of "light" as a way of speaking about God as true or the truth. In John's Gospel, we read that Jesus was the informing Word and "in him was the life, and the life was the light of all people. The light shines in the darkness, and the darkness did not overcome it."[24] The 1 John passage says, "This is the message we have heard from him and proclaim to you, that God is light and in him there is no darkness at all." Once again we come across an "is" statement about God; "God is light." We now have three: God is love; God is spirit; and God is light.

God Is Just

It is very likely that Jesus, drawing upon his rich heritage of the Hebrew Bible and the history of Hebrew people, would have thought and taught about the omnipresent God as love and truth, or to say it in a more experiential way, God is always with us in loving and truthful ways. In addition, as he read his Bible and listened in the synagogues of Galilee, he would have heard that *God is also just*. God treats every person and all peoples fairly and justly. God holds all humans, whether in their personal behavior or in their corporate actions, accountable. Jesus, in his identity as a prophet would directly speak about the need for justice.[25] There is a description of Jesus in the historical accounts that is not the gentle Jesus of the Bethlehem crib or the one who is meek and mild in the corridors of power. He did not arrogate this power to himself, but attributed it to God and deeply believed that God called him to a prophetic message. In his mind, Jesus would reflect on the covenant in which God promises blessing but expects righteous behavior in return. He would remember the Law with its strong ethical codes, and he would see himself in the line of the great prophets who warned kings that God expects justice. The demand for faithful obedience lived in the soul of Jesus and was at the center of his understanding of how to respond to God.

It is quite common in reading the accounts of the teaching of Jesus to see the place and importance of God's justice in the common life of the people with whom he associated. It is evident in the heart of his teaching recorded for us in the Sermon on the Mount. He clearly states that the law

23. John 15:1–11.

24. John 1:4.

25. Schillebeeckx, *Jesus*, 126–39, underlines the influence of the prophet John the Baptist on Jesus.

is an expression of justice and the law is to be honored and followed.[26] Matthew quotes Jesus as saying, "Do not think that I have come to abolish the law or the prophets; I have come not to abolish but fulfill. For truly I tell you, until heaven and earth pass away, not one letter, not one stroke of a letter, will pass from the law until all is accomplished."[27] He underlines his respect for justice by giving a specific example in the case of divorce. Again, Matthew's Gospel has Jesus saying, "It was also said, 'Whoever divorces his wife, let him give a certificate of divorce.' But I say to you that anyone who divorces his wife, except on the ground of unchastity, causes her to commit adultery; and whoever marries a divorced woman commits adultery."[28] These words, spoken in that context, call attention to the easy way that women were mistreated in a marriage and easily caste aside. Jesus calls them to the ideal of marriage in which the law is honored and all are treated fairly. Later he says, "In everything do to others as you would have the do to you; for this is the law and the prophets."[29] It is the "golden rule" which emerges from this passage as the guide to justice in all matters, and its influence across the centuries would be hard to overstate.

In a subsequent passage in Matthew's Gospel, as the author collects the prophetic sayings of Jesus, we read about the less than meek and mild Jesus. Jesus is quoted as saying to those in power: "The scribes and the Pharisees sit on Moses' seat; therefore do whatever they teach you and follow it; but do not do as they do, for they do not practice what they teach."[30] In the same section in Matthew, we read: "Woe to you, scribes and Pharisees, hypocrites! For you tithe mint, dill, and cumin, and have neglected the weightier matters of the law: justice and mercy and faith. It is these you ought to have practiced without neglecting the others. You blind guides! You strain out a gnat but swallow a camel!"[31]

I quote one other passage in order to hear the primary teaching of Jesus about justice and love, and their interrelationship. "When the Pharisees heard that he had silenced the Sadducees, they gathered together, and one of them, a lawyer, asked him a question to test him. 'Teacher, which commandment in the law is the greatest?' He said to him: 'You shall love the Lord your God with all your heart, and with all your soul, and with all your

26. Or an approximation of justice. Jesus does occasionally question parts of the law and especially interpretations of the law when it became rigid moralistic codes and the spirit of the law was missed.

27. Matt 5:17–19.

28. Matt 5:31–32.

29. Matt 7:12.

30. Matt 23:2–4.

31. Matt 23:23–24.

mind.' This is the greatest and first commandment. And a second is like it: 'You shall love your neighbor as yourself.' On these two commandments hang all the law and the prophets."[32]

God Is Sovereign

We turn now to one final category to describe Jesus' understanding of God, and I do not mean to say that these are the only categories from which we might choose. But they do seem to contain, taken together, many of the qualities of the divine that guided the life and teachings of Jesus. Our final category, sovereign, is intimately connected to the primary theme and mission of Jesus, the kingdom of God.[33] The use of the term kingdom is somewhat problematic in that there are few ruling leaders in the contemporary world who claim royalty, and it does have patriarchal overtones. Many of those who carry the title of king or queen may have some influence on shaping policy and the quality of life for citizens, but they are not vested with the authority and power of ancient kings and queens and would not be described as sovereign. The Hebrew Bible does not hesitate to describe God as like a king, as for example in Psalm 47:7, "God is the king." The same point is made in Psalm 103:19, "The Lord has established his throne in the heavens and his kingdom rules over all." Jesus would have had this understanding, that God, like a king, occupies the unique position of lordship and actively reigns. There are passages in the Hebrew Bible in which the rule occasionally hints at being tyrannical or arbitrary, at least by modern standards.[34] But in general, those other qualities of love and justice are in evidence, as for example in the same Psalm quoted above, Psalm 103:8, "The Lord is merciful and gracious, slow to anger and abounding in steadfast love."

Jesus speaks and teaches about a sovereign God in the language of the kingdom of God, or the "kingdom of heaven" as it appears in Matthew's Gospel. The language of kingdom has a political overtone and makes reference to power and its use. It is identified as the purpose of the vocation of Jesus in the opening of the Gospel of Mark: "Now after John was arrested, Jesus came to Galilee, proclaiming the good news of God and saying: 'The time is fulfilled, and the kingdom of God has come near, repent, and believe the good news.'"[35] The good news or gospel to which Jesus refers is that the

32. Matt 22:34–39.

33. Schillebeeckx, *Jesus*, 140–54.

34. Noted Old Testament scholar Brueggemann, in *Theology of the Old Testament*, addresses these issues in "Israel's Countertestimony," 313–403.

35. Mark 1:14–15; Matt 4:17.

time has come when God will reign, that is, God's power and presence is now available to all. The mission is to proclaim this gospel, that all should repent (change direction) and believe (receive the full presence of God in their lives). It is clear from this passage and the use of the language of kingdom that Jesus understands his mission in life is to proclaim this good news that God will reign in our lives as we open our hearts to receive the divine presence and power.[36]

In the Sermon on the Mount, the author of Matthew underscores that the power and presence of God is available to all and especially to those who feel powerless and marginalized.[37] For example, it is available to the "poor in spirit, for theirs is the kingdom of heaven." The power and presence of God is present and available to them. It is available to "the pure in heart, for they will see God." It is especially available to "those who are persecuted for righteousness, for there is the kingdom of heaven." The state of blessedness or the divine goodwill is there for them and results in deep contentment, joy, and peace. Later in the sermon of Jesus, Matthew says for them to pray, "Our Father in heaven, hallowed by your name. Your kingdom come, your will be done, on earth as it is in heaven."[38] Pray that the sovereign God will bless you with the divine presence and power.[39]

The Understanding of Transcendence in the Contemporary Setting

Our question at this point is whether the radical understanding of God that Jesus had is credible and persuasive in the contemporary world. And it is this world in which we live and about which we speak; we now live in a global context where a wide range of beliefs about the divine exists. The Christian understanding of the divine may not be the primary way people in many

---

36. We have discussed the meaning of the kingdom of God more fully in ch. 5, and at this point, we merely underscore the way it points to Jesus' understanding of God as sovereign.

37. Matt 5:3–12. Note that Luke 6:20 says, "Blessed are you who are poor, for yours is the kingdom of God." This passage may be earlier than the one in Matthew and is more likely the way Jesus spoke this blessing.

38. Matt 6:9–10.

39. There has been an extended conversation over many decades about whether Jesus understood the coming of the kingdom of God as apocalyptic in character and referring to the end of history. There are certainly traces of this theme in the words attributed to him, but there is no doubt that the kingdom was coming in his presence. I continue to prefer the "already / not yet" point of view in my interpretation of the kingdom of God.

parts of the world perceive the divine. But for a great many people within the Christian community, such an understanding of the divine as love, presence, truth, just, and sovereign continues to be convincing and comforting. Variations of this range of beliefs about God in the larger Abrahamic family, Judaism and Islam are also acceptable to the adherents of these religious traditions as it is with those American religious traditions which are not a part of the traditional expressions of Christian faith such as Mormonism and Jehovah's Witnesses. But even within these families of faith there are those who struggle with the traditional understanding of God, as it is taught in churches, synagogues, and mosques. Is such an understanding of the divine really credible in contemporary life, or is it just a needed psychological projection of another being that happens to have greater powers than we have and who can help us out of difficulties and bring us peace and meaning?

In addition, there are the other great religious traditions that understand transcendence in quite different ways. A dominant view within Buddhism, for example, would not understand transcendence in terms of a personal God and would speak of transcendence in terms of universal principles such as karma. Many others from all parts of the world, influenced by the Enlightenment frame of reference, the rise of science, and the development of critical-historical understanding, find nearly all forms of belief in God or a more abstract transcendence hard to accept. And of course there are those who simply find religion and its ethical demands out of keeping with the quests for power, wealth, and sensual fulfillment and therefore ignore or reject it. A brief introduction to some of these views may help us gain a perspective on how we might find a way to understand the divine and discover an authentic spiritual pathway.

Cogent Alternative Views: Indigenous Wisdom Traditions

One pattern of religious belief and practice that continues to hold sway with many people of the world would maintain that the divine is more imminent than transcendent. This view understands the divine differently than Jesus' understanding of God and offers an attractive alternative for thoughtful seekers who simply cannot accept a view of the divine that is just another being with greater powers than humans. This point of view is especially pervasive in the great *indigenous wisdom traditions* that have been present across human history and are currently present all across the globe.[40] What

40. See an account of these traditions in my book *Exploring the Spirituality of the World Religions*, 23–77.

may be thought of as having a divine dimension is present in nature and culture or social and governmental structures or leaders. One might easily relegate these religious beliefs to an earlier time and to less advanced or primitive cultures but it would be an inaccurate assessment.[41]

The early generations of humans did face extraordinary challenges that forced them to give attention to birth, subsistence, and death. With a life expectancy of less than half of our own, these first humans were concerned about survival in a threatening environment. There were practical steps taken to insure survival, but what also emerged were beliefs and practices that dealt with fear, the ravages of nature, and conflict with other tribal groups. There is evidence that these people turned to religion as a means of coping. They sensed that there were sources of power rooted in Mother Nature and even in ruling leaders that might be used to control the negative forces in life. A way of viewing the natural world and exercising some influence on it developed in these cultures and had several characteristics. As we speak about these common elements, we will focus more on the sense of the divine in nature in these traditions than the belief that political leaders may be divine. We know better.

In most of these traditions, there were sacred stories that described how the world was created and sacred powers within this created world that were integral to all of nature. Human life was viewed as a part of the chain of nature, connected to the plants and animals and the seasonal cycles. Religious practices developed which were thought to have the power to influence and affect human life. Often the tribal leaders were thought to be endowed with divine powers and rights, and religious leaders called shamans were called upon to help people make contact with the spirits that existed in this other level of reality. For instance, ancestors were seen as part of this spirit world and needed to be contacted and asked for help. In short, it was and is a complex worldview filled with sacred spaces, sacred times, and sacred ways.

With the rise of the modern world and its penetration to tribal regions of the world, many of these practices have disappeared or been altered as indigenous people have attempted to cope with the challenges to their way of life. In a recent trip to Africa (Zambia) I was privileged to visit a traditional native village and saw these beliefs and way of life in an evolving stage. What I observed was partially sad, but also encouraging as I spoke with these people about the ways they were preserving their sacred values

41. The language of "less advanced and more primitive cultures" is unacceptable in my judgment, but many hold such views and they were certainly a dominant view in the nineteenth century as people from Europe and America explored other parts of the world.

while integrating their way of life into contemporary society. It is these values that are being preserved and being lifted up in the "advanced" countries of the world as necessary if not to human survival, then certainly to human well-being. These values represent a persuasive religious outlook that can be an alternative to traditional monotheism or, as is happening in many cases, joining with and enriching the practices of the monotheistic religions. Let me illustrate with three examples:[42]

1. As a general rule, the indigenous wisdom traditions have *great respect for nature* and teach ways that human life may be integrated into the natural order rather than be exploitive of it. This outlook, while not always described in scientific categories, is still ecological in character and has a great deal to teach advanced cultures that view nature as theirs to use for their own ends. These people know that they belong to nature, and they live their lives in a way that honors the patterns and the order of the universe. It is a way of life that respects what is thought to be divine and lends a perspective to the ways which creation might be better understood in the monotheistic religions.[43]

2. It is also the case that the indigenous wisdom traditions of the world have *a way of life that is more centered and less fragmented and alienated than life in the first world.* This pattern of life is ordered around accepted values and ways of living that are congruent and holistic in tone. Their lives, while filled with all the challenges of their changing and challenged culture often have a spiritual center grounded in the belief that there is a divine vital force running through all of reality and especially evident in nature and the natural order. Again this outlook can bring wisdom to those within the monotheistic religions who often fragment their lives into separate categories with one spiritual in worshipping a transcendent God in another realm, and another part of life that is quite secular in keeping with the basic values and beliefs of a materialistic culture.[44]

3. As a general rule the indigenous wisdom traditions understand *the divine as fully present and integral to all of human life.* The divine is not somewhere else and separated by a divine being so "wholly other" and

---

42. Ferguson, *Spirituality of the World Religions*, 36–37.

43. Christopher, *Holy Universe*, speaks persuasively to those who see themselves as spiritual but not religious and integrates ancient wisdom and modern knowledge which invites us to be "at home" in the universe and to care for it.

44. Woodley, *Shalom and the Community of Creation*, speaks directly and thoughtfully to the centered way of life among the indigenous people and how it might teach the majority culture.

our sin being so pronounced that union with the divine is difficult and dangerous because of access and divine judgment. To be sure, there are personified projections of the divine taking form in a variety of ways in these wisdom traditions, with some being distant and judging, but the ideal of these traditions is to offer a spiritual way that gives direct access to the divine. There is not the excessive dualism that separates a transcendent God from nature and humankind, but an attempt to see the present world, its people and the natural order that they inhabit and the divine as unified. There are ways for immediate access through the "the practice of the presence," that the presence of the divine can be enhanced by incorporating the spiritual disciplines of prayer, music, meditation, reflection, and active rituals.[45]

As one is exposed to the great indigenous wisdom traditions, it is possible to see how they may complement the teaching of Jesus and offer guidance for alternative ways of living and addressing ethical issues. Remarkably, many have found good ways of integrating the beliefs and practices of both traditions.[46]

Cogent Alternative Views: Transcendent Monism

A large number of the people of the world would identify with the religions which began and developed in South and East Asia; they include Hinduism, Buddhism, Confucianism, Taoism, and many with a mixture which includes beliefs and practices which one might identify as more closely connected with the indigenous wisdom religions.[47] In these great religious traditions, the conception of the divine or transcendence is rooted in the belief that all of reality is essentially one. These traditions would differ from the commonly shared view of God in the Abrahamic and monotheistic religions in which the divine is understood as one subject among many, although qualitatively and quantitatively different. The spiritual quest in these Asian religions is to gain a viewpoint from transcendence however it might be understood and find harmony with the One; in some cases the One is personal and in some cases the One is more of a principle or a pattern of truth in reality.[48]

45. Fox, *One River, Many Wells*, 15–97, draws out the deep spiritual insights from many religious traditions, but speaks directly about the wisdom traditions and the foundation of creation as the ground of spirituality.

46. Woodley, *Shalom and the Community of Creation*, is a fine example.

47. Shinto, a religion practiced primarily in Japan, is an example.

48. Ferguson, *Spirituality of the World Religions*, 79–136.

Hinduism is the oldest and largest of these grand religions, a movement that evolved and developed in a pattern that has been followed by other religions with only slight differences. Hinduism in its early development had a preliterate phase, moving then to oral traditions, and then to written scripture and recorded history. The concern for survival and the well-being of the clan, respect for nature and its power, and elements of animism and the role of the shaman were present in its early phase. In time, the sense of the omnipresence of the sacred emerged, and with it came creation stories, rituals and ceremonies, and patterns of life in keeping with the values embedded in the understanding of transcendence. As the oral traditions evolved, they were written down and sacred writing preserved the norm for beliefs and practices. The oldest of these were the Vedas that became the Hindu scriptures.

A similar pattern is present in the development of Buddhism, a preliterate phase, the evolution of an oral tradition, and then written sacred scripture. The scripture in Buddhism is called the *Tripitaka*, which consists of several writings that provide guidance to the community of faith (Sangha). In China, the writings of Confucius become normative, and the small classic, Lao Tzu's the *Tao Te Ching*—with Tao meaning way, Te meaning power, and Ching meaning essence—was followed by a smaller segment of society.

In these religions, the understanding of the divine is diverse and includes elements of both imminence and transcendence. In the case of Hinduism, the more advanced thought of the scholarly Brahmins or priestly class put the primary emphasis on Brahman, a universal being which was not personal as in the Abrahamic religions, but the source and energy of the universe. More popular Hindu practice made room for two major gods, Indra and Varuna, which were expressions and personifications of power in human emotions and behavior.[49] Hinduism, often referred to as the religion of many gods, made room for manifestations of Brahman in a pantheon of thousands of divine expressions more rooted in nature and often depicted in icons or statues attached to individual homes and places of worship. Across the vast and diverse family of Hinduism, the spiritual goal is for the *atman*, the soul or essence of one's self, to overcome ignorance and alienating behavior which keeps one locked into the karma-samsara cycle and find ultimate union with Brahman.[50]

---

49. The pattern has some similarity with the Greek pantheon of gods.

50. The Hindu religion is quite complex and many-sided and short paragraph summaries run the risk of over-simplification.

Siddhartha Gautama founded Buddhism and lived sometime between the sixth and fourth centuries BCE (some place his birth at 563 BCE).[51] His life story, although often recounted with some mythological elements, is nevertheless profound and informative. Early in his life, he was influenced by the tribal religions existing in North India and Hinduism that still had an influence on the people of the region. As a young man he longed for a more meaningful life, left his family and the privileged life of a prince and sought a spiritual way. He experimented with the extreme asceticism of a group of Brahmins, but found this way unsatisfactory even as he had the more materialistic and sensuous life as a prince. He observed suffering and death and thought there must be some escape from these tragic aspects of human experience. In time, he sought a middle way between extreme asceticism and self-gratification that was a life of meditation and service. It is the pattern of life that became the way of Buddhism. As one becomes committed to Buddhism, one enters the stage of being a Bodhisattva, a person who aspires to attain enlightenment in order to relieve the suffering of others. It is a life in which one must practice compassion and heal the suffering of others, and in time one may reach Nirvana or enlightenment. For Buddha, there was no personal God, but the goal of life was to overcome ignorance and suffering, the cycle of karma-samsara, and find enlightenment or unity. It is to enter into the world of no-birth and no-death, no permanence and no impermanence, no self and no non-self. Nirvana is the complete silencing of all concepts as one merges into the oneness of reality.[52]

The Four Noble Truths and the eightfold path that undergird the practice of Buddhism have a great appeal in the modern Western world. They teach ways of managing suffering, ways of overcoming ignorance and grasping reality, and offer guidance for diligent practices that lead to a more enlightened and peaceful way of life. In the original and more stringent forms of Buddhism, there is no personal Being who is divine, unlike the monotheistic traditions, but primarily a way of life that leads to serenity and the practice of compassion. In other forms of Buddhism, there is a belief in a transcendent order and even a more personal and relational sense of divinity, but the goal remains to find unity (nirvana) with ultimate reality whether it is ordered reality or personal divinity.

The tradition of Confucianism speaks less directly to the divine and more to an ideal way to order society. It is even debated whether the Confucian way should be thought of as a religious outlook or a spiritual pathway.

51. An excellent biography of Siddhartha is Bloomfield, *Gautama Buddha*.

52. The same caution about over-simplification applies to Buddhism, as well. Other branches within Buddhism do have elements of transcendence that are more tangible.

But it is likely that Confucius thought of his pattern of ordering family and society with the model of respect for others and the practice of civility in government as universal in character and reflecting the ideals inherent in the larger reality or self-evident in the world, as we know it. Such a way has in the language of Confucius "the Mandate of Heaven." He taught that respect should characterize family life, respect for the spouse, the siblings, and the elders. The family structure was the microcosm of society, and these same values that should be practiced in family life should take the form of neighborliness, hospitality, and reciprocity in the local region, city and state. He taught that these values should characterize government relations as well, and that if they are not present, then the people have the right to change governments.

These values, which in the mind of Confucius were universal and not limited by the time and place of their origin, appear now to us as grand ideals but limited in time and to a particular culture. But his thought does raise questions about whether there are transcendent values that are universal in character and whether ideals such as compassion and justice might have application across the history of the human family. Jesus' understanding of God as love, truth, and just might point to some form of transcendent law written into the ways humans behaves and governs their affairs.[53]

A similar sort of question arises in the Taoist tradition. In fact, it is more clearly stated that Tao is nature's way, although it has a mysterious character. "The Tao that can be followed is not the eternal Tao. The name that can be named is not the eternal name."[54] It is often said in Taoism, following Lao Tzu, that if you think you understand the Tao, then you don't. Even with this caution, we might say that while it is hard to fully grasp, it is nevertheless the way of ultimate reality, the way of the universe, and the ideal way of human life. The Tao does remain mysterious and must always be studied and honored. It is the nature of life's journey that we discern the pattern of the Tao and connect with it. As a religious tradition (and it is quite varied as one would suspect with its limited definitions or boundaries), it teaches a way life that is less prescriptive than Confucianism, one that is more intuitive and one that is found within experience and not taught or read about. It is lived from the soul rather than by adhering to society's norms and expectations. There are those within the tradition, who have developed a community of religious life with the elements of priests, temples, rituals, and ceremonies, but there is also a following that is more philosophical and reflective and less organized as a movement. The goal is

53. See Ferguson, *Exploring the Spirituality of the World Religions*, 118–36.
54. Lao Tzu, *Tao Te Ching*, 2.

to preserve one's inner power and to always be on the way to living wisely and well. It is a way of not getting into conflict and useless activities, but to focus on the quiet and peaceful life drawing upon the internal resources or gift of the Tao.[55] While this pattern is not as well known in the Western world as similar traditions in Buddhism, such as Zen, it still does have appeal across cultures and time. It speaks to what may be divine within us. The teaching of Taoism, while elusive, does invite its adherents to focus on personal peace and serenity and living in harmony with nature and others. These ideals have great appeal to those who live lives of "quiet desperation" in contemporary Western society.

Many of the values, ideals, and practices of the religions of transcendent monism may be accepted and practiced within the religions of monotheism. It is not uncommon, for example, to visit a progressive synagogue, church, or mosque that offers programs in Zen meditation (Buddhism), life-changing yoga (Hinduism), and ways of leading a simple and peaceful life (Taoism).

Cogent Alternative Views: The Scientific Worldview

I have suggested that it is possible to find some common ground among the world religions. There are a wide variety of beliefs and practices, spread across time, cultures, and languages, but a sympathetic understanding of them invites dialogue and collaboration, especially in the areas of the quest for a just peace and in spiritual formation. It is also possible to find common ground with those who see no compelling evidence to endorse a transcendent explanation for the cosmos and remain content with the quest of science to understand reality in all of its many forms.[56] Others, out of the disciplines of the humanities and social sciences, are inclined to trace the rise of the scientific worldview and the rise of modernity that is essentially secular in nature.[57] It is clear that there has been a "swerve" from premodern to modern, and a more recent rise of postmodern and postcritical perspectives. These developments have their origin in the rise of science and the

55. Ferguson, *Spirituality of the World Religions*, 128–39.

56. The life work of Wilson represents the best of those who remain content with a scientific understanding of the cosmos while remaining open to dialogue with those who look beyond the natural world for explanations and meaning. His later books point to his efforts for understanding that goes beyond a particular study of some part of the natural order, such as *Consilience* and *Meaning of Human Existence*.

57. See Greenblatt's National Book Award–winning volume, *Swerve*.

development of evolutionary and critical historical understanding that do not draw upon religious ideas for explaining reality.

Along with this new consciousness have come fundamental questions about religion and the general belief in transcendence and specific religious views that maintain a belief in a personal God. There are wise and carefully researched arguments and books which offer ways to bring the worlds of science and religion together, if not into harmony, at least to the point of thoughtful and helpful dialogue. The outcome of many of these conversations has tended to point to ways in which the two "worlds" have agreed that they speak about different realms and use different language. It is also hoped, as these conversations occur, that each side will listen and understand with empathy or have an attitude that might lead to more harmony and cooperation. Ken Wilbur, a scientist and philosopher whose books are too easily placed in the "new age" category at bookstores, has made a major attempt at integration.[58] From another perspective is the work of Thomas Berry, who titles one of his books *The Sacred Universe* and points to ways of the integration of earth, spirituality, and religion in the twenty-first century.[59]

Still others have worked on specific questions that bring science and religion into the same room. Ian Barbour's *Religion and Science* is sort of a classic in the field and extremely helpful for suggesting language and categories that clear away the cobwebs. Nancy Murphy and George F. R. Ellis skillfully invite a review of the issues in terms of cosmology,[60] and Michael Dowd, with a sort of evangelistic spirit, works diligently to integrate belief in God with evolutionary thought.[61] An earlier book brings together a conversation between an interpreter of historical thought, Fritz Capra, and a Benedictine monk, David Steindahl-Rast, with a title that explains their goal, *Belonging to the Universe: Explorations on the Frontiers of Science & Spirituality.*[62] The distinguished German philosopher Jürgen Habermas in many of his writings speaks about ways of seeing a larger frame of reference in the dialogue between science and religion.[63]

But the debate between the worldviews, the scientific and the religious, continues and in some cases the dialogue gets quite heated. Richard Dawkins, in *The God Delusion* and many of his other books,[64] does not

---

58. See, e.g., from among his many books, *Theory of Everything*.

59. There is a new and revised version.

60. Murphy and Ellis, *On the Moral Nature of the Universe*.

61. Dowd, *Thank God for Evolution*.

62. This volume is quite helpful and persuasive.

63. See, e.g., his small volume entitled *An Awareness of What Is Missing*.

64. Richard Dawkins' several books have the tendency to be quite critical of popular

mince words and speaks of religious thought and belief in God as he says in the title, as a clear delusion. Sam Harris, in *The End of Faith: Religion, Terror, and the Future of Religion*, is quite pointed in calling religion, and especially its radical side, dangerous.[65] In a more personal book and one that was a National Book Award finalist, Christopher Hitchens, a prolific author who recently passed away, is completely uninhibited as was his style of addressing the issue. His book *God Is Not Great: How Religion Poisons Everything* sums up his point of view.[66]

There have been equally as many books, also with some deep conviction, on the other side. I will not review them all, but would suggest David Bentley Hart's books, one of which I mentioned earlier, for their well-reasoned arguments for belief in God and a spiritual way of life.[67] The point in reviewing this literature is to introduce the current debate about the divine, the arguments for and against belief in God, and whether in fact a credible case can be made for faith in God and a commitment to a spiritual life. There are clear alternatives to the belief in God even in a broad sense and participation in a spiritual community within the larger family of faith. It is my contention that Jesus and his radical understanding of God provide a credible and life-giving direction for thoughtful seekers.

A Contemporary Response

Over the past several decades with the rise of a modern and postmodern consciousness there has been a steady production of very thoughtful and scholarly works on the question of the existence of God.[68] And if God exists, in what ways might we understand the divine and use appropriate language that points in helpful directions, even if there is still humility before the mystery of the divine and the knowledge that our language is approximation? These thoughtful contributions to religious thought and life have been especially sensitive to the "swerve" from a premodern to a modern consciousness and the emerging new consciousness that has come from

religion, a legitimate target, but I often wish his comments were more interactive with scholarly religious thought.

65. His writing tends to be quite personal.

66. This volume reflects past experience with religion that has been hurtful.

67. *The Experience of God*, and an earlier book, *Atheist Delusions*. This latter volume takes direct aim at Richard Dawkins whom David Hart may see as the most persuasive of those who hold the opposite point of view.

68. These studies have been developed in most of the religions of the human family. I have been aware of them across the spectrum, but have focused my attention more among those that have come from within the Abrahamic religions.

our rapidly changing global world. A review of these studies and schools of thought would take us far beyond the scope of our study, but a brief glance may point to some of the constructive approaches that have been taken. The distinguished Catholic theologian Hans Küng addressed the issues directly in his volume entitled *Does God Exist?* He thoroughly reviews the range of challenges to belief in God in the contemporary world. With a careful study of the many challenges to belief, he finds his way to a Christian understanding akin to our brief description of Jesus' understanding of God. It has been an important question for Karen Armstrong as well and her viewpoint points in the direction of the need to understand the issue as it has been "lived" by millions of people across the span of history.[69] Facing squarely the inevitable problem of evil as one speaks of God as good and sovereign, Schubert Ogden and his many colleagues, learning from Alfred North Whitehead and Charles Hartshorne, explore process theology and ways that God might be understood as involved in the evolutionary processes of the cosmos.[70] I was especially helped in my struggle with the question by Sally McFague in her book *The Body of God: An Ecological Theology*, in which she places our understanding of the divine within the drama and responsibility of our era, namely how to live in healthy way with the earth.[71] Also drawing upon drama of our time (indeed the whole twentieth century) Jürgen Moltmann explores the way a personal and loving God identifies with human suffering.[72] In a more recent book, Douglas F. Ottati, while writing for a progressive segment of the church, maintains that we must place the issue within the conversation of current ecological understanding.[73] A representative of the scientific community, Stuart A. Kauffman, proposes a new understanding of natural divinity based on a scientifically based worldview. He maintains that the qualities of divinity that we hold sacred—creativity, meaning, and purposeful activity—are in fact properties of the universe that can be investigated scientifically.[74] In his writing we hear the echoes of Einstein and Stephen Hawking. Kaufman's thought also suggests that all of truth cannot be found with a single epistemology (scientific empiricism) and implies the need for multiple epistemologies.

There are many possible directions for thinking about how we might understand the divine in the language, thought, and the realities of our time.

69. See *A History of God*, and *The Battle for God*.

70. See, e.g., his book, *Reality of God*.

71. She also wrote a very helpful book entitled *Models of God*.

72. Moltmann, *Crucified God*.

73. Ottati, *Theology for Liberal Protestants*.

74. Kauffman, *Reinventing the Sacred*.

In closing this chapter, I want to return to the thought of David Bentley Hart who takes on the questions from a more classical starting point.[75] He is an Eastern Orthodox scholar of religion and draws upon his great heritage to speak about the reality and experience of God. His argument (and it is an argument) is subtle and tied to human experience as well as philosophical concepts. He explores how the great intellectual traditions of philosophical and theological thought articulate an approach to understanding the divine mysteries. He speaks about the way which thoughtful and sensitive human beings have moments of clarity and deep feeling that put them in touch with ultimate reality.[76] These moments are being (we exist), we are aware (consciousness), and we feel deep contentment (bliss), and these moments have an essential contingency and continuity with ultimate reality. Over against the scientific worldview (not science), a deist concept of a distant God, and a fundamentalist view of the Bible, Hart gives us a thoughtful alternative which invites the reader to reflect about the profound experience of beauty and love which reflect reality and a God who is love, present and personal, the truth, just, and sovereign.[77]

We turn now to an exploration of the ways that we might find to encounter transcendence, building upon the teaching of Jesus.

Study Resources

Discussion Questions

1. In what ways does our understanding of God affect our faith and spirituality?

2. Which of the categories used to describe Jesus' understanding of God (love, presence, truth/light, just, sovereign) is most persuasive and meaningful to you?

3. Do you think there is a transcendent reality beyond the cosmos that created the world and now gives it order and meaning?

4. Do you think the understanding of transcendence/divine in the indigenous wisdom traditions and transcendental monism might be integrated into monotheism and Christianity in particular? Is there some common ground?

75. Hart, *Experience of God*.
76. Martin Heidegger spoke of poetry as the closet way that words describe Being.
77. These comments reflect my categories more than Hart's.

5. Do you think that the scientific approach to knowing and understanding can explain all of reality?

6. What are the best arguments for and against the existence of God or transcendence?

Terms and Concepts

1. Anthropomorphic: When we define and understand God or another reality by describing it as like a human being in some way.

2. *Via Negativa:* An argument used to define God or another reality by saying what it is not like.

3. Abba: An Aramaic term which means father, used to address God.

4. Indigenous Wisdom Traditions: The wisdom, often about transcendence, which developed in the cultures of people who originally lived in those areas or were indigenous to a region.

5. Transcendent Monism: The view that postulates that all reality, including the divine or transcendent, is one.

Suggestions for Reading and Reference

Berry, Thomas. *The Sacred Universe: Earth, Spirituality, and Religion in the Twenty-First Century.* New York: Columbia University Press, 2009.

Christopher, David. *The Holy Universe: A New Story of Creation for the Heart, Soul, and Spirit.* Santa Rosa, CA: New Story, 2014.

Dawkins, Richard. *The God Delusion.* Boston: Houghton Mifflin, 2006.

Ferguson, Duncan. *Exploring the Spirituality of the World Religions: The Quest for Personal, Spiritual and Social Transformation.* New York: Continuum, 2010.

Hart, David Bentley. *The Experience of God: Being, Consciousness, Bliss.* New Haven: Yale University Press, 2013.

Swimme, Brian Thomas, and Mary Evelyn Tucker. *Journey of the Universe.* New Haven: Yale University Press, 2012.

Wilber, Ken. *A Theory of Everything: An Integral Vision for Business, Politics, Science, and Spirituality.* Boston: Shambhala, 2001.

Wilson, Edward O. *The Meaning of Human Existence.* New York: Liveright, 2014.

8

God's Presence in the World

The Human Response

The Radical Proclamation of Jesus

WE BEGAN BY SAYING that the teaching of Jesus is of great importance
to humankind. Perhaps no other teacher in history has spoken with
such compelling wisdom and insight. We underlined that access to the
teaching of Jesus is more difficult than it would appear. The New Testament and the Gospels in particular are the primary source of accessing
his teaching, but they must be read with care in that these documents
were written several years after he engaged in his public ministry and
were designed to meet the variety of needs of the newly forming church.
They were not intended primarily to be a historical record in the modern
sense of critical-historical scholarship but spiritual guidance. Of course
the guidance was based on his life and teaching, but by the time of the
writing of the Gospels, beliefs about the meaning of Jesus' life had begun
to develop and the "Christ of faith" had some priority over the "Jesus
of history." Well-educated and faithful teachers and scholars across the
modern era have developed ways of speaking about the differences between the two and using historical methods to discern between the two.
We spoke about these ways in chapter 1.

We have focused our attention more on the life and teaching of Jesus,
although the quest to understand the identity of Jesus and the meaning of
his life, death, and resurrection are of great importance.[1] We have touched

1. It is difficult to separate the Jesus of history from the Christ of faith; it is one

on these topics surrounding the "Christ of faith" or the post-Easter Jesus, but another volume would be needed to do them justice, and there is excellent literature at all levels and varied points of view available that address the issues of the meaning of Jesus' life, death, resurrection, and divine identity.

We went on in section 1 to speak about the historical setting of the life of Jesus. Our conviction in this endeavor is that we are all children of our time and place in history, and that Jesus was not an exception, although we noted that his teaching points to universal truths that transcend language, culture, and history. But we do learn about Jesus and his teaching from the historical context of his life. It sheds light on his teaching and why he acted and made decisions as he did. In particular, we observed the variety of ways that Jesus was influenced by his surroundings. He lived, spoke, and taught within the framework of first-century Judaism, the political realities of Palestine, the influence of Hellenistic culture, and the presence of the alien government of Rome. We also spoke about how Jesus understood his vocation in that context; he felt called by God to his mission as a teacher (Rabbi), healer, and prophet. Many identified him as the promised messiah and first generations of Christians, influenced by the Apostle Paul thought of him as Lord and Savior.

In section 2, we turned our attention directly to his teaching. We explored the method of his teaching that was charismatic in style and creative in approach. One special feature of his approach, and there were many, was his use of parables as a way of stimulating the imagination of his listeners. Many of his wise aphorisms have been passed down to the present such as the golden rule. We then turned to his primary message that was the coming of the kingdom of God, and how in his proclamation of the coming kingdom, he asked people to repent (change directions) and receive the power and presence of God in their lives. It was not only by words that he taught, but also through his sense of and commitment to his mission and the way his actions illustrated his teaching. He practiced what he taught; few would dare to question his integrity. He identified with the suffering of the people whom he met, healed them, and called on those in power to offer a religious way that was life-giving and to govern justly.

We turned in section 3 to the deep belief of Jesus that God was active in the world. For Jesus, God was not distant and abstract. Jesus was not a detached philosopher, although extraordinarily wise. Nor do I think that his view of God can easily be relegated to the view that it was merely a psychological projection of human need. For Jesus, God is the Creator who made

person about whom we speak. But it is not possible to do justice to this issue in this one brief account. I have appreciated the way that Edward Schillebeeckx has written two volumes, one called *Jesus* and one call *Christ*.

and sustains all there is. God does stand behind it all, but also enters into the human drama. Jesus draws upon his Jewish heritage and stresses what the Hebrew people had experienced across their history, that God is love, is present for us, the great Truth which lights our way through the darkness, always just and fair, and sovereign over all. All that we have said so far points to the proclamation of Jesus: he asks his listeners then and now that they give a full and dedicated response to God's approach to and relationship with human beings, an interaction which Jesus called the kingdom of God.

The Human Response: Repent and Believe the Good News

The message in the proclamation of Jesus as he began his public ministry was that salvation has come to the human family. In partial contrast to the message of John the Baptist who spoke of the coming judgment of God, Jesus had a joyous message that God's reign is at hand. Jesus did learn from John about judgment, but shifts the emphasis to *gospel*, the good news that we can repent or change the direction of our lives, our way of thinking, and our way of living (*metanoia*). The actions that violate the will and way of God and on which we will be judged will be forgiven, and we are empowered to change our way of life. Repentance consists of a radical transformation of our attitude, our point of view, and the way we live our lives. Jesus invites his listeners to accept and endorse the good news (*evangel*). This good news is that God's rule is at hand and available to not only his listeners, but to his followers across history. It is the announcement by Jesus that God's unconditional love and forgiveness are present; there is clemency; there can be reconciliation; there can be joyful reunion with God, love for all in the human family, and respect for the created world. What John preached about judgment is helpful background, but salvation has come and with it there is empowering grace to go in a new direction.[2] A first generation Christian, the Apostle Paul sums it up in his letter to Roman Christians: "For the kingdom of God is not food and drink but righteousness and peace and joy in the Holy Spirit."[3] The kingdom of God, the loving and transforming power of God is now present. It is beginning in the coming of Jesus and it points to an eschatological end when all of creation is transformed and reconciled to the Creator.

---

2. This message appears in the all the Gospel sources, the Q community, the Marcan tradition, in the source peculiar to Matthew, in the source particular to Luke, and in the Johannine tradition. Schillebeeckz, *Jesus*, 140.

3. Rom 14:17. It is not about the divisive legalism regarding food and drink customs, but about God's presence as the Holy Spirit.

Jesus' Way of Inviting People to Respond

Jesus proclaimed the message of the coming of the kingdom of God in word and deed. He did it in a way that was creative and persuasive. He was both the medium and the message, and what he did and how he acted are inseparable from what he said. For modern people to understand the message of the kingdom of God, they must go with Jesus as he encounters people in his ministry. The message becomes clear and compelling as we walk with Jesus on the dusty trails of Palestine. But it is not all that easy to "get there" in that we hear the message second hand.

The question is whether this message can jump over the two thousand years, the languages and cultures, and be relevant, meaningful, and transforming for contemporary people. There are various ways which contemporary people proclaim, teach, and share this message, and in many cases, as it was with Jesus, the medium becomes the message. People agree or reject the message to some extent on whether they like the presenter and the nature of the presentation. They may in fact miss the message in that they are so preoccupied with the messenger. In addition, people respond in different ways depending upon who they are and what they value. Further, a presentation may be effective or offensive depending upon how it fits within the culture or the subculture in which it is presented. Some do respond to an emotional appeal and an emphasis on human sin and need. The style of John the Baptist has its place. Others depend more on a thoughtful explanation with a range of options and choices, one that I endorse. I have spent a good many years in a progressive church community and an academic culture in which thoughtful discussion and choice are present, and I have found that my understanding of Jesus and his teaching is more in keeping with my experience. It jumps the two thousand years for me *because of his method and his message.* I find it persuasive; it offers a spiritual way for me as I live out my life in the vast complexity of the contemporary world.

I do not mean to imply that it is easy for us from a different time and place in history to grasp in detail the way Jesus taught his message about the kingdom of God. But there are many clues that guide us. What is most likely the case is that he taught about God's love and forgiveness in ways his listeners could understand, and they were then enabled to make thoughtful and wise choices and commitments. Our goal is to read these accounts in a careful and sensitive way. My reading of his message and his presence as a teacher and his style of teaching suggest several primary characteristics about Jesus and the way that he taught. The first and perhaps the most obvious quality that epitomized Jesus as a teacher and healer was that he was a *loving and compassionate as he taught about God's love and compassion.* And his love was available to all.

There are several accounts of Jesus' encounters with people who were on the edge of society, even outcasts because of their condition, their profession, or their ethnic identity. There is, for example, the account of Jesus meeting the leper, cleansing him of the disease, and asking him to see the authorities to get a clean bill of health.[4] Lepers, those with a skin disease, were thought to be contagious, were unattractive, and were marginalized by placing them outside towns and villages. In general, they had little participation in the normal give and take of social life. Jesus demonstrates the quality of acceptance of the leper as a full human being with great value by allowing him to approach and make his request. It was a radical break with the norms of society. In boldness and perhaps some desperation, he approaches Jesus and gets directly to the point: "If you choose, you can make me clean." Jesus responds with a touch signaling that the approach was received in a loving way. Jesus offered the leper unconditional acceptance, a central component of the love called *agape* in the New Testament. Jesus then feels genuine compassion, that quality which motivates one to relieve the suffering of others: "Moved with pity, Jesus stretched out his hand and touched him, and said to him, 'I do choose. Be made clean.'" Jesus then acts for the safety and security of the leper, another dimension of love and compassion. He warns him of the risk of moving back into society: "After sternly warning him he sent him away at once, saying to him, 'See that you say nothing to anyone; but go, show yourself to the priest, and offer for your cleansing what Moses commanded, as a testimony to them.'" Jesus advises him to get legal clearance, but unfortunately, the leper was so excited that he began to tell everyone he saw about his healing, and it did cause some difficulty for Jesus who was constantly approached for help and healing: "But he went out and began to proclaim it freely and to spread the word, so that Jesus could no longer go into a town openly, but stayed out in the country; and people came to him from every quarter."

A second characteristic of Jesus as he interacted with people and taught them was *empathy*. It is a quality closely related to love and compassion and may be integral to them, but it often has its own distinctive dimensions. Empathy is that characteristic which is able to identify with and feel the pain and suffering of others. Jesus wants his listeners to know that God is present for them in their pain and suffering. There is an account in the Gospels that speaks about Jesus and the disciples who were fatigued, hungry, and needing

4. Mark 1:40–45; Matt 8:1–4; Luke 5:12–16.

rest. They went to a deserted place "to rest a while."[5] But they were unable to get away from the crowds: "Now many saw them going and recognized them and they hurried there on foot from all the towns and arrived ahead of them." There were many people who sought to hear Jesus (estimated at five thousand) and they, too, were hungry. Jesus had compassion for them, sensing that they had profound needs and were hungry. He taught them, and out of *his deep empathy for them*, asked the disciples to assist in providing food for them. They considered going to the market and getting adequate food, but knew it was logistically impossible. They found five loaves and two fish, and Jesus in prayer asked that it be multiplied in order to feed his followers. The passage does raise the question of miracles and may even be a reference to the developing practice of the Eucharist. But the point I want to make is that in his teaching, he has empathy for the needs of his learners and finds a way to respond that reflects God's empathy for them. Some have suggested that the initial act of sharing by Jesus and his disciples caused others in the crowd to begin sharing what they had so that all were fed. Whatever the case, it was the full expression of the golden rule which is empathy in action.

Still another characteristic of the teaching (and healing) of Jesus was that he often spoke and responded to a *felt need*. There were times when he may have spoken to his contemporaries about concerns for which his listeners did not have intense emotions. But Jesus appeared to be keenly aware that those with *felt* needs were responsive and eager to learn if they knew that their needs and concerns were being addressed. There is, for example, the story of the rich man who ran up to Jesus, knelt before him, "and asked him, 'Good Teacher, what must I do to inherit eternal life?'"[6] Jesus, sensing the earnestness of the question and the felt need behind it, responds in a teaching mode to address the concern. He says, "Why do you call me good? No one is good but God alone." He goes on to speak of each of the commandments. In turn, the rich man says, "Teacher, I have kept all these from my youth." Jesus then says, "You lack one thing, go sell what you own, and give the money to the poor, and you will have treasure in heaven; then come, follow me." The man went away grieving for he had great possessions. Jesus speaks directly to the rich man's need to be reassured of eternal life, senses the sincerity of the question, and therefore does not mince words. He makes it clear that to be truly with God (eternal life), one must put God first. Possessions can so easily distract us. In fact, Jesus says: "It is easier for a camel to go through the eye of a needle than for someone who is rich

5. Mark 6:30–44; Matt 14:13–21; Luke 9:10–17; John 6:1–14.

6. Mark 10:17–22; Matt 19:16–30; Luke 18:18–30.

to enter the kingdom of God."[7] Jesus made it clear that it was a matter of priorities, not that there was something sinful in having the wealth. He teaches that it is God's will and way which must be first, loving others not far behind, and then managing one's wealth which can be done to help the poor. The risk, Jesus told the rich man and then the disciples who asked some questions, is that we too easily and often put wealth first, neglect others, and do not follow the will and way of God. This rich man suffered from what Augustine called "disordered love" and went away sorrowful for he had great possessions which were his top priority. The rich man learned about God through the teaching of Jesus.

A fourth quality, which characterized Jesus as teacher was that he *lived in solidarity with his learners*. His life demonstrated what he was teaching. He did not stand behind his importance and remove himself to a way of life different from those who came to him for guidance and help. Rather, *he went to them* as Mark describes: "In the morning, while it was still very dark, he got up and went out to a deserted place, and there he prayed. And Simon and his companions hunted for him. When they found him, they said to him, 'Everyone is searching for you.' He answered, 'Let us go on to the neighboring towns, so that I may proclaim the message there also; for that is what I came out to do.' And he went throughout Galilee, proclaiming the message in their synagogues and casting out demons."[8] He went without wealth, without authoritative titles, walking with his companions. As he encountered people, he spoke with them as one of them, a carpenter from the Galilean village of Nazareth. On his travels, he meets a leader of the synagogue, likely in Capernaum.[9] The man's name was Jairus, and he asks Jesus to heal his daughter who is very ill. Jesus does not say that he is too busy or that there are others who need his attention, although as he goes to the home of Jairus he does meet others along the way in need.[10] As Jesus and Jairus approach the home of Jairus, they are met by those who say, "Your daughter is dead. Why trouble the teacher any further?" Jesus intervenes and says to Jairus, "Do not fear, only believe." Jesus goes with Jairus and the disciples into the home where there is the presence of deep grieving over what they fear is the death of the child. Jesus comforts them: "Why do you make a commotion and weep? The child is not dead but sleeping." The people of the home doubt what Jesus says, but Jesus takes her by the hand and says, "Little girl, get up!" She does and begins to walk. Jesus takes time

---

7. Mark 10:25.

8. Mark 1:35–39; Matt 4:23–25; Luke 4:42–44.

9. Mark 5:21–43; Matt 9:18–26; Luke 8:40–59.

10. A woman suffering from a hemorrhage, Mark 5:25–34.

out of a busy day, goes in solidarity with this family and these people, and shares their life, their fear, and their grief. And he shares their joy as the little girl wakes up. Jesus teaches that God heals.

Still another quality, which is characteristic of his teaching and healing, is the way in which he speaks with those whom he encounters and *works within their language, conceptual framework, and customs of their culture.* Often, this feature is difficult for contemporary readers of the Gospel stories because the ways in which these events are recorded express the beliefs of the culture and an outlook that is premodern. It is, for example, filled with miracles and "spirits." It is not the way we might explain what is going on in our setting. These were categories of the contemporaries of Jesus that described and explained what was happening. There may be other ways of explaining what occurred, ones that we would likely use given our modern understanding of reality. Let me illustrate the differences with a story from the Gospels.

On one occasion, as Jesus traveled across the large lake, often called the Sea of Galilee, he encounters a deeply troubled man. His disciples did not attempt to prevent the man from approaching Jesus, and as he did, it become obvious that he was profoundly troubled. The man shouts to Jesus, "What have you to do with me, Jesus, Son of the Most High God: I adjure by God do not torment me."[11] Jesus responds to his illness or possession with the command that the demon come out of the man. Jesus speaks to the demon: "What is your name?' The reply is 'My name is Legion; for we are many.'" Jesus frees the man from his torment and sends the "unclean spirits" into a herd of swine. I select this passage on purpose even though it is a difficult one to interpret. There are the complex issues of demon possession and removing these demons into the swineherd, descriptions that are difficult for us to accept as accurate explanations of the behavior. But the passage does underline our concern, which is to show Jesus as he was—one who lived, acted, and spoke in the context of first-century Palestine. In addition, it is also important to note that he easily became a part of the lives of those whom he served, understanding their concerns, feeling their suffering, and responding in ways that were appropriate to their culture. The outcome of the story is even mixed in that because of what happened, the pigs were drowned. I admit to having difficulty with the concept of demon possession, and therefore have some questions about exorcism. What is clear about the passage, however, is that a troubled man was healed by his encounter with Jesus. Jesus demonstrates God's healing power and speaks about it in a way

11. Mark 5:1–13; Matt 8:28–9; Luke 8:26–39. The passage likely records an actual incident but may also include the belief of the early church in the phrase "Son of the Most High God."

that could be understood in first-century Palestine; those who were present could understand.[12]

There is still another arresting quality that was characteristic of Jesus in his teaching and his way with people. *He was a person of great integrity.* He spoke and acted in accord with his beliefs and values. He was consistently authentic, true to himself, and was therefore trusted by those who encountered him. Even those who may have disagreed with him or are threatened by him do not expect him to back down or change his values. Jesus, perhaps because he was spiritually nurtured in a setting of Hellenistic Judaism, demonstrates some flexibility about the interpretation of Torah. His views often differ from the strict interpretations of the Pharisees. Jesus, sharing with the Pharisees a great respect for the law, understood it as a way for people to live in accordance with God's expectations. But he resisted a rigid legalism and understood that God wanted the spirit of the law to inform and enrich the lives of people, not bind them in technical legal disputes. I call attention to two stories early in the Gospel of Mark in which Jesus opts for behavior that improves the life of those with whom he is engaged. They both have to do with what one can do on the Sabbath. The first story is about Jesus walking with his disciples on a Sabbath day, and the disciples, as they pass a grain field, pluck heads of the grain for sustenance.[13] The Pharisees notice this activity and call them into account for violating a Sabbath ordinance. Jesus responds with a biblical precedent: "Have you never read what David did when he and his companions were hungry and in need of food? He entered the house of God, when Abiathar was high priest and ate the bread of the Presence which is not lawful for any but the priests to eat, and he gave some to his companions." He reminds the Pharisees that "the Sabbath was made for humankind, and not humankind for the Sabbath." Jesus, out of his deep concern for human welfare, has the integrity to defend his disciples who ate some grain.[14]

A similar situation occurs when Jesus heals the man with a withered hand on the Sabbath.[15] This story appears to be less coincidental and more intentional on the part of Jesus. The healing takes place in a synagogue, and Jesus was carefully watched as he approached the man. He asks, "Is it lawful to do good or to do harm on the Sabbath, to save life or to kill?" The Pharisees and Herodians who were present remained silent in their negative response. The story continues: "He looked around at them with anger; he

---

12. I will continue to ponder what happened and how it happened.

13. Mark 2:23–28; Matt 12:1–8; Luke 6:1–5.

14. The passage does insert at the end, "so the Son of Man is lord even of the Sabbath," which may reflect a later period, early in the church's life.

15. Mark 3:1–6; Matt 12:9–14; Luke 6:6–11.

was grieved at their hardness of heart and said to the man, 'Stretch out your hand.' He stretched it out and his hand was restored." His detractors left and conspired "how to destroy him." Even in the context of the synagogue and in the presence of the religious leaders, Jesus had complete integrity with his conviction that the Law, and the Sabbath law in particular are for human well-being.[16] The message of the kingdom is that God heals people, liberates them, and makes them joyful.

These passages also point to another characteristic of Jesus' way with people, whether they are those with political and religious authority or the common people he encountered daily. The integrity of Jesus *gave him complete freedom*. This quality of Jesus is reflected across the profile we get of him in reading the Gospels, and it is particularly in evidence as he encounters those in authority in the last week of his life. One incident, placed in the last week of his life by the Synoptic Gospels and early in his ministry by the Gospel of John, is especially poignant in demonstrating the freedom Jesus had; he was fearless. The incident is called "the cleansing of the temple" and it is a passage that has been interpreted in two primary ways with many variations within these ways.[17] A traditional and more orthodox way of understanding the incident is that Jesus is challenging the whole temple system as the means of guiding belief and practice. In a sense he was saying that the temple system and the Law in particular are now going to be replaced by faith and grace, a way that becomes the Christian way. Another view and one that I am inclined to affirm is that Jesus is not so much challenging the orthodoxy of the temple system or rejecting the Law, but is calling into question the orthopraxis of the system. I view the incident as more the action of the radical prophet, much in keeping with the teaching of John the Baptist that the practice of Judaism had deteriorated, but that its basic beliefs were still valid. Jesus, whether early in his ministry as the Gospel of John suggests,[18] or at the end of his ministry as the Synoptic Gospels suggest, does challenge the practices present in the temple system, and in so doing, makes it clear what God desires.

Mark, in his typically brief descriptive style, has Jesus going directly to the temple when he enters Jerusalem: "Then they came to Jerusalem. And he entered the temple and began to drive out those who were selling and those who were buying in the temple, and he overturned the tables of the money changers and the seats of those who sold doves, and he would not

16. Again, this passage may reflect a later post-Easter period, but likely is an accurate reflection the way Jesus understood the Law.

17. Mark 11:15–18; Matt: 21:12–17; Luke 19:45–48; John 2:13–22.

18. Some place the action of Jesus early in his public ministry while he is still partially influenced by John the Baptist.

allow anyone to carry anything through the temple." This action of Jesus, almost out of character for him or at least our stereotypes of him, points directly to his integrity and the freedom he has to act within his convictions and identity. He knows there will be a price to pay, likely one of arrest and punishment, but growing out of his prophetic call and the traditions of the great prophets of Israel, Jesus acts out in symbolic form his convictions and his mission as an eschatological prophet from God.[19] He teaches as he acts in freedom, and in this case, he is speaking to the larger Jewish community. Other interactions during this final week of his life also illustrate the extraordinary freedom and courage of Jesus as he lives the kingdom's message at the end of his life.

Another characteristic of Jesus as teacher (and healer and prophet), and one closely associated with freedom is that *Jesus spoke directly and boldly to the central issue under discussion*. He has a way of moving the conversation toward what is really being said and what is important. He is not inclined to allow his contemporaries to get off the subject or to dodge important issues with a hidden agenda. Of course, it needs to be acknowledged that the recorded conversations in the Gospels were placed there in order for the author to make a point and to shape the teaching of Jesus in a way that would address the needs of the early Christian community. Once again, we are asked to read the text with a critical eye, as well as an open mind, and assess whether the incident, as part of a growing oral tradition that preserved logions which were part of the effort to remember and preserve the teaching of Jesus. But there are many pericopes with an authentic pedigree that describe Jesus speaking directly and boldly to an issue. Some of them come later in his public ministry as his critics challenge Jesus.

In one case, at the end of his public ministry, Jesus has his authority questioned as he speaks directly and boldly about certain religious issues.[20] The authority to speak on these kinds of issues was often rooted in a biblical precedent or status in the religious community such as a scribe whose primary responsibility was to be an expert on the Hebrew Bible as it existed and interpreted at the time. Jesus was not a scribe, but he did use biblical precedent on occasion. The account begins in the following way: "Again they came to Jerusalem. As he was walking in the temple, the chief priests and the scribes came to him and said, 'By what authority are you doing these things? Who gave you this authority to do them?'" Jesus goes directly to the issue and, as he often did, asks them a question that puts them on the spot. He says, "I will ask you a question; answer me, and I will tell you by what

19. See Schillebeeckx, *Jesus*, 243–49.

20. Mark 11:27–33; Matt 21:23–27; Luke 20:1–8.

authority I do these things. Did the baptism of John come from heaven, or was it of human origin? Answer me." After some discussion and discomfort with the question, they decide that they should not answer the question because whichever way they answer it, they will cause a reaction from the crowd. If the say, "from God" it means they agree with what he taught or if they answer that John did not have the authority to speak as a prophet, they risk a negative reaction from the crowd which liked the message and mission of John. So they say, "We do not know." Jesus, not intimidated, says in response, "Neither will I tell you by what authority I am doing these things." His point is that he has the same heavenly authority as John the Baptist in the role of a prophet that they will not acknowledge. It is often difficult to hear the message of the prophet in our midst because the message will mean a deep and profound change.

It is vitally important that the change, which Jesus in his prophetic role is describing, is framed in a way that is *insightful and liberating*. This element is also characteristic of Jesus the teacher and his teaching. He does not ask that people change just to please him or to accommodate to the expectations of a particular group that needs homogeneity and adherence to their rules and practices. Jesus is more interested in transformation, both of the individual and the groups in which individuals participate as part of their normal life.[21] He consistently focuses on insight, that way of understanding that enlightens and shows people a life-giving way to understand. Insight liberates people from ignorance, fears, and prejudice.[22] Jesus has a way of taking his students to the point where they can say, "Ah, now I understand and I can move forward."

There are many examples of the insightful and liberating teaching of Jesus from the Gospels. One example is from the Sermon on the Mount, that section in Matthew that has placed many of the sayings of Jesus in a collection arranged partly by subject.[23] There is, for example, his teaching about prayer, a spiritual discipline that is difficult for most people and most likely was for his listeners. Then as now it was easy to wonder if one's public prayers are really to impress an audience or sincerely offered to God; it is to wonder whether even the private prayers ever get higher than the ceiling. In the account in Matthew, Jesus teaches that prayers must be sincere.[24] The

21. We will say more about the way in which Jesus, the teacher and prophet, spoke about associations of people, structures, and political systems in the next chapter.

22. In this pattern of the teaching of Jesus, we see similarity with the teaching of Buddha.

23. The sources for this sermon are partly Q, Mark, and some material that is particular to Matthew.

24. Matt 6:5–13; Luke 11:2–4.

passage begins, "And whenever you pray, do not be like the hypocrites; for they love to stand and pray in the synagogues and at the street corners, so that they may be seen by others." Rather, Jesus teaches, "When you pray, go into your room and shut the door and pray to your Father who is in secret; and your Father who sees in secret will reward you." The insight comes: "Oh, now I see, prayers are not to impress others and demonstrate my spiritual IQ, but need to be an honest expression of who I am." Insight liberates. So leave aside empty phrases, and "pray then in this way: Our Father in heaven, hallowed be your name, your kingdom come, your will be done, on earth as it is in heaven." The insight comes: honor and respect God in your prayers, and ask that the divine will and way (kingdom) will prevail in your life, in your setting, and in your world, just as it does in heaven.

Then one can move on to some basic needs. "Give us this day our daily bread, and forgive us our debts, as we also have forgiven our debtors." The prayer is simple: help us to sustain our lives by having our daily needs met. It is not out of order to ask that basic needs be met. And we need to be forgiven, both for sins of omission (debts) and our sins of commission (trespasses). The insight is so profound, that if we are forgiven, we are liberated, and we then are empowered to forgive others as well. To be forgiven is to get a fresh start, to be free of deception and guilt, and be enabled to extend ourselves in ways that are helpful to others.

But life can be so difficult and we say, "If you only knew what I was going through!" Jesus teaches us to pray: "And do not bring us to the time of trial, but rescue us from evil." Another insight! I am so easily drawn away into self-destructive and harmful behavior, trapped then by my guilt and shame, and forced to be deceptive around others. There are the added phrases to the Lord's Prayer, not a part of the original manuscripts, but in keeping with them. "For the kingdom, the power, and the glory are yours now and forever. Amen." With liberating insight and grace, we acknowledge our dependence upon God and give God the glory.

There is at least one other quality or characteristic of Jesus' way with people and how he communicates with them. It too is somewhat different than the way of John the Baptist. Jesus is a gracious host and invites people to *celebrate and enjoy life with him*. The gospel is a joyous gift and life's goodness can and should be enjoyed. Early in Mark's Gospel, we read about this characteristic of Jesus in a conversation about fasting.[25] "Now John's disciples and the Pharisees were fasting; and people came to him, 'Why do John's disciples and the disciples of the Pharisees fast, but your disciples do not fast?'" It is a good question in that then as well as now the truly religious

25. Mark 2:18–22.

are often expected to have an ascetic lifestyle. "Jesus said to them, 'The wedding guests cannot fast while the bridegroom is with them, can they? As longs as they have the bridegroom with them, they cannot fast. The days will come when the bridegroom is taken away from them, and they will fast on that day." The wedding day has arrived, the good news has come in the person of Jesus, and we can experience the power and presence of God and celebrate. Jesus goes on to explain, "No one sews a piece of unshrunk cloth on an old cloak; otherwise, the patch pulls away from it, the new from the old, and a worse tear is made. And no one puts new wine into old wineskins; otherwise, the wine will burst the skins, and the wine is lost, and so are the skins; but one puts new wine into fresh wineskins." The living presence of Jesus brings joy and sets his disciples free. The disciples and those present in this exchange are caught off guard with his profound humanness. The disciples in particular adore him because they have been set free to enjoy the gift of God's full presence and God's generous gift of life.

We learn from this pericope about the joy felt by Jesus of eating and drinking in fellowship with his own. But what is startling is that he also enjoys being with outcasts, tax collectors and sinners. Jesus has come with freedom and salvation for all. Luke emphasizes this characteristic of Jesus as he describes a meal that Jesus shares with a Pharisee. A sinful woman in the city comes in during the meal to pay homage to Jesus, wanting to treat his feet with ointment (a wonderful gift in an age of sandals and dusty roads). As she does so, she cries and wants to dry his feet from her tears with her hair. The Pharisee is chagrined with this horrendous break of protocol, perhaps understandably. But Jesus defends her and points to the difference in her behavior and that of the Pharisee and says, "Therefore I tell you, her sins, which were many, have been forgiven; hence she has shown great love."[26] It is hard to be sad in the presence of the great gift of love.[27] Jesus is the human face of God.

The Nature of the Transformed Life

An integral part of the radical teaching of Jesus is that embracing the reign of God in one's life is transforming. In his proclamation, Jesus says repent and believe by which he means that we need to change directions, our values, and our way of life and receive the power and presence of God. The two, to repent and believe, go together. We are asked to change directions and then be open to receiving the empowering grace of God. These actions set

26. Luke 7:36–50.
27. See Schillebeeckx, *Jesus*, 200–210.

a new course in life and help us sustain it. Once again, I want to draw upon incidents in the life and teachings of Jesus that illustrate this transformation. As Jesus lives what he teaches, people hear him and sense the grace of God. They are transformed in a variety of ways.

Jesus stresses the need for this transformation as he talks with a Pharisee named Nicodemus. Nicodemus was fascinated by Jesus and came to him at night because he was somewhat cautious about how his Pharisee colleagues might interpret such a visit.[28] Nicodemus respects Jesus as a teacher (rabbi) and asks him: "Rabbi, we know that you are a teacher who has come from God; for no one can do these signs that you do apart from the presence of God." Jesus answers in the words that have unfortunately almost become a cliché: "Very truly I tell you, no one can see the kingdom of God without being born from above." To which Nicodemus replies, "How can anyone be born after growing old? Can one enter a second time into the mother's womb and be born?" Jesus, creative with his metaphors, replies, "Very truly, I tell you, no one can enter the kingdom of God without being born of water and the spirit. Do not be astonished that I said to you, you must be born from above [again, anew]." Jesus underlines the need to be forgiven and transformed by the power and presence of God.

One dimension of the new life which he describes to Nicodemus, and which welcomes one into the commonwealth of God, is that *they were forgiven*. They were able put the harmful and self-destructive behavior behind them and begin a new way of life, "born of the Spirit." And it was just a beginning for them, a process that was starting. Not all of the guilt and shame for past behavior immediately disappeared nor did the actions that caused these feelings. Those who embraced the power and presence of God began the process of claiming forgiveness and the sense of reconciliation. So it is with us as we make a similar decision; it will take time, time to erase painful memories and time to claim the forgiveness on a daily basis as we make mistakes and violate ourselves and hurt those around us.

The Gospels record situations in which people are forgiven and restored to health and wholeness. Early in his public ministry, Jesus would receive those who needed his wisdom and healing, and they would come to him at his location in Capernaum. Often it was crowded and on one occasion, friends brought a paralytic man. Because it was not possible to access Jesus, in part because of the crowds and because of the man's paralysis, they lift the man to the roof of the house and let him down on a mat near Jesus.[29] Obviously, these friends desperately wanted Jesus to heal the para-

28. John 3:1–10.
29. Mark 2:1–12; Matt 9:2–8; Luke 5:17–26.

lytic man, but, somewhat unexpectedly, Jesus responds to the man in terms of forgiveness. He says to him, "Son, your sins are forgiven." Later, after a debate with some scribes about the authority of Jesus to forgive sins, Jesus heals the man: "I say to you, stand up, take your mat and go to your home. And he stood up, and immediately took the mat and went out before all of them; so that they were all amazed and glorified God, saying, 'We have never seen anything like this!'" There is the question about Jesus' authority to forgive, but what I want to stress in this story is that Jesus places forgiveness first, and then physical healing. To be forgiven is life-giving and liberating, and the healing of the paralysis speaks to the way that Jesus cares for the total health of the person. The man leaves Jesus being forgiven and healed by the power and presence of God.

A second component of inviting God to reign in one's life following the experience of forgiveness is one already mentioned, but needs to be stressed: one is *empowered by the presence of God*. The power and presence of God is often expressed in the language of Spirit or Holy Spirit, and it is quite common in the writing of Paul.[30] It appears less frequently in the accounts of Jesus in the Gospels, but is mentioned in Mark's Gospel with a reference to John the Baptist. The author of Mark quotes John as saying, "I have baptized you with water; but he will baptize you with the Holy Spirit."[31] The passage is somewhat problematic in terms of authenticity, but it does reflect the conviction that Jesus' ministry will frame the kingdom transformation as the presence of the Holy Spirit. The Gospel of Luke makes a similar point about empowerment in speaking about being able to make the right defense and find the right words when being questioned about one's faith before authorities. The passage reads: "Do not worry about how you are to defend yourselves or what you are to say: for the Holy Spirit will teach at that very hour what you ought to say."[32]

In the Gospel of John we read about the promise of Jesus that his followers will be empowered by the presence of the Holy Spirit. The passage may be more a comforting and a guiding sermon than the actual words of Jesus, but again it reflects the first generation's belief that God does not leave us alone, but is present with us in our struggles. The author of John places on the lips of Jesus the following: "And I will ask the Father, and he will give you another Advocate to be with you forever. This is the Spirit of truth . . . But the Advocate, the Holy Spirit, whom the Father will send in my name,

30. See Levison, *Filled with the Spirit*, for an excellent treatment of the subject the Holy Spirit.

31. Mark 1:8.

32. Luke 12:11–12.

will teach you everything, and remind you of all that I have said to you."[33] The Apostle Paul, reflecting this same thought, says that the "fruit of the Spirit is love, joy, peace, patience, kindness, generosity, faithfulness, gentleness, and self-control."[34]

The passage from Paul's Letter to the Galatians suggests the kinds of qualities that characterize the life transformed by the power and presence of God. Much could be said about each of these "fruits" of the Spirit, but I'll just briefly refer to the first three, love, joy, and peace. They are the products of being forgiven and empowered, and they point to the transformation that is taking place. Jesus underscores by word and deed that *love is foundational* in the new life. It is the essence of the Law, as he says to a scribe who asks him: "Which commandment is first of all?" Jesus answered, "The first is, 'Hear, O Israel: the Lord our God, the Lord is one; you shall love the Lord your God with all your heart, and with all your soul, and with all your mind, and with all your strength.' The second is this, 'You shall love your neighbor as yourself.' There is no other commandment greater than these."[35] Jesus' word, translated into the verb form of *agape*, expresses unlimited and selfless love, given freely and totally, without conditions.[36] Stephen Post provides the following definition of *agape*: "The essence of love is to affectively affirm and to gratefully delight in the well-being of others; the essence of unlimited love is to extend this form of love to all others in an enduring, intense, effective, and pure manner."[37]

There are many stories in the Gospel that describe the ways that Jesus demonstrated love to others. Matthew's Gospel has an excellent summary: "After Jesus had left that place, he passed along the Sea of Galilee, and he went up the mountain, where he sat down. Great crowds came to him, bringing with them the lame, the maimed, the blind, the mute, and many others. They put them at his feet and he cured them, so that the crowd was amazed when they saw the mute speaking, the maimed whole, the lame walking, and the blind seeing. And they praised the God of Israel."[38] Jesus, filled with compassion and empathy, loves each of these people, and they are healed. Note that it is God who is praised, as Jesus had opened his heart and soul to the empowering grace of God. He does model for his followers the ways in

33. John 14:16, 25–26.

34. Gal 5:22.

35. Mark 12:28–34.

36. See my book *Lovescapes*, 29–52. The classic study of *agape* is by the Swedish scholar Nygren, *Agape and Eros*. Jesus spoke in Aramaic, but the passion carries the meaning of *agape love*.

37. Post, *Unlimited Love*, 19.

38. Matt 15:29–31.

which the kingdom life can and should be lived. It is first and foremost a life of love in which one reaches out to others in need with the goal of serving them and does so yielding to the empowering grace of God's Spirit.

Another outcome of changing directions and opening one's life to the power and presence of God is that *it fills us with joy and happiness*. In the opening section of the Sermon on the Mount, Jesus speaks to his followers about the "blessed" life, a section referred to as the Beatitudes.[39] He draws again upon his Jewish heritage and speaks about what it means to be blessed by God. As one receives from the hand of God those gifts in life that are most precious, it is often described as being blessed. In Psalm 144, for example, a life blessed by God is described: "May our sons in the youth be like plants full grown, our daughters like corner pillars cut for the building of a palace. May our barns be filled with produce of every kind; may our sheep increase by thousands, by tens of thousands in our fields, and may our cattle be heavy with young. May there be no breach in the walls, no exile, and no cry of distress in our streets" (vv. 12–14). As Jesus speaks about the blessed life full of joy and happiness, he talks especially to those for whom life has been difficult and who seek the divine will and way. He speaks to the poor (or poor in spirit),[40] those who mourn, those who are humble, those who hunger and thirst to live the righteous life, those who are merciful, those who are pure in heart, those who are peacemakers, and those who are persecuted and says that they will be blessed. He is saying that they may not have all the privileges of wealth and power, but if they are pure in heart, merciful, and seek peace, they will be blessed. Their life will be filled with joy and deep happiness, a contentment that only comes in union with God. It will be like going to a banquet in which the rich and busy people were unable to attend, but the poor, the crippled, the blind, and the lame came and were invited to "eat bread in the kingdom"[41] and experienced bliss.

Still another outcome of the kingdom life is being *given peace and serenity*, regardless of our external circumstances. The Apostle Paul, in writing to new Christians in Philippi about their faith and about the life dedicated to God, exhorts them to "rejoice in the Lord always," to be gentle with one another, not to worry, and to pray with thanksgiving.[42] If we live in that fashion, then "the peace of God, which surpasses all understanding, will guard your hearts and your minds in Christ Jesus." He continues to exhort his

---

39. Matt 5:1–11.

40. There is a difference between the version in Matthew and Luke. It is likely that Luke's version speaking about the poor is the most authentic.

41. Luke 14:15–24.

42. Phil 4:9.

followers to focus on the just, the pure, and what is of great value, and says, "The God of peace will be with you." The author of John's Gospel addresses a similar theme as he attempts to reconstruct Jesus' closing comments to his disciples. Jesus is recorded as saying to his disciples who are worried that he may leave them: "Peace I leave with you; my peace I give to you. I do not give to you as the world gives. Do not let your hearts be troubled, and do not let them be afraid." It is not power and possessions nor fame and status that will bring you peace of mind, but the kingdom of God which will bring peace. Jesus teaches that such a blessing is what is most important: "The kingdom of heaven is like a treasure hidden in the field, which someone found and hid; then in his joy he goes and sells all that he has and buys the field."[43] Further, "the kingdom of heaven is like a merchant in search of fine pearls; on finding one pearl of great value, he went and sold all that he had and bought it."[44] There is nothing of greater value.

There are many other dimensions of this new adventure guided by the Spirit of God. I want to call attention to three of them that seem indispensable to sustaining a faithful life as a "subject" of the kingdom of God. The first is that as one is called to this new life, *one joins a supportive community of like-minded people* who comfort, guide, and complement the gifts one brings to this new undertaking. This new fellowship of committed people will be called the church (*ecclesia*). It is not likely that Jesus was the founder of the Christian church as we have come to know it, but his life and teaching started a movement. It was one linked to the Jewish community initially, but as differences arose, it gradually became separated. But by the time of the writing of Matthew's Gospel, the term would be used in reference to the Christian community.[45] Luke in Acts and Paul in his epistles use the term, as well.[46] Acts speaks about Paul prior to his conversion "ravaging the church by entering house after house, dragging off both men and women."[47] Later Paul is serving the church as he sends Timothy to aid the church in Corinth.[48] Paul also gives us vivid analogies for the church, and especially insightful is the way that he calls the church "the body of Christ" and describes each member as having a gift to give to the body, even as each part

---

43. Matt 13:44.

44. Matt 13:45–46.

45. Matt 16:18; 18:17.

46. Acts 5:11; 1 Cor 4:17; 14:12.

47. Acts 8:3. This incident would be quite early in the formation of the Christian community.

48. 1 Cor 4:17.

of the body contributes to the body's health.[49] We all belong to this new community, find support and guidance in it, and are called to serve in collaboration with others. We find community and life-giving fellowship.

It is within the church that we are guided in our spiritual lives. This new adventure of being Christian asks of us that *we dedicate ourselves to a spiritual way*. To pursue a spiritual way is the sincere effort, empowered by the Holy Spirit, to incorporate all of the elements of this new endeavor into a pattern which provides guidance in life, leading to the formation of the person which brings wholeness (holiness), insight, serenity, and responsible living.[50] These new Christians were asked to give up old ways such as the worship of idols[51] and sexual immorality.[52] They are asked to live a moral life, one that honors the principles expressed in the Law and summarized in the Ten Commandments.[53] It is one described by the double-love commandment, to love God fully and love one's neighbor as oneself.[54] It is a way of life characterized by the practice of the golden rule: "In everything do to others as you would have them do to you; for this is the law and the prophets."[55] This new life involves a range of spiritual practices and disciplines such as worship,[56] prayer,[57] study,[58] and service.[59]

One final dimension of this new way of life offered as one embraces the power and presence of God is that it brings *purpose and focus to one's life*. The first generation of followers of Jesus was preoccupied with just living, a task not all that easy, especially for the less privileged and those on the margins of society. A great deal of one's time had to do with making a living and caring for the family, and to do so without the efficiencies of modern

---

49. 1 Cor 12.

50. Ferguson, *Spiritual Pathways*, 3–19. Foster, in *Streams of Living Water*, describes several patterns of spiritual practice, and in another book, *Celebration of Discipline*, lists twelve spiritual disciplines in the categories of inward disciplines (meditation, prayer, fasting, study); outward disciplines (simplicity, solitude, submission, service); and corporate disciplines (confession, worship, guidance, and celebration).

51. 1 Cor 10:14.

52. 1 Cor 5:1–5.

53. Deut 5:1–21.

54. Mark 12:30–33.

55. Matt 7:12.

56. Luke 4:8.

57. Luke 11:1.

58. Acts 2:42.

59. 1 Cor 12:5. The Greek word for service is *diakonia*. It has the meaning of "waiting at table" but emphasizes service in genuine love (1 Cor 16:15). See Kittel, *TDNT*, 2:87.

life as we know it in the first world. For many people living in first-century Palestine, the purpose of life often focused on survival with the hope of a measure of happiness and contentment. Jesus invited those who listened to him to continue their basic responsibilities but also to link them with transcendence. This linkage was offered and described in a variety of ways in their culture, but given clear definition in the teaching of Jesus. He says: "Therefore, do not worry, saying 'What will we eat?' or 'What will we drink?' or 'What will we wear?' For it is the Gentiles who strive for these things; and indeed your heavenly Father knows that you need all these things. But strive first for the kingdom of God and his righteousness, and all these things will be given to you as well. So do not worry about tomorrow, for tomorrow will bring worries of its own. Today's trouble is enough for today."[60]

Jesus teaches that there is a transcendent purpose in life, one that reaches beyond the immediate needs of the present, and one that puts these needs in the context of the power and presence of God. One undertakes the daily tasks in the spirit of doing the will and way of God. One gains a positive outlook by understanding the day's tasks as a God-given responsibility and to do them in the spirit of love and service. I do the will of God by being responsible in my daily tasks and caring in a loving way for my family and those with whom I associate. My purpose in life to do the will of God and my focus from day to day is love and care for those within my circle of associations. We seek first the reign of God in our lives, and then find that the other dimensions of life fall into place. We serve God and focus on loving service.

We have focused our attention in this chapter on the ways that endorsing the kingdom of God transforms individual lives. We turn now to the implications of Jesus' teaching for creating a more just and peaceful society and world.

Study Resources

Study Questions

1. What is the radical proclamation of Jesus? What makes it radical?

2. What does it mean when Jesus says, "Repent and believe?"

3. How would you describe Jesus' way of inviting people to respond to his message?

4. How does Jesus differ from the Pharisees in his understanding of the Law (Torah)?

60. Matt 6:31–34.

5. In what ways does Jesus speak about transformation and what are the outcomes of this change?

Terms and Concepts

1. Metanoia: A fundamental change of direction for our lives, our way of thinking, and our ways of living.

2. Agape: A type of love that is unlimited and unconditional.

3. Empathy: The quality in one's life that is able to identify with the pain and suffering of others.

4. Insight: That way of understanding our lives which enlightens us and shows us a life-changing way to understand.

5. Blessed: To have been given a special gift, to receive all that one needs in life which brings happiness and deep contentment.

Suggestions for Reading and Reference

Ferguson, Duncan S. *Lovescapes: Mapping the Geography of Love*. Eugene, OR: Cascade, 2012.
Foster, Richard J. *Streams of Living Water*. New York: HarperOne, 1998.
Levison, John R. *Filled with the Spirit*. Grand Rapids: Eerdmans, 2009.
Nygren, Anders. *Agape and Eros*. Translated by Philip S. Watson. London: SPCK, 1953.
Post, Stephen G. *Unlimited Love: Altruism, Compassion, and Service*. Philadelphia: Templeton Foundation, 2003.

9

God's Presence in the World

Go and Do Likewise

Jesus' Understanding of God

WE HAVE DISCUSSED THE way Jesus understood and related to God. For Jesus, God was intimately present; he referred to God as Abba, an affectionate term for father in Aramaic. There is a sense in which Jesus was a revolutionary mystic.[1] He understood God as active in the history of his people and in his surroundings and circumstances. He experienced God as loving and compassionate, the ground of all truth, just and fair in his dealings with humankind, and sovereign over all. Jesus felt called by God to the mission of announcing that the kingdom of God was dawning, and that his vocation was to proclaim this message by inviting his contemporaries to repent (change directions), believe in this good news (gospel), and receive the power and presence of God into their lives. Jesus was true to his vocation, sharing the good news with all who came his way as a charismatic teacher, a compassionate healer, and a radical prophet. Many, especially in his region, the region of Galilee, enthusiastically received his message but there were detractors who saw Jesus and his message as a threat and misguided. His life reached a climax in Jerusalem where he encountered those who opposed him; the Sanhedrin judged him harshly, and the Romans crucified him.

---

1. Adyashanti, *Resurrecting Jesus*, makes a strong case for understanding Jesus as a mystic. See also Harvey, *Mystics*, 169–216.

The human family now has the legacy of his faithful life, given to us in the Gospels and all of the New Testament. We see from these documents how his life and teachings were understood by the first generations of Christians, and we now have the challenge of discerning their meaning and following their pattern in our time. In the previous chapter we spoke about how his contemporaries responded to his life and teaching, and how they used ways of describing him and understanding his mission. We are now offered guidance by their reflections. As we read these reflections in their writings, we are told that we too may be born anew, forgiven, empowered by God's Spirit, and have lives filled with love, joy, and peace. They were able to join with others in the community of the church and dedicate themselves to the way of Jesus that gave focus and purpose to their lives. We too have a similar invitation to join others in the way of Jesus within the contemporary community of the church.

As we expose ourselves to this great legacy, we are invited to ponder ways that we might respond. There is the personal response of praying, "Your kingdom come, you will be done on earth as it is in heaven."[2] We open our hearts to the reign of God and find that our lives are transformed. We discover that love may become our way of life and that serenity and happiness fill us even if we are challenged by the troubles and difficulties of our lives. As we reflect about how to respond, we also become aware of the way that the life and teachings of Jesus ask us to partner with God in *building a more just and humane world*, even if it is only in one small corner of the world. It is to this theme that we now turn. Perhaps in the spirit of Jesus as a teacher, we might reflect on a story from the passage in Luke's Gospel that is called the Good Samaritan. In the story, Jesus is asked by a lawyer how he can receive eternal life, to which Jesus replies, "Love God fully and love your neighbor as yourself." The lawyer responds with the question, "And who is my neighbor?" Jesus then tells the story of a man who is robbed and left in a ditch as he traveled on the road from Jerusalem to Jericho. A busy priest, perhaps rushing to a meeting and then by a Levite bound by custom and protocol and therefore unable to help, pass him on the other side of the road. But a Samaritan (an outsider) stops, treats his wounds, takes him to an inn, and gives him some money. Jesus asks: "Which of these three, do you think, was a neighbor to the man who fell into the hands of robbers?" The lawyer had to respond, "The one who showed him mercy." Jesus says, "Go and do likewise."[3]

---

2. Matt 6:10.

3. Luke 10:25–37. The word mercy may be occasionally translated as compassion.

Go and Do Likewise: A Brief History

There is a marvelous heritage left by those who have reflected on this passage and its many ways of being asked and expressed. Across history the human family, often within the context of its many individual groups (whether religious, ethnic, regional, or national identity), has raised the questions of ethics: What is the good life? How should we live our lives? Is there a moral truth? What is virtue?[4]

It is not possible to review all of these theories in depth, although they are very helpful as we assess our concern to understand the ethical teaching of Jesus.[5] But a brief review of those arising within the church community will illustrate the issues and concerns.[6] I will describe five historical periods of Christian history that address the ethical responsibility of the church in reference to the social realities of their time and attempt to describe the primary tone of their ethical position.[7]

The first period we might call *From the Hellenistic Context to Christian Formation* (40–400 CE). Christianity was born in the Near East and soon spread in several directions. The growth may have gone as far as India to the East, to Britain to the West, to Northern Africa in the South, and to Germany in the North. Each of these settings had different languages, different social realities, and different ethical challenges. What they had in common was the reality and control of the Roman Empire and the influence of Hellenism, a lingering worldview that might be understood as ancient Greek thought, its values, customs, and patterns of life. But no broad generalization

4. There are many accounts of the history of ethics. One that has served as a good introduction for me, not just to the history of reflection about these questions, but suggesting a way to put together a thoughtful answer is Maguire, *Ethics*. Three other volumes, slightly dated, and which are in the form of textbooks for courses in ethics, have exceptional summaries and explanations of the complex issues surrounding the study of ethics: Albert and Peterfreund, *Great Traditions in Ethics*; Grasson, *Moral Reasoning*; and Velasquez and Rostankowski, *Ethics*. These three are somewhat representative of the scores that are available.

5. Of course there are many which have addressed the more specific question of Christian ethics and the several issues needing ethical consideration such as the environment, peace and justice, war and nonviolence, economics, abortion, and the issues in personal relationships such as marriage and divorce. I have been helped by Gustafson, *Ethics from a Theocentric Perspective*; Thielicke, *Theological Ethics*; many of the books of Hauerwas, which provoke thought, such as *Peaceable Kingdom*; and the several books by Sider, including *Rich Christians in an Age of Hunger*. I will be referring to several others that have been published more recently.

6. The popular book by McLaren, *Secret Message of Jesus*, provides a very accessible summary of Jesus' message, understood as the kingdom of God. See ch. 15, "Kingdom Ethics," 129–37.

7. Each of these eras of church history deserves a full book.

quite captures the diversity of ethical outlooks across this wide expanse. Life in Egypt was different than life in Corinth and life in Rome was different than in Constantinople. Though varied, there were ethical norms in all of these regions and the Christian message challenged the social milieu and offered an alternative, even a challenge to what was considered a permissive society across the Roman Empire.[8] Initially, the Christian movement was slightly below the radar of the empire, and its influence spread with only the occasional persecution. Christians did speak out and act against what was considered superstitious idolatry and moral corruption, and the Christian way increased in influence and became not just an offer to individuals to endorse a new way of life, but a social message and movement as well. The Christian community became concerned for those who suffered, offered charity, invited people to follow the teachings of Jesus, and to accept that love was the law of life.[9]

In time, the Christian emphasis on ethics had profound impact on both those inside the Christian community as Christian formation, and to a slightly lesser extent, on those outside as a moral apologetic.[10] While both the Christian community and the external context were moving targets, there was a steady stream of proclamation and writing about Christian standards for behavior. In many ways, the emphasis in this post-apostolic period was on *developing a Christ-like character with less reliance on empowering grace and more reliance on one's own effort.* The standards were set high: the simple life rather than one of luxury, the life of love and the avoidance of hate, union within the Christian churches over conflict, the centrality of finding the truth over against heretical thought, and sexual morality over against permissive sexual expression. These themes appear in the *Didache*, a short guidebook for Christians written in Greek called "The Teaching of the Lord through the Twelve Apostles." Scholars place this document, discovered 1875, in a very early period, perhaps as early as 100 CE. It describes two ways, the way of life and the way of death. Contained in the document are regulations, ordinances, and guidelines for baptism, fasting, and prayer. The tone borders on moralism, stressing the need to be perfect.

Other writings from this early period focus on church discipline, the relationship of Christian ethics to Jewish ethics, and the way that Christian ethics often stand over against the values of the culture and the norms of society. There is a sense of self-protection, the need for preservation from

---

8. White, *Christian Ethics*, 9–25.

9. It was not always the case that Christians always followed their own teaching; hypocrisy is a constant companion.

10. White, *Christian Ethics*, 26–27.

the threat of the world, and an almost sectarian removal from the culture.[11] What emerges alongside of this sectarian spirit is a growing antipathy toward marriage and procreation, a point of view that did not exist among first-century Christians. It was not easy for Christians in this early period to preserve their identity and way of life in the encounter with so many other influences and forces in their cultures. There were powerful pressures and the leaders of the church felt the need to make extraordinary adjustments to survive and thrive.[12] They had to deal with several critical issues and concerns with guidance from Scripture, but without the precedents of centuries of interpretation and tradition. For example, they had to address the ethical questions surrounding the use and abuse of wealth, the place of slavery in the economy, how to relate to the state and its power, whether to engage in military service, and whether to approve of capital punishment.[13]

The second period of the church's reflection about ethics we might call *The Middle Ages: From a Protective Moralism to Christian Moral Philosophy*, a period lasting from about 400–1500 CE. It was an age in which the Christian church and its teaching became the primary guide and motivating force for ethical behavior, especially in Europe. Roman Emperor, Constantine (288–337 CE) declared the Christian religion to be the religion of the Roman Empire and with this declaration there was the emergence of religious freedom for Christians and substantial growth of the church. For the next several centuries, Europe came under the influence of the church, and many of the church's thoughtful interpreters reflected on the nature of Christian ethics. In time this era in European history, under the rule of Charlemagne (742–814) who ruled a vast region of Eastern and Western Europe, would be referred to as the Holy Roman Empire.

As the Roman Empire began to crumble and with it the structures of society, much of the population turned to more regional and local organizational systems. The church in the early phase of the Middle Ages also became more regional and local, although some infrastructure for the church across what was the Roman Empire did exist. There were two ways in which the church responded to its new environment. One was to turn toward the ascetic-monastic way of life, a pattern that had elements of the

---

11. Names of those offering guidance through their writing include Clement of Rome, Clement of Alexandria, Tertullian, and Origen. Each one is distinctive in emphasis and persuasive in argument, but the net result is a description of a self-conscious community that must guard against worldly values and exist with its memory of the Christ-event, the mission to the world, and hope in a common destiny.

12. The study of Christian ethics in this period is fascinating, although somewhat disturbing.

13. White, *Christian Ethics*, 52–80.

mystical tradition as well. In many ways this movement was a turn away from a worldly life with its compromises and distributions of power, and toward living in an isolated retreat community of like-minded people. The second way of responding to the environment of the medieval world was to be engaged in reflecting on this environment in terms of developing a moral philosophy that guided life in such a context. The questions addressed in this movement were how to engage in ecclesiastical statesmanship and how to apply Christian ethics to the prevailing political conditions.[14]

The first tendency found support in the New Testament for the ascetic life. There were the descriptions of the conflict between the flesh and the spirit in the teaching of Paul, as well as his counsel to live the celibate life if possible. Jesus spoke of fasting, and his single life of public ministry became a model. Those who led the ascetic-monastic life read the early church teachers such as Justin Martyr, Clement of Alexandria, and Tertullian about costly discipleship requiring sacrifice, discipline, and living the simple life. It followed that those that sought to live an ascetic and disciplined life could do so more easily by joining others in monastic communities. Benedict in the sixth century called people into the monastic life around a comprehensive *Rule* that emphasized routine labor, study, moderate asceticism, and prayer. Other groups across the centuries of this medieval period followed such as the Dominicans, Jesuits, and the Franciscans, each with a slightly different identity and ethos. Groups formed for women as well, and some of the church's finest spiritual teachers came from these movements.[15]

Others whose names are well known, such as Augustine, Abelard, and Aquinas, at different times in the medieval era offered more reflective philosophical and theological guidance for living the ethical life. Augustine (354–430) wrote about the whole range of subjects within theological reflection, and addressed ethical questions within his theological frame of reference. For example, he said that there are many levels of being, and we are to make appropriate responses to these various levels. There is a response to ultimate Being or God that is worship and devotion, to humans that is love and respect, and to created things to which we respond with proper use. He argued that our tendency, rooted in our sinful nature, is to engage in disordered love; we are inclined to ignore God, use others, and to place created objects at the center of our lives. Objects in the created world can be very attractive in that God creates many of them. The way to maintain appropriate order in our love and loyalty is to draw strength from the reality that

14. Ibid., 81–92.

15. See, e.g., the writing of the mystic theologian Julian of Norwich, *Showings*. Jantzen describes Julian's life and work in her biography, *Julian of Norwich*.

we are created in the image of God and can be empowered by the grace of God. Augustine speaks as well about governments and the rule of law, arguing that there are two "cities," the City of God concerned with our spiritual destiny and the City of this world concerned about our material existence. Human beings are often caught and conflicted by living in both cities; there is a complex interaction between the two, and this interaction becomes the story of personal and corporate ethics.

Peter Abelard (1079–1192), from a different time and place, is more committed to enlightened reason than to the Augustinian emphasis on human limitations. He is committed to and teaches that human beings should carefully reason in order to understand the ever-present dialectical choices in life. We are in fact continually in situations that require us to say "yes and no" (*Sic & Non*—the title of his book). Struggling himself with his romantic love affair and marriage to Eloise, he affirms that within our human freedom, we make moral judgments, and that the quality of an act lies not in the act itself, but in its intention. In stressing intention, Abelard introduces the psychological character of ethical decisions. He and Eloise had the best of intentions even though he left his monastic vows for the life of married love.

Thomas Aquinas (1225–1274) also speaks about reason, human freedom, and the human capacity to make right choices. His theological system is vast and comprehensive, well beyond the scope of our discussion, and his ethical teaching fits within and should be viewed as part of this larger system of thought. He maintains that the highest good is the happiness and peace that comes from our understanding and love of God. We begin this process here on earth, but it will only be completed in eternity. Our ethical responsibility in this life consists of pursuing the highest good by practicing faith, hope, and charity, and living the cardinal virtues of prudence, courage, temperance, and justice. He speaks as well about corporate ethics and maintains that the state exists to maintain the well-being of the human family. However, there is the tendency of the state to be tyrannical, and when this happens, it is appropriate for there to be an intervention by the people. He assumes the presence of royalty to lead countries, but he does open the door to the questions of democracy and civil disobedience.

The third era in the development of the development of Christian ethics may be called *New Perspectives Arising from the Reformation and the Enlightenment* (1400–1750). The leading Reformers, Martin Luther (1483–1546) in Germany and John Calvin (1509–1564) in Geneva, both place their views of Christian ethics within the larger context of their understanding of how it is that human beings find reconciliation with God. Luther's story begins with him struggling as a young man to please God. Educated at the University of Erfurt and in the monastery of the Augustinian order, he became very familiar with medieval theology with its stress on practicing the Christian faith in the pattern of Jesus himself. He finds this challenge quite difficult, and the harder he tried, the more he realized his inability to measure up to all the expectations of God. He was a teacher of Scripture, and while teaching Paul's Letter to the Romans, he senses that it is not human effort that reconciles one to God, but faith in what God has done in the redemptive acts of Jesus. Soon, he is proclaiming the message of "justification by faith" and as he did, he encountered some opposition from the established church. But his genie was out of bottle, and it could not be replaced. He then moved to his conversation about Christian ethics, saying that being saved by grace through faith frees the human being and empowers the believer to follow the way of God.[16] One is empowered by the Holy Spirit to be able to follow the guidance of God contained in Scripture. In this new life, one is not bound by the Law, in the sense of Jewish teaching, but enlightened by Scripture and given the grace to be obedient to God. Luther raises in a quite dramatic way the healthy tension between those who say that humans have that innate capacity to follow the teachings of faith, and those that say that humans need to receive empowering grace and to be transformed in order to follow the teachings given to us in Scripture.

John Calvin, another major voice in the Reformation (and there were many), is not too distant from Martin Luther in his view of Christian ethics. Calvin shades the view of human nature more strongly toward original sin, arguing that are we are "depraved." Our inherent knowledge of God is "stifled or corrupted, ignorantly or maliciously."[17] He stresses, perhaps even more than Luther, the need to be saved by grace through faith, and justification by faith becomes one of the central themes of his theology. He argued that we must be vigilant in our new faith orientation to follow the teachings of Scripture. He put less emphasis on human freedom even in our redeemed state than Luther, and maintained that we must be empowered by God's Spirit and diligently follow the teachings Scripture. As was Luther, Calvin emphasized the sovereignty of God, but more than Luther, he stressed that God is fully in control and that we were chosen (elected) by God to be saved. As he developed this theme, he put less confidence in human freedom and the capacity of humans, even in a redeemed state, to make wise ethical choices.[18] He, like Luther, was a distinguished scholar of the Bible, and across his lifetime, he wrote a commentary on all of the books of

---

16. Luther, *Three Treatises.*

17. Calvin, *Institutes,* 1:46–71.

18. Ibid., 453–59.

the Protestant Bible. For both Calvin and Luther, the Bible becomes central in guiding the church and the behavior of Christians.

Another Christian scholar who is often placed in the category of Reformer is Desiderius Erasmus (1466–1536). He did not, however, hold the same views as Luther and Calvin and did not leave the Roman Catholic Church. He like Luther was an Augustinian, but preferred literary and scholarly study in the academy to life in a conflicted church. His contribution to Christian ethics was limited, but he did serve as a bridge between the Reformation and the Renaissance and moved the discussion of ethics more toward humanism and the capacity of the human mind to reason and the human will to choose the ethical way. He spoke about the Christian soldier and the Christian life as warfare, and the primary enemy is human beings themselves.[19] He spoke of our animal nature but says that we can overcome our tendency to violate God's way and call upon God as our great Ally. We are capable of following the divine way but reason must regain authority in our lives. We must cultivate a reasoned-based outlook and complement it by turning to deep piety, charity, and compassion. He also moved beyond personal ethics and called upon the church to engage in social ethics. He maintained that it is possible to transform society, and in his teaching, he anticipates the values of the eighteenth and nineteenth centuries in their "faith in progress." As he spoke about creating a more just society, he underlined the corrupting challenges of wealth and called for the simple life. He also argued that rulers should be just in their exercise of power, and he fundamentally opposed war.

Sharing with Erasmus in the belief that human beings have the capacity to live an ethical life were those who actually took the Reformation beyond Luther and Calvin. Moving away from the authority of a hierarchical church, but without the emphasis on original sin, several writers explored new patterns in ethics emphasizing human capability. One part of this new movement, drawing to some extend on the Enlightenment's affirmation of human value and worth were those who spoke of the human endowment with conscience and reason, and a second spoke more about psychological endowment and stressed "the inner light" or spirit of God within human beings.[20] First, then a word about being *endowed with conscience,* and an able spokesperson for this point of view was Joseph Butler (1692–1752). In his book *Sermons on Human Nature and the Analogy of Religion* (1733), Butler argued that the basis of morality is the conscience, which is part of

---

19. His book is entitled *Handbook for the Christian Soldier.*

20. I will follow the outline of White, *Christian Ethics,* in this very brief review that leads to the modern era.

every human being. The conscience guides humankind with the voice of authority, and as we listen to our conscience, we must follow it without regard for consequences. Its voice is clear and immediate, not like that produced by only thoughtful reasoning. The human conscience, however, needs to be sensitized by religious teaching, although it is not rooted in religion.

Many philosophers could be mentioned who discuss the place of reason in discerning the right ethical practice, and we have already introduced a few of them. But it is Immanuel Kant (1724–1804) who most persuasively provided a foundation for the place of reason in ethical judgment.[21] Kant explained that morality is concerned with the highest level of conduct that requires discerning what is the greatest good or the highest principle for guidance. He searched for this principle that can become a universal for all human behavior, a maxim that may stand as a universal law. As a result of this search, he discovered that respect for others is the major factor in discerning what might become a universal law. He maintained that we must never regard another person as a means to an end, but always the final end. In addition to reason, we are also guided to treat others as an end in themselves by an exposure to great ethical principles of previous ethical teachings such as the Decalogue. He continued in the development of his ethical theory to maintain that practice of ethics is governed by the exercise of a good will; human beings should not driven by pleasure but by duty, duty that is discovered and known by the use of reason.

For Kant, there is the guidance of conscience and discernment by reason to know what is ethical, but there are those, while not denying the role of conscience and reason, who speak with a slightly different language than Kant, and emphasize the inner presence of the divine to guide ethical behavior. The Puritan movements of the sixteenth and seventeenth centuries, in Great Britain as well as in the American colonies, appealed to an inner divine experience that guided them in their behavior.[22] The name of the Puritans had its origin in their attempt to purify the church, and perhaps their greatest contribution was in the field of practical ethics. The sternness of their views and way of life need to be acknowledged, and we should not miss their emphasis on the need to struggle against evil and a personal devil that could easily lead one astray. John Bunyan's books *Holy War* and *Pilgrim's Progress* captured the seriousness with which they taught moral

21. His books on this subject are *Foundations of the Metaphysic of Morals* and *Critique of Practical Reason*.

22. The books of Miller are especially helpful in understanding the Puritan movement. See Miller and Jefferson, *Puritans: A Sourcebook of Their Writings*, for a good introduction.

rectitude. Life must be centered upon God, and one must be empowered by God to live up to the divine expectations.

Another group, representing the left wing of the Reformation, the Society of Friends, took the emphasis on inner illumination to its logical conclusion. The Quakers, as they become known, put their emphasis less on original sin and predestination, themes of John Calvin, and more on the divine presence that opens the heart and empowers one to understand the will and way of God. George Fox (1624–1691) was more of a mystic than earlier Reformers, and he followed the teaching found in John 1:9 that there is a "true light, which enlightens everyone, was coming into the world."[23] He also spoke of the promise of the coming of God's Spirit that brings the light, and that Christians must open their hearts to the presence of God's Spirit. Over against other teachers such as Butler and Kant, he said that we need not be overly dependent upon an endowed conscience and natural reason because we have the very direct guidance of God. In terms of ethical emphasis, the Society of Friends gave a high priority to social compassion, and in many ways their commitment to a more just and peaceful society and world has been an extraordinary contribution to the life of the larger church. They of course speak about social compassion in their literature, but in a special way have put their ideals into practice. For example, their fearless devotion to ambulance work on major battlefields demonstrates the integrity of their commitment to peace and their uncompromising opposition to war.

In some ways, the model of the Society of Friends, with it emphasis on social responsibility, leads into a fourth period of Christian ethics, one that we might call *The Modern Period: From Inner Transformation to Social Responsibility* (ca. 1750–1950). New perspectives about and applications of Christian ethics, even though changing because of facing new situations in the passing of time, often retain many of the insights that came from pervious eras. As we explore the changes that occur in the eighteenth and nineteenth centuries, and on into the twentieth century, we view new influences on Christian ethics arising in response to major economic and political changes, not the least of which was the industrial revolution. Coupled with these major changes was the rise of the social sciences that enabled alternative ways of understanding social realities. We observe the church bringing foundational commitments to these new realities and, in many cases, integrating them into the quest for societal change by using the insights of psychology, sociology, anthropology, and economics.

In the area of personal ethics, we turn to the teaching of John Wesley (1703–1791). Influenced by the Reformers and the Puritans, he accepted

---

23. See *Journal of George Fox*, 1924.

their foundational theology, but dialed the ethical compass in a slightly different direction with his emphasis on how society shapes human behavior. He retained the Reformed emphases on justification by faith, and the Puritan teaching about discipline and inner asceticism, but placed more emphasis on human freedom and choice. He spoke about being a total Christian, one who habitually and methodically practices self-discipline and the continual renewal of one's soul and mind, as created in the image of God. In this emphasis, he did not ignore social ethics, but taught that one who seeks holiness will naturally be concerned about challenging social injustice and practicing charity. His teaching stressed the need for simplicity, generosity, honesty, and a circumspect life. Such a life with its emphasis on compassionate love will naturally lead to engagement in social reform, economic justice, and the pursuit of peace.[24] If one loves others, one will care about the conditions in which they live, and in his life Wesley devoted himself to those who were addicted to alcohol and captive to slavery.

Another British voice in the rise of Christian social ethics in this period was F. D. Maurice (1805–1872) who sought to apply Christian teaching to the rise of industrialism and its many negative consequences for achieving a just social order. Maurice was acquainted with French socialism, and he found inspiration in these writings for his application of Christian ethics to industrial and economic conditions caused by the deep and profound changes in British society. He was the first to coin the phrase "Christian socialism" and strongly affirmed that the uniting center of a socialized community was the will of God expressed in the teachings of Jesus about the kingdom of God. In the ongoing discussion about the human capacity to be ethical or the need for the empowerment of grace, he leaned toward being optimistic about the capacity of human initiative in making positive change. He underlined that God is present (immanent) as an educative influence in human life. With this divine influence, often expressed as being created in the image of God, humans have the capacity and will to be responsive to the way of God. Other socialists of his era were doubtful of what Maurice advocated, in part because of his use of religious language. They questioned whether religious motivation led to a true expression of socialism, but did have to acknowledge that the influence of Maurice on the church's commitment to social justice in England was significant.

During this period in the United States, the same concern for turning Christian ethics toward social justice was present.[25] People such as Wash-

24. I have found the reading of Wesley's journal especially inspirational and perspective about how humans are shaped by their social environment. See the version entitled *Journal of John Wesley*, abridged by Idle, published in 1966.

25. White, *Christian Ethics*, 290–99.

ington Gladden, Walter Rauschenbusch, Shailer Matthews, and in first half of the twentieth century, Reinhold Niebuhr, were among those who gave voice to Christian social ethics. Gladden (1836–1918), a pastor, spoke about the local church's responsibility in pursuing social justice within its sphere of influence. He used such language as "Christianising" society and the need for social transformation. He spoke prophetically about how the church should lead in the ministry of reconciliation and bring people from all classes and ethnicities together.[26] Walter Rauschenbusch (1861–1918) was also committed to using Christian teaching to guide in social reform. A bit more radical than Gladden, Rauschenbusch saw that church going beyond reconciliation of classes and ethnicities. He saw the goal of racial reconciliation as important, but urged the church to take further steps and identify with those who are marginalized and the working class in particular. The church must live and work in solidarity with those who are victims of social injustice. Working as a pastor in New York's West Side, he saw firsthand the terrible effects of poverty, unemployment, malnutrition, disease, and crime. In his work and with his writing, he framed a theological foundation for what was called the Social Gospel.[27] Shailer Matthews (1863–1941) was even more radical than his predecessors in that he was less concerned about remaining mainline in his theology and advocated a theology more grounded in the new disciplines of social studies, more evolutionary in character, and one that applies the teaching of Jesus to the society, economic life, and social institutions.[28] His work points forward to the mission and ministry of Martin Luther King Jr.

One of the most subtle and influential voices in articulating Christian social ethics in the first half of the twentieth century was pastor and professor Reinhold Niebuhr (1892–1971). He represented a generation following the social gospel movement and called into question the inherent and optimistic idealism of the social gospel in large part because of what he saw in the industries of Detroit as a young pastor and his reflections on the harsh realities of war as he observed World War I.[29] Niebuhr invited the church, certainly in the United States, but well beyond, to reclaim some of the classical themes of Christian thought.[30] He did not disdain the application of

26. See his books entitled *Working Men and Their Employers* and *Applied Christianity.*

27. His writings include *Christianity and the Social Crisis* (1907), *Christianising the Social Order* (1912), and *Theology for a Social Gospel* (1918).

28. His book *Social Teaching of Jesus* (1897) was widely read and influential in the development of the social gospel movement.

29. See his personal statement in *Leaves from the Notebooks of a Tamed Cynic.*

30. He was often grouped with other theologians of his generation by the term

Christian teaching to society, but cautioned against a naive view of human perfection and the inevitable progress of history. He argued that history does not necessarily go in the direction of progress, even though individuals may seek to create a more just and peaceful social order.[31] Corporate entities such as political parties, industries, corporations, and countries do not have a conscience; they seek their own development and progress in order to survive. What is needed from the church is a tough-minded Christian realism about the nature of evil in many forms.[32] He strongly urged that a Christian ethic be developed and followed, one that will attempt to reconcile the Christian ideal of unlimited love with the pride and injustice of human society and national states.[33]

In many ways, it is Reinhold Niebuhr, and many of his contemporaries such as Dietrich Bonhoeffer, the Christian martyr, who pushed the church to a more global perspective in Christian ethics. Our fifth and final period in the development of the church's response to the teaching of Jesus may be called *The Contemporary Period: From Regional Concerns to a Global Outlook* (from 1950 to the present). In some ways, the Christian church has always been global in its outlook, at least in terms of sharing the Christian message and in compassionately caring for those who were less fortunate. Never completely free from mistakes in judgment and attitude, nor from criticism by those who saw that church as ideological and exclusive with its message, the church nevertheless, even with its limitations went beyond its borders and tried to help. There is in the church the deep conviction that Christians are called to love their neighbor in wise and constructive ways, and the global context clearly suggests that our neighbor is the entire human family. And the problems faced by humankind in this era are challenging, perplexing, alarming, and daunting. "Finding solutions has and will require the best minds and finest spirits within the global human family cooperating across all boundaries to see a way forward at this critical moment in the earth's history."[34] In fact, the earth is in peril, increasingly interdependent and fragile, and "calls" us to work toward a preferable future by coming together and using the marvelous diversity of the world's many cultures and religions to find solutions to problems that seem overwhelming in scope and magnitude. We must commit ourselves to a "deep respect for nature, the

---

neoorthodoxy.

31. See Niebuhr, *Moral Man and Immoral Society.*

32. See Niebuhr, *Christian Realism & Political Problems.*

33. See *Interpretation of Christian Ethics.* His most comprehensive treatment of the human condition may be found in *Nature and Destiny of Man.*

34. Ferguson, *Lovescapes,* 254.

protection of human rights, the quest for economic justice, and the building of just and peaceful world."[35]

Christian ethics has turned in this direction, and as it does, Christian leaders must realize that it helps by joining hands with many others, most of whom begin with somewhat different presuppositions.[36] The church lends a hand in humility and with the knowledge that it does not have all the answers or the resources. Christian ethical perspectives move then to make a contribution and should guard against the arrogant assumption that they bring the answer. Rather, they join with others in discovering answers, while being guided and motivated by the teaching of Jesus. The list of issues needing ethical wisdom and service has many entries including those surrounding ecology such as global warming and global infrastructure; those in the category of overpopulation and the related issues of poverty, hunger, and disease; the issues dealing with global economics and the distribution of wealth; the issues of regional, national, and global governance including the rule of law and the concerns of equitable treatment by the law, racial and gender equality, access to education, and good health care; and issues dealing with war and conflict, often provoked by ancient tribal prejudices; the need for natural resources; lack of interreligious literacy, understanding, and cooperation; and the use of nuclear arms. This is but a sample of the global concerns, and there are just as many facing regions, families, and individuals who must make ethical decisions. This list is long and the issues complex. They include such concerns as abortion, addiction, euthanasia, the death penalty, sexism, racism, the treatment of animals, and those mentioned above such as health care and education.

We can only hint at the ways that the teaching of Jesus provides guidance for the appropriate responses to these ethical concerns. Let me suggest four overarching categories of ethical concern and illustrate possible responses by referring to those people and organizations, which have felt called to respond. I borrow from "The Earth Charter" in describing these categories:[37]

1. Creating an earth community with ecological integrity

---

35. Ibid.

36. Fletcher, in his book entitled *Situation Ethics*, while not speaking to the global questions, did underline that our ethical positions tend to be and can be situational in character.

37. The Earth Charter was crafted well over a decade ago by a gathering of people with expertise and compassion, and the Earth Charter International Secretariat, based in San Jose, Costa Rica, now manages its use. I used material from the Earth Charter in *Lovescapes*, 254.

2. Creating an earth community of care and respect

3. Creating a global culture of social and economic justice

4. Creating a global context of participatory governance, nonviolence, and peace

We turn first to the daunting task of creating an earth community with ecological integrity.[38] All of us and our fellow creatures live on this earth, and we must find ways to preserve it and keep it healthy. How have the Christian church and its teachers of ethical responsibility guided its adherents in response to the ecological crisis in which we find ourselves? Part of the answer is "not easily" because of the resistance of powerful groups with vested interest and cultures with long and deeply rooted practices that hurt the earth and those who live on it and in it. It is also not easy to find a direct quote form Jesus that speaks to a contemporary issue understood and described in current scientific language. But there is in Jesus a deep love for the earth, its beauty and its bounty. He has read his Bible about the creation and human responsibility for creation. He would have read in Genesis: "God saw everything that he had made, and indeed, it was very good."[39] He cautions his followers not to worry about what they wear and says: "Consider the lilies of the field, how they grow; they neither toil not spin. Yet I tell you, even Solomon in all his glory was not clothed like one of these."[40] He illustrates the need to be an example by using an analogy drawn from the resources of the earth: "You are the salt of the earth; but if salt has lost its take, how can saltiness be restored?" Again he says: "You are the light of the world"[41] and underscores the need to light the way for others. He speaks about "hearers and doers" and their different responses to his guidance by referring to a part of creation: "Everyone who hears these words of mine and acts on them will be like a wise man who built his house upon a rock. The rain fell, the floods came, and the winds blew and beat on the house, but it did not fall, because it had been founded on a rock."[42] In his parables, Jesus speaks about the sower who plants seeds, the weeds among the wheat, the mustard seed that grows, and yeast that enables bread to rise.[43] Again and again, Jesus draws examples from creation to illustrate his teaching.

38. I will follow to some extent my own discussion of these categories in *Lovescapes*, 254–61.

39. Gen 1:31.

40. Matt 6:28–29.

41. Matt 5:13–14.

42. Matt 5:45.

43. Matt 13.

Jesus appears to care deeply for the earth and, if alive today, would want to preserve it for its own sake because it has inherent value, but also for all of its creatures who call it home. And if it is not cared for and abused, the radical prophet would speak and call on his followers to save the sacred universe.[44] It follows that we should be good stewards of the earth and concerned about the following:[45]

1. We must respect the earth in all of its diversity, grasp the rarity of our interdependence upon all that exists, recognize that all of life has value, and that we live in a sensitive ecological system which is interconnected, but delicately balanced and calibrated.

2. We must shift our understanding of the role of the human family, discarding older points of view that saw humans as the lords of creation and that understood nature as the enemy that must be conquered. We need to shift our orientation and learn to respect the rights of other life on earth, not just because we are dependent upon it, but because it too is the creation of God and has intrinsic value. We must recognize what Einstein said, that no problem could be solved by the consciousness that caused the problem in the first place. So we need to learn how to live with Mother Nature, even with all of her challenges; she is our mother and we live as dependent children in her home.

3. We need to change our focus from looking exclusively at our immediate needs and turn our attention to long-term ecological sustainability. Time is running out, and there is a pronounced urgency about harnessing global science and encouraging the centers of science to focus on food production and distribution, the improvement of health, and the management of the environment from the perspective of a healthy global infrastructure.

So much more could be said and has been said, and we should be informed and responsible citizens of the earth, but it is our more limited purpose in this context only to suggest an attitude and direction.

A second theme in our partnership with God in *creating a more just and peaceful world is to create an earth community of care and respect*. It is not difficult to find in the teachings of Jesus the guidance to give our lives to compassion for others. We are not only to love our neighbor as we love ourselves, but to love our enemy as well. He says, "You heard that it was said, 'You shall love your neighbor and hate your enemy.' But I say to you,

---

44. See Berry, *Sacred Universe*, and *Dream of the Earth*.

45. See the books of Brown of the Earth Policy Institute, such as *World on Edge*.

Love your enemies and pray for those who persecute you."[46] In response, we should put emphasis on the following:

1. We will need to learn how to respect the rights of others, acknowledge their differences of belief, culture, and customs, and insure their rights to a good life. There will be conflict, but there are peaceful ways of resolving conflict without the resort to violence, although these approaches often seem inadequate in the face of such profound challenges. We live in age filled with fear of "the other" and it is hard to understand how this fear, in so many parts of the world, could lead to the preoccupation of changing others against their will, and target others as enemies that must be eliminated. These conflicts, of course, are entangled in the need for land, the quest for economic sustainability, and zealotry and xenophobic attitudes behind deep religious prejudices. We need to ponder the insight of Martin Luther King Jr. in his "Letter from the Birmingham Jail": "We are caught in an inescapable network of mutuality tied in a single garment of destiny. What affects one directly affects all indirectly."

2. In order to respect the rights of others, we must be converted to the teaching of Jesus that all people are created in the image of God and have inherent worth and dignity. We need to learn that the diversity of the human family can teach and enrich the whole family. We must learn how to seek the common good, not just our own good over against others who may threaten us. In abiding by this foundational affirmation, we are able to become a part of the solution and not contribute to the problem. Others need not be just like us and follow our customs and adhere to our culture and values as long as their way is peaceful and just. So we follow the counsel of Pope John XXIII: "In essentials unity, non-essentials liberty, and in all things charity."

3. An essential part of respecting the rights of others and their inherent worth and dignity is to become advocates for forms of government that enable all to participate and have the potential to empower those who are on the margins. We do not need to impose Western governance systems and create little Americas or little Frances. This risk is very real in the ways we intervene and attempt to solve conflicts around the world. Western countries have their own array of problems. It is possible to respect the history and culture of other groups and nations and encourage governance that is participatory in nature and promotes justice and peaceful solutions to conflicts. Realistic in our appraisals and

46. Matt 5:43.

tough-minded in our assessments, we should not give in to cynicism, but find ways to encourage peaceful solutions that ensure security and economic justice that enables an acceptable standard of living for all.[47] And we must remember that we too easily try to impose our version of order over the demonstration of compassion in order to ward off exceptions to our views of how life should be organized.

The emphasis on principle two leads directly to a third overarching goal, that of creating *a global culture of social and economic justice*. It is easy to observe in what we can know about the life and teachings of Jesus to find examples of his commitment to social and economic justice. He was a student of the great prophets of the Hebrew Bible who spoke profoundly about justice and saw himself in their company. He would have read the opening chapter of Isaiah: "Learn to do good; seek justice, rescue the oppressed, defend the orphan, and plead for the widow."[48] Or perhaps he would have read Hosea: "Hold fast to love and justice."[49] Toward the end of his life, he laments the condition of Jerusalem, the seat of government and religious leadership, and says, "Jerusalem, Jerusalem, the city that kills the prophets and stones those who are sent to it."[50] He consistently reaches across the barriers of prejudice and custom, offering living water to the Samaritan woman, healing to the leper, and eating with tax collectors. In his own home of Nazareth, he speaks in the synagogue and quotes from the prophet to illustrate his mission: "The Spirit of the Lord is upon me, because he has anointed me to bring good news to the poor. He has sent me to proclaim release to the captives and recovery of the sight to the blind, to let the oppressed go free, to proclaim the year of the Lord's favor."[51]

As we speak about creating a global culture of social and economic justice, it is important to be clear about the meaning of the word "culture." We are using the word to describe an integrated pattern of human knowledge, belief, and behavior, and set of shared attitudes, values and goals.[52] Because there are so many different regions of the world, each with their own culture, it is necessary to find the particular way that the more universal values of social and economic justice take form. But whatever the culture, the following components should be present:

47. I write these sentences in midst of the conflict between Israel and Hamas in Gaza and the rise of ISIS and the range of conflicts in Syria and Iraq.

48. Isa 1:17.

49. Hos 12:6.

50. Matt 23:37.

51. Luke 4:18–19.

52. Ferguson, *Lovescapes*, 258.

1. A primary goal of creating a culture of social and economic justice is to eradicate poverty that carries with it so many damaging consequences.[53] As Jesus feeds the five thousand, so we must find ways to help people in poverty-stricken areas of the world to have access to clean water and sufficient food. They must also have ways of making a living, educational opportunities, and adequate health care.[54]

2. Efforts must also be made to shape economic policies and tax structures to help all people have access to a livelihood. Careful not to remove the ways and motivations to create wealth, an effort must nevertheless be made to create a more equitable distribution of wealth. The recent initiatives of America's most wealthy people, including Warren Buffet and Bill Gates, are pioneering ways of distributing wealth apart from government action.

3. Even with the strong cultural resistance, we must find ways to achieve racial and gender equality. Jesus resisted the norms of his culture as he honored and respected the women in his life and among his followers.[55] Nelson Mandela, in the midst of his transforming work in South Africa said: "Freedom cannot be achieved unless the women have been emancipated from all forms of oppression."[56] The 2014 social unrest in Ferguson, Missouri, points to the reality that civil rights have miles to go.[57]

A fourth and final overarching goal that I will mention for followers of the way of Jesus is to *create a global context of participatory governance, nonviolence, and peace.* While Jesus was unafraid of conflict, he pursued his goals with a clear commitment to peace. He affirmed this commitment in the Beatitudes: "Blessed are the peacemakers, for they will be called the children of God."[58] The word "peace" speaks of several dimensions of life. The Hebrew word, *shalom* and its Greek counterpart in the New Testament *"eirene"* mean wholeness, well-being, and serenity in the individual, and not only cessation of war in society but a state of health, prosperity, and security. Again, we can only point to attitudes and directions for achievement

---

53. See Sachs, *End of Poverty.*

54. A recent book by Karr-Morse with Wiley, *Scared Sick*, cites several studies that show how the conditions of poverty cause severe childhood trauma.

55. See the excellent small book by Hiers, *Women's Rights in the Bible.*

56. On a sign and postcard I recently purchased in Cape Town.

57. See the article in *Presbyterians Today*, September 2014, 24–35.

58. Matt 5:9.

of participatory governance, nonviolence, and peace and would underline the following:

1. Efforts should be made in all countries and regions of the world to foster participatory institutions that empower people to shape their common life. The people of the world must have ownership for the decisions that impact the quality of their lives and insure that they will be treated with fairness and justice. People need to have the rights to gather in groups, discuss their needs and strategies for the common good, and to hold those in power accountable for insuring equal rights, education, and adequate health care.

2. To shape a culture committed to these values, they must be taught in the schools. The children of the world have in their curriculum the ways and means of achieving a more democratic government and the resolution of conflicts without the resort to violence. There should be an exposure to the life of Mahatma Gandhi, Nelson Mandela, and others who found ways to empower people through nonviolent means.[59] Perhaps to partially overstate, "we must educate or perish." It is through education that we will achieve a just peace and create a society that serves the common good.

3. To reaffirm a point already made, we will need to create a culture that accepts and even celebrates the differences within the human family. As far as possible, we must find peaceful ways to resolve conflicts, and when necessary, use statesmanship to resist the intrusion of our regions and countries by foreign powers. We need to explore every possible way to negotiate the differences that cause conflicts, making our mother earth a just and peaceful place to live and work.

Jesus' Command to Go and Do Likewise: Contemporary Issues

We have uncovered a broad range of issues in our very modest survey of the ways that the Christian community has responded to statement of Jesus to the inquiring lawyer who heard the story of the Good Samaritan. It is my hope that a brief summary of these issues will serve as a guide for those committed to partner with God in seeking a more just and peaceful world. I would once again confess that to follow the guidance of Jesus in our

59. See the fine book edited by Helmick and Peterson, with a foreword by Desmond M. Tutu, *Forgiveness and Reconciliation: Religion.*

regions, countries, and globally is complex and difficult challenge. Books have been written and libraries have been filled with descriptions of the ways we should "go and do likewise" and we can only suggest the kind of directions we might follow in our effort to be responsive to the call of Jesus to have compassion for those in need. As we seek to partner with God in this endeavor, I will stress five issues about which we should have clarity, knowing that there were many others that have been present in the multitude of groups who have sought to "go and do likewise." These five then will be suggestive though not exhaustive.

1. There is a foundational premise that guides us in our desire to "go and do likewise." We go with the same conviction and purpose as Jesus by seeking *to invite others to embrace the kingdom of God*, or to say it another way, to accept the power and presence of God in one's life, and to find ways to join with God in affirming the will and way of God in every aspect of our lives and in all of groups and associations. I would add that this invitation takes different forms in the settings in which it is practiced, with some quite intentional about converting others (evangelism) and some more inclined to be clear about what Jesus taught, but open to the ways of others and always respectful of the beliefs and dignity of others.

2. There are foundational values that are inherent and integral to our endeavor; *we go in love and compassion and seek justice and a good life for all.* The love we demonstrate is limitless, but also wise and appropriate, not sentimental and driven by romantic fantasy. The compassion we demonstrate cares for the suffering of others and finds ways of reducing their suffering. In that effort, we seek to build a just society that works for the well-being of all its citizens.

3. One fundamental issue arising from this premise and these values is *whether we have within us the capacity to carry out this mission or whether we must be led and empowered to implement this mission.* We saw advocates of both views, arguing, for example, that we are endowed with reason and a conscience and the capacity to follow the will and way of God. This point of view also is inclined to speak about natural law, an order and structure in the world that may be discerned by reason and conscience. Others, including the Reformers stressed our need to be graced by the Holy Spirit in order to follow the will and way of God. God must transform us in order to have the will and the capacity to do the will of God. I see no need to make the choice, even though I come from the Reformed tradition, but learned from John

Wesley that we should pray like it all depends upon God and live like all depends upon us. We must also take into account that it is a process, and that our spiritual formation lasts across the years of our lives.

4. Another fundamental issue arising from our survey is *the nature of our approach* or strategy in carrying out the mission to "go and do likewise." There were those who argued that education and spiritual formation were essential as we equip ourselves to be faithful in our service to God. Others believed, especially in the challenge of creating a more just society, that we should be prophetic in speaking truth to power. Still others believed, especially in the challenge of creating a more just society, that we should go beyond political advocacy and live in solidarity with those who suffer, following in the patterns of Mother Teresa and Martin Luther King Jr. In the case of M. L. King, there are issues of whether we should use civil disobedience and nonviolence in our strategies. Others argued that much of our theology is rooted in the past and is not relevant to the challenges of the present. They maintained that every generation must rethink its theology, especially that which is connected to mission, in that every generation and every region and country faces different challenges. We would argue that all of these approaches are valid, depending upon our gifts, skills, and resources, and the key is to be discerning and faithful.

5. Another issue that arose in our survey is *the way in which we relate and cooperate with those who are different from us.* We learned that there are strong feelings about this issue, with some on the more conservative side saying that we must not compromise our beliefs and practices by joining with those who do not believe as we do and who have different goals and practices in their mission. There are those on the more progressive side of the Christian community who argue that we now live in a global context, are connected worldwide by digital processes, unlimited communication opportunities, the ease of transportation, and the globalization of knowledge and information. I do not see a time when this debate will stop, but one practical way of not getting bogged down in the debate and getting on with the mission is to do what is appropriate in our regional settings. We can cooperate with others on achieving fair laws, providing good schools, and ensuring adequate health care, but it may be more difficult if we want to post the Ten Commandments at city hall or to have a crèche in front of a public building at the Christmas season. On the more national and global level, there is great wisdom in working across ethnic, national, and religious boundaries on the most pressing issues of peace and justice.

In the religions domain, it is possible to find ways of expanding religious literacy, reducing stereotypes and caricatures by enabling people to observe other religious services, and joining in spiritual practices such as prayer and meditation that are present and practiced in nearly every religious tradition.[60]

We close this chapter and the book with the goal of aiding contemporary seekers to understand the way of Jesus. He was a charismatic teacher, a compassionate healer, and a radical prophet whose message of the kingdom of God is available to all who seek a spiritual center.

Study Resources

Study Questions

1. On reading the Parable of the Good Samaritan, what do you think Jesus meant when he said to the lawyer, "Go and do likewise"?

2. How optimistic are you about the human capacity for making constructive changes in society through democratic processes? Should one resort to civil disobedience?

3. Do you think that people are primarily endowed with the motivation and capacity to do good in the world or do they need to be empowered by an external force such as the grace of God?

4. What is the place of reason and conscience in discerning how we should live our lives?

5. How much should we cooperate and collaborate with those who fundamentally differ from us without losing our identity and values and making compromises?

Terms and Concepts

1. Hellenistic or Hellenism: A worldview that was rooted in Greek thought which incorporated the values, customs, and patterns of life of ancient Greece.

2. Empowering Grace: The presence of God's Spirit in one's life which enables them to be motivated and have the capacity to do the will of God.

---

60. See the book of his Holiness, the Dalai Lama, *Toward a True Kinship of Faiths.*

3. Ascetic-Monastic: A lifestyle in the medieval world that was Spartan and disciplined and which was lived in a community (monastery) of like-minded people.

4. Disordered Love: The view of Augustine that it is easy for us to love the wrong object, as for example, to love objects in the world, exploit or use those around us, and to not give honor and worship to God. In Augustine's view, we are to give love to God with our whole being, love our neighbor as ourselves, and to wisely use objects in the created world.

5. Culture: An integrated pattern of human knowledge, belief, behavior, and a set of shared attitudes, values, and goals.

Suggestions for Reading and Reference

Berry, Thomas. *The Sacred Universe: Earth, Spirituality, and Religion in the Twenty-First Century*. New York: Columbia University Press, 2009.

Maguire, Daniel C. *Ethics: A Completed Method for Moral Choice*. Minneapolis: Fortress, 2010.

Niebuhr, Reinhold. *An Interpretation of Christian Ethics*. New York: Meridian, 1956.

Spohn, William C. *God and Do Likewise: Jesus and Christian Ethics*. New York: Continuum, 2000.

White, R. E. O. *Christian Ethics*. Atlanta: John Knox, 1981.

Bibliography

Abernathy, David. *Understanding the Teaching of Jesus*. New York: Seabury, 1983.

Achtemeier, Paul A., ed. *Harper's Dictionary of the Bible*. San Francisco: Harper & Row, 1985.

Adyshanti. *Resurrecting Jesus: Embodying the Spirit of a Revolutionary Mystic*. Boulder, CO: Sounds True, 2014.

Albert, Ethel M., et al. *Great Traditions in Ethics*. New York: Van Nostrand, 1975.

Allison, Dale C. *Constructing Jesus: Memory, Imagination, and History*. Grand Rapids: Baker, 2011.

Armstrong, Karen. *The Battle for God*. New York: Ballantine, 2000.

———. *A History of God*. New York: Ballantine, 1993.

Alter, Robert, and Frank Kermode, eds. *The Literary Guide to the Bible*. Cambridge: Belknap of Harvard University Press, 1987.

Aslan, Reza. *Zealot: The Life and Times of Jesus of Nazareth*. New York: Random House, 2013.

Augustine. *The City of God*. Translated by Marcus Dods. New York: Modern Library, 1950.

———. *The Confessions of St. Augustine*. Translated by E. B. Pusey. New York: Dutton, 1907.

Bailey, Kenneth E. *Jesus through Middle Eastern Eyes: Cultural Studies in the Gospels*. Downers Grove: InterVarsity, 2008.

Baillie, D. M. *God Was in Christ*. New York: Scribner, 1948.

Barbour, Ian G. *Religion and Science: Historical and Contemporary Issues*. San Francisco: HarperSanFrancisco, 1997.

Barkley, William. *Jesus as They Saw Him*. New York: Harper & Row, 1962.

Barth, Karl. *Church Dogmatics*. 4 vols. Translated by G. W. Bromiley and T. F. Torrance. Edinburgh: T. & T. Clark, 1957.

Bawer, Bruce. *Stealing Jesus: How Fundamentalism Betrays Christianity*. New York: Three Rivers, 1997.

Beasley-Murray, G. R. *Jesus and the Kingdom of God*. Grand Rapids: Eerdmans, 1986.

Bellah, Robert. *Religion and Human Evolution*. Cambridge: Belknap of Harvard University Press, 2011.

Berry, Thomas. *The Dream of the Earth*. San Francisco: Sierra Club, 1988.

————. *The Sacred Universe: Earth, Spirituality, and Religion in the Twenty-First Century.* New York: Columbia University Press, 2009.

Bloomfield, Vishvapani. *Gautama Buddha: The Life and Teachings of the Awakened One.* London: Quercus, 2011.

Boff, Leonardo. *Jesus Christ Liberator: A Critical Christology for Our Time.* Translated by Patrick Hughes. Maryknoll: Orbis, 1984.

Bonino, Jose Miguez. *Faces of Jesus: Latin American Christologies.* Translated by Robert R. Barr. Maryknoll: Orbis, 1977.

Borg, Marcus. *Jesus: Uncovering the Life, Teachings, and Relevance of a Religious Revolutionary.* San Francisco: HarperSanFrancisco, 2006.

————. *Meeting Jesus Again for the First Time.* San Francisco: HarperSanFrancisco, 1995.

Borg, Marcus, and John Dominic Crossan. *The First Paul: Reclaiming the Radical Visionary behind the Church's Conservative Icon.* New York: HarperOne, 2009.

Bornkamm, Günther. *Jesus of Nazareth.* New York: Harper & Row, 1960.

Bourgeault, Cynthia. *The Wisdom Jesus.* Boston: Shambhala, 2008.

Brown, Lester R. *World on the Edge: How to Prevent Environmental and Economic Collapse.* New York: Norton, 2011

Brown, Raymond E. *The Birth of the Messiah: A Commentary on the Infancy Narratives in Matthew and Luke.* Garden City: Doubleday, 1977.

Brueggemann, Walter. *Theology of the Old Testament: Testimony, Dispute, Advocacy.* Minneapolis: Fortress, 1997.

Buchanan, John M. "Editor's Desk." *Christian Century,* April 2, 2014.

Bultmann, Rudolf. *The History of the Synoptic Tradition.* Translated by Kendrick Grobel. New York: Harper & Row, 1963. First published 1923.

————. *Jesus and the Word.* Translated by Louise Pettibone Smith and Erminie Huntress Lantero. London: Collins: Fontana, 1958.

————. *The Theology of the New Testament.* 2 vols. Translated by Kendrick Grobel. London: SCM, 1952, 1955.

Bunyan, Paul. *The Pilgrim's Progress.* New York: Grosset & Dunlap, no date given (Bunyan lived 1628–1688).

Cadbury, Henry J. *The Peril of Modernizing Jesus.* London: SPCK, 1962.

Calvin, John. *Institutes of the Christian Religion.* 2 vols. Translated by Henry Beveridge. Grand Rapids: Eerdmans, 1957.

Capra, Fritjof, and David Steindl-Rast. *Belonging to the Universe: Explorations on the Frontiers of Science and Spirituality.* San Francisco: HarperSanFrancisco, 1991.

Charlesworth, James H. *Jesus within Judaism: New Light from Exciting Archaeological Discoveries.* New York: Doubleday, 1988.

Chilton, Bruce. *Rabbi Jesus, An Intimate Biography: The Jewish Life and Teachings That Inspired Christianity.* New York: Doubleday, 2002.

Christopher, David. *The Holy Universe: A New Story of Creation for the Heart, Soul, and Spirit.* Santa Rosa, CA: New Story, 2014.

Connick, C. Milo. *Jesus: The Man, the Mission, and the Message.* Englewood Cliffs, NJ: Prentice-Hall, 1974.

Conzelmann, Hans. *Jesus.* Translated by Raymond J. Lord. Philadelphia: Fortress, 1973.

Crossan, John Dominic. *The Historical Jesus: The Life of a Mediterranean Jewish Peasant.* San Francisco: HarperSanFrancisco, 1991.

————. *Jesus: A Revolutionary Biography.* San Francisco: HarperSanFrancisco, 1994.

Crossan, John Dominic, and Jonathan L. Reed. *In Search of Paul: How Jesus's Apostle Opposed Rome's Empire with God's Kingdom.* San Francisco: HarperSanFrancisco, 2004.

The Dalai Lama. *Towards a True Kinship of Faiths: How the World Religions Can Come Together.* New York: Doubleday, 2010.

Davies, A. Powell. *The First Christian: A Study of St. Paul and Christian Origins.* New York: Mentor, 1957.

Dawes, Gregory W., ed. *The Historical Jesus Quest: Landmarks in the Search for the Jesus of History.* Louisville: Westminster John Knox, 1999.

Dawkins, Richard. *The God Delusion.* Boston: Houghton Mifflin, 2006.

Dibelius, Martin. *Jesus.* Philadelphia: Westminster, 1949.

Dodd, C. H. *The Founder of Christianity.* London: Collins, 1971.

Dowd, Michael. *Thank God for Evolution.* New York: Plume, 2009.

Duling, Dennis C. *Jesus Christ through History.* New York: Harcourt Brace Javonovich, 1979.

Dunnett, Walter M. *The Interpretation of Holy Scripture.* Nashville: Nelson, 1984.

Echegarary, Hugo. *The Practice of Jesus.* Translated by Matthew J. O'Connell. Maryknoll: Orbis, 1980.

Edersheim, Alfred. *The Life and Times of Jesus the Messiah.* 2 vols. Grand Rapids: Eerdmans, 1950.

Eckardt, A. Roy. *Reclaiming the Jesus of History.* Minneapolis: Fortress, 1992.

Ehrman, Burt. *Does Jesus Exist? The Historical Argument for Jesus of Nazareth.* New York: HarperOne, 2012.

———. *Misquoting Jesus: The Story behind Who Changed the Bible and Why.* New York: HarperOne, 2005.

Eliade, Mircea. *From Primitives to Zen.* New York: Harper & Row, 1977.

———. *A History of Religious Ideas.* 3 vols. Chicago: University of Chicago Press, 1978–1985.

Farrar, Frederic W. *The Life of Christ.* New York: Burt, ca. 1870.

Ferguson, Duncan S. *Biblical Hermeneutics: An Introduction.* Atlanta: John Knox, 1986.

———. *Exploring the Spiritual Pathways of the World Religions.* New York: Continuum, 2010.

———. *Lovescapes: Mapping the Geography of Love.* Eugene, OR: Cascade, 2012.

Feuerbach, Ludwig. *The Essence of Christianity.* Translated by George Eliot. New York: Harper Torchbooks, 1957. First published 1841.

Fletcher, Joseph. *Situation Ethics: The New Morality.* Philadelphia: Westminster, 1966.

Foster, Richard J. *Celebration of Discipline: The Path to Spiritual Growth.* San Francisco: Harper & Row, 1978.

———. *Streams of Living Water.* New York: HarperOne, 1998.

Fowler, James W. *The Stages of Faith: The Psychology of Human Development and the Quest for Meaning.* San Francisco: Harper & Row, 1981.

Fox, George. *The Journal of George Fox.* Revised by Norman Perry. New York: Dutton, 1924.

Fox, Matthew. *The Coming of the Cosmic Christ.* San Francisco: Harper & Row, 1988.

———. *One River, Many Wells.* New York: Tarcher / Putnam, 2000.

Fredriksen, Paula. *From Jesus to Christ: The Origins of New Testament Images of Christ.* New Haven: Yale University Press, 1988.

Funk, Robert W. *Honest to Jesus.* San Francisco: HarperSanFrancisco, 1996.

Gadamar, Hans-George. *Truth and Method.* New York: Crossroad, 1975.

Grant, Michael. *Jesus: An Historian's Review of the Gospels.* New York: Scribner, 1977.

Grant, Robert M. *A Short History of the Interpretation of the Bible.* With David Tracy. Philadelphia: Fortress, 1984.

Grant, Robert M., and David Noel Freedman. *The Secret Sayings of Jesus.* New York: Barnes & Noble, 1960.

Grassian, Victor. *Moral Reasoning: Ethical Theory and Some Contemporary Problems.* Englewood Cliffs, NJ: Prentice-Hall, 1981.

Greenblatt, Stephen. *Swerve: How the World Became Modern.* New York: Norton, 2011.

Grillmeier, Aloys. *Christ in Christian Tradition.* Vol. 1. Translated by John Bowden. Atlanta: John Knox, 1975.

Gutierrez, Gustavo. *A Theology of Liberation.* Translated by John Eagleson and Caridad Inda. Maryknoll: Orbis, 1973.

Gustafson, James M. *Ethics from a Theocentric Perspective.* 2 vols. Chicago: University of Chicago Press, 1981 & 1984.

Habermas, Jürgen. *An Awareness of What Is Missing: Faith and Reason in a Post-Secular Age.* Translated by Ciaran Cronin. Malden, MA: Polity, 2010.

Harris, Sam. *The End of Faith: Religion, Terror, and the Future of Reason.* New York: Norton, 2005.

Hart, David Bentley. *Atheist Delusions: The Christian Revolution and Its Fashionable Enemies.* New Haven: Yale University Press, 2009.

————. *The Experience of God: Being Consciousness, Bliss.* New Haven: Yale University Press, 2013.

Harvey, A. E. *Jesus and the Constraints of History.* Philadelphia: Westminster, 1982.

Harvey, Andrew. *Mystics: The Soul's Journey into Truth.* Edison, NJ: Castle, 1996.

Hauerwas, Stanley. *The Peaceable Kingdom: A Primer in Christian Ethics.* Notre Dame: University of Notre Dame Press, 1983.

Helmick, Raymond G., and Rodney L. Peterson, eds. *Forgiveness and Reconciliation.* Philadelphia: Templeton, 2001.

Henry, Patrick. "Ferguson, Missouri." *Presbyterians Today* 104 (2014) 24–35.

Hiers, Richard H. *Women's Rights and the Bible: Implications for Christian Ethics and Social Policy.* Eugene, OR: Pickwick, 2012.

Hitchens, Christopher. *God Is not Great: How Religion Poisons Everything.* New York: Hatchette, 2007.

Horsley, Richard. *The Prophet Jesus and the Renewal of Israel.* Grand Rapids: Eerdmans, 2012.

Jantzen, Grace M. *Julian of Norwich: Mystic and Theologian.* New York: Paulist, 1988.

Jasper, David. *A Short Introduction to Hermeneutics.* Louisville: Westminster John Knox, 2004.

Julian of Norwich. *Showings.* Translated by Edmund Colledge and John Walsh. New York: Paulist, 1978.

Karr-Moore, Robin. *Scarred Sick: The Role of Childhood Trauma in Adult Disease.* With Meredith S. Wiley. New York: Basic, 2012.

Kauffman, Stuart A. *Reinventing the Sacred: A New View of Science, Reason, and Religion.* New York: Basic, 2008.

Keller, Timothy. *Jesus the King: The Life and Death of the Son of God.* New York: Riverhead, 2011.

Kittel, Gerhard. *Theological Dictionary of the New Testament* [*TDNT*]. 10 vols. Edited by Gerhard Kittel and Gerhard Friedrich. Translated by Geoffrey W. Bromiley. Grand Rapids: Eerdmans, 1964–1976.

Kung, Hans. *On Being a Christian*. Translated by Edward Quinn. Garden City: Doubleday, 1976.

Ladd, George E. *Crucial Questions about the Kingdom of God*. Grand Rapids: Eerdmans, 1952.

Lao Tzu. *Tao Te Ching*. New York: Barnes & Noble, 2005.

Levison, John R. *Filled with the Spirit*. Grand Rapids: Eerdmans, 2009.

Lohfink, Gerhard. *Jesus of Nazareth: What He Wanted, Who He Was*. Translated by Linda Maloney. Collegeville, MN: Liturgical, 2011.

Lonergan, Bernard. *Method in Theology*. New York: Seabury, 1972.

Luther, Martin. *Three Treatises*. Philadelphia: Muhlenberg, 1960.

Maguire, Daniel. *Ethics: A Complete Method for Moral Choice*. Minneapolis: Fortress, 2012.

Manson, T. W. *The Teaching of Jesus: Studies in Its Form & Content*. Cambridge: Cambridge University Press, 1967.

Martin, James. *Jesus: A Pilgrimage*. New York: HarperOne, 2014.

McFague, Sallie. *The Body of God*. Minneapolis: Fortress, 1993.

———. *Models of God*. Philadelphia: Fortress, 1987.

McIntire, C. T., ed. *God, History, and Historians: Modern Views of History*. New York: Oxford University Press, 1974.

McLaren, Brian D. *The Secret Message of Jesus*. Nashville: Nelson, 2006.

Meier, John P. *A Marginal Jew*. 4 vols. New York: Doubleday, 1991 (vol. 1), 1994 (vol. 2); New Haven: Yale University Press, 2001 (vol. 3), 2009 (vol. 4).

Meyers, Robin R. *Saving Jesus from the Church: How to Stop Worshiping Christ and Start Following Jesus*. New York: HarperOne, 2009.

Miles, Jack. *God: A Biography*. New York: Vintage, 1996.

Miller, Perry, and Thomas H. Johnson, eds. *The Puritans: A Sourcebook of Their Writings*. 2 vols. Rev. ed. New York: Harper & Row, 1963.

Moltmann, Jürgen. *The Crucified God*. Translated by R. A. Wilson and John Bowden. New York: Harper & Row, 1974.

Murphy, Nancey, and George F. R. Ellis. *On the Moral Nature of the Universe: Theology, Cosmology, and Ethics*. Minneapolis: Fortress, 1996.

Neill, Stephen. *Jesus through Many Eyes: Introduction to the Theology of the New Testament*. Philadelphia: Fortress, 1976.

Nerburn, Kent, ed. *The Wisdom of the Native Americans*. Novato, CA: New World Library, 1999.

Nicholson, Adam. *God's Secretaries: The Making of the King James Bible*. New York: HarperCollins, 2003.

Niebuhr, Reinhold. *Christian Realism & Political Problems*. London: Faber & Faber, 1954.

———. *An Interpretation of Christian Ethics*. New York: Living Age-Meridian, 1956.

———. *Leaves from the Notebooks of a Tamed Cynic*. New York: Living Age-Meridian, 1957.

———. *Moral Man & Immoral Society*. New York: Scribner, 1932.

———. *The Nature and Destiny of Man*. New York: Scribner, 1949,

Nygren, Anders. *Agape and Eros*. Translated by Phillip S. Watson. London: SPCK, 1953. First published 1932.

Ogden, Shubert, M. *The Reality of God*. New York: Harper & Row, 1964.

Ottati, Douglas F. *Theology for Liberal Protestants: God the Creator*. Grand Rapids: Eerdmans, 2013.Pagels, Elaine. *Beyond Belief*. New York: Random House, 2003.

————. *The Gnostic Gospels*. New York: Vintage, 1979.

Parini, Jay. *Jesus: The Human Face of God*. Boston: Houghton Mifflin Harcourt, 2013.

Pelikan, Jaroslav. *Jesus through the Centuries*. New Haven: Yale University Press 1985.

Polanyi, Michael. *The Tacit Dimension*. London: Routledge & Kegan Paul, 1967.

Post, Stephen G. *Unlimited Love: Altruism, Compassion, and Service*. Philadelphia: Templeton, 2003.

Powell, Mark Allan. *Jesus as a Figure in History: How Modern Historians View the Man from Galilee*. Louisville: Westminster John Knox, 1998.

Prothero Stephen. *American Jesus: How the Son of God Became a National Icon*. New York: Farrar, Straus & Giroux, 2003.

Rahner, Karl. *Foundations of Christian Faith*. Translated by William V. Dych. New York: Seabury, 1978.

Ramsey, Paul. *Basic Christian Ethics*. Chicago: University of Chicago Press, 1950.

Ratzinger, Joseph [Pope Benedict XVI]. *Jesus of Nazareth*. Vol. 2, *Holy Week: From Entrance into Jerusalem to the Resurrection*. Translated by Philip J. Whitmore. San Francisco: Ignatius, 2011.

————. *Jesus of Nazareth*. Vol. 3, *The Infancy Narratives*. Translated by Philip J. Whitmore. New York: Image, 2012.

Rauschenbush, Walter. *The Social Principles of Jesus*. New York: Association, 1918.

Renan, Ernest. *The Life of Jesus*. London: Watts, 1947. First published ca. 1861.

Reventlow, Henning Graf. *The Authority of the Bible and the Rise of the Modern World*. Translated by John Bowden. Philadelphia: Fortress, 1985.

Richardson. Alan, *History Sacred and Profane*. London: SCM, 1964.

Riches, John. *The World of Jesus: First-Century Judaism in Crisis*. Cambridge: Cambridge University Press, 1990.

Rohr, Richard. *Jesus' Plan for a New World: The Sermon on the Mount*. Cincinnati: Franciscan, 1996.

Sachs, Jeffrey D. *The End of Poverty: Economic Possibilities for Our Time*. New York: Penguin, 2005.

Sanders, E. P. *The Historical Figure of Jesus*. London: Penguin, 1993.

————. *Jesus and Judaism*. Philadelphia: Fortress, 1985.

Schillebeeckx, Edward. *Christ: The Experience of Jesus as Lord*. Translated by John Bowden. New York: Seabury, 1980.

————. *Jesus: An Experiment in Christology*. Translated by Hubert Hoskins. New York: Seabury, 1979.

Schleiermacher, Friedrich. *On Religion: Speeches to Its Cultured Despisers*. Translated by John Oman. New York: Harper & Row, 1958.Schüssler Fiorenza, Elisabeth. *In Memory of Her: A Feminist Theological Reconstruction of Christian Origins*. New York: Crossroad, 1988.

Schweitzer, Albert. *The Mystery of the Kingdom of God*. Edited an translated by R. H. Hiers and D. L Holland. Philadelphia: Fortress, 1971. First published 1892.

————. *The Quest of the Historical Jesus: A Critical Study of Its Progress from Reimarus to Wrede*. Translated by W. Montgomery. New York: Macmillan, 1948. First published 1906.

Sheldon, Charles M. *In His Steps: What Would Jesus Do?* Chicago: Laird & Lee, 1897.

Sider, Ronald J. *Rich Christians in an Age of Hunger.* Downers Grove: InterVarsity, 1977.

Singer, Irving. *The Nature of Love.* Chicago: University of Chicago Press, 1984 (Vols. 1 [2nd ed.] & 2,), 1987 (vol. 3).

Sobrino, Jon. *Christology at the Crossroads: A Latin American Approach.* Translated by John Drury. Maryknoll: Orbis, 1984.

Sorokin, Pitirim A. *The Ways and Powers of Love.* Philadelphia: Templeton, 2002. First published 1954.

Spohn, William L. *Go and Do Likewise: Jesus and Ethics.* New York: Continuum, 2000.

Stein, Robert H. *The Method and Message of Jesus' Teachings.* Philadelphia: Westminster, 1978.

Stella, Tom. *Finding God beyond Religion: A Guide for Skeptics, Agnostics & Unorthodox Believers Inside & Outside the Church.* Woodstock, VT: Skylight Paths, 2013.

Swimme, Brian Thomas, and Mary Evelyn Tucker. *Journey of the Universe.* New Haven: Yale University Press, 2011.

Tatum, W. Barnes. *In Quest of Jesus.* Nashville: Abingdon, 1999.

Theissen, Gerd, and Annette Merz. *The Historical Jesus: A Comprehensive Guide.* Translated by John Bowden. Minneapolis: Fortress, 1996.

Theissen, Gerd, and Dagmar Winter. *The Quest for the Plausible Jesus: The Question of Criteria.* Translated by Eugene M. Boring. Louisville: Westminster John Knox, 2002.

Thielicke, Helmut. *Theological Ethics.* 3 vols. Translated by John Doberstein. Grand Rapids: Eerdmans, 1964, 1966, 1969.

Tillich, Paul. *Systematic Theology.* Vol. 1. London: Nisbet, 1953.

Tracy, David. *The Analogical Imagination: Christian Theology and the Culture of Pluralism.* New York: Crossroad, 1981.

Velasquez, Manual, and Cynthia Rostankowski. *Ethics: Theory and Practice.* Englewood Cliffs, NJ: Prentice Hall, 1985.

Vermes, Geza. *Jesus in His Jewish Context.* Minneapolis: Fortress, 2003.

———. *The Religion of Jesus the Jew.* Minneapolis: Fortress, 1993.

White, R. E. O. *Christian Ethics.* Atlanta: John Knox, 1981.

Wilber, Ken. *A Theory of Everything: An Integral Vision for Business, Politics, Science, and Spirituality.* Boston: Shambhala, 2001.

Williams, Daniel Day. *The Spirit and the Forms of Love.* New York: University Press of America, 1981.

Wilson, Edward O. *Consilience: The Unity of Knowledge.* New York: Knopf, 1998.

———. *The Meaning of Human Existence.* New York: Liveright, 2014.

Woodley, Randy S. *Shalom and the Community of Creation: An Indigenous Vision.* Grand Rapids: Eerdmans, 2012.

Wright, N. T. *The Original Jesus: The Life and Vision of a Revolutionary.* Grand Rapids: Eerdmans, 1996.

———. *Simply Jesus: A New Vision of Who He Was, What He Did, and Why He Matters.* New York: HarperOne, 2011.

———. *Who Was Jesus.* London: S.P.C.K., 1992

Wright, Robert. *The Evolution of Religion.* New York: Little, Brown, 2009.

Zeitlin, Irving M. *Jesus and the Judaism of His Time.* Cambridge, UK: Polity, 1988.

Index